Critical Essays on
CARSON McCULLERS

CRITICAL ESSAYS
ON
AMERICAN LITERATURE

James Nagel, General Editor
University of Georgia, Athens

Critical Essays on

CARSON McCULLERS

edited by

BEVERLY LYON CLARK
and
MELVIN J. FRIEDMAN

G.K. Hall & Co.
An Imprint of Simon & Schuster Macmillan
New York

Prentice Hall International
London   Mexico City   New Delhi   Singapore   Sydney   Toronto

G. K. Hall & Co.
An Imprint of Simon & Schuster Macmillan
1633 Broadway
New York, NY 10019

Library of Congress Cataloging-in-Publication Data

Critical essays on Carson McCullers / [edited by] Beverly Lyon Clark and Melvin J. Friedman
        p.   cm. — (Critical essays on American literature)
    Includes bibliographical references and index.
    ISBN 0-7838-0037-1
    1. McCullers, Carson, 1917–1967—Criticism and interpretation.
    2. Women and literature—Southern States—History—20th century.
    3. Southern States—In literature.   I. Clark, Beverly Lyon.
    II. Friedman, Melvin J.   III. Series.
    PS3525.A1772Z594   1996
    813'.52—dc20   95-43272
                                                                              CIP

The paper used in this publication meets the minimum requirements of American National Standard for Information Sciences-Permanence of Paper for Printed Library Materials. ANSI Z39.48-1984. ∞™

10   9   8   7   6   5   4   3   2   1

Printed in the United States of America

To Judy
—M. J. F.

To Roger
and in memory of Mel
—B. L. C.

Contents

General Editor's Note

♦

This series seeks to anthologize the most important criticism on a wide variety of topics and writers in American literature. Our readers will find in various volumes not only a generous selection of reprinted articles and reviews but original essays, bibliographies, manuscript sections, and other materials brought to public attention for the first time. *Critical Essays on Carson McCullers,* edited by Beverly Lyon Clark and Melvin J. Friedman, is the most comprehensive collection of essays ever published on one of the most important modern writers in the United States. It contains both a sizable gathering of early reviews and a broad selection of more recent scholarship as well. Among the authors of reprinted articles and reviews are Richard Wright, May Sarton, James Agee, Dorothy Parker, Nadine Gordimer, Tennessee Williams, Kay Boyle, Louis D. Rubin Jr., Sandra M. Gilbert and Susan Gubar, and Irving Howe. In addition to a substantial introduction by Lisa Logan, there are four original essays commissioned specifically for publication in this volume: a special tribute by William Trevor; and new studies by Suzanne Morrow Paulson on the chain gang in *The Ballad of the Sad Café,* Thadious M. Davis on ethnicity in *The Member of the Wedding,* and Lori J. Kenschaft on homoerotics in McCullers's fiction. We are confident that this book will make a permanent and significant contribution to the study of American literature.

JAMES NAGEL
University of Georgia

Publisher's Note

♦

Producing a volume that contains both newly commissioned and reprinted material presents the publisher with the challenge of balancing the desire to achieve stylistic consistency with the need to preserve the integrity of works first published elsewhere. In the Critical Essays series, essays commissioned especially for a particular volume are edited to be consistent with G. K. Hall's house style; reprinted essays appear in the style in which they were first published, with only typographical errors corrected. Consequently, shifts in style from one essay to another are the result of our efforts to be faithful to each text as it was originally published.

Introduction

♦

LISA LOGAN

McCullers's fiction . . . can speak to the adolescent reader in very intense fashion, for what it conveys is the frustration and pain of being more than a child and yet not an adult . . .

—Louis D. Rubin Jr.[1]

Carson had great vitality and she was quite beautiful in that already decaying way. She was like a fairy. She had the most delicate kind of tinkling, dazzling little way about her . . . like a little star. Like a Christmas, she was like an ornament of a kind. She had no mind and she could make no philosophical statements about anything; she didn't need to. She said far-out, wonderfully mad things, that were totally disarming and for a while people would say, "I'll go wherever you go."

—William Goyen[2]

Most critics tend to agree that Carson McCullers was concerned with human isolation and loneliness, and with the inability to mediate this condition through love. They tend to agree that she conveyed these ideas through her use of freaks, misfits, and adolescents, or what is sometimes termed, after the tradition of Southern writers, the grotesque. They compare her to Katherine Anne Porter, Flannery O'Connor, and Eudora Welty, to Sherwood Anderson and Thomas Wolfe, and even, although less flatteringly, to William Faulkner. As the epigraphs suggest, critics find consensus on McCullers's themes and

1

Peter Pan image, a consensus reinforced by Virginia Spencer Carr's ground-breaking work on McCullers's life and private vision.[3] They are less certain, however, about what to do with her work and about how to reconcile the disturbing ideas it expresses with their image of the boyish genius. They can't quite decide if she is a major or a minor writer, a modernist or a regionalist, or if the work of this Southern *wunderkind* declined or grew more ambitious with age, illness, and distance from her Georgia home. And although the oft-rehearsed explanations of McCullers's theory of love and loneliness do much to explain her work on an abstract and symbolic level, they do little to address its particularities. Far less agreement exists, therefore, as to what exactly McCullers was about when she addressed androgyny, homosexuality, sexual awakenings, racial and class oppression, and the complexities of the sociopolitical context in which she wrote. One might trace in the history of critical responses to Carson McCullers a sense of initial approval and consensus, followed by increasing disagreement. Most recently, critics have begun to question as insufficient and even dismissive arguments that rely strictly on McCullers's theories of love and loneliness and to challenge the comforting myth of "child-genius" with readings that advance her gendered identity.

I. THE CRITICAL RECEPTION

These are not popular ideas. They do not flatter the reader. They are uncomfortable to live with. We are reluctant to acknowledge that they may correspond to reality—and our very reluctance may be evidence of a sneaking suspicion that they do.

—Oliver Evans[4]

McCullers was introduced to the literary scene at age twenty-two, when her novel *The Heart Is a Lonely Hunter* (1940) was published after the manuscript outline won a Houghton-Mifflin writing contest. The novel received wide praise, and McCullers was touted as a young genius. In this work, set in 1930s Georgia, McCullers established her reputation for unusual characters, employing among her cast a deaf mute, a tomboy, a black physician, and a carnival worker. Critics noted McCullers's theme of loneliness and lauded her for her "astonishing perception of humanity."[5] Positive comments on McCullers's accomplishments were frequently paired with remarks about her age. For example, Louis B. Salomon wrote that her "character-perception" is "quite remarkable" in a "girl of twenty two."[6] For Richard Wright, McCullers's accomplishment lay in her realistic portrayal of Southern African Americans. He wrote, "To me the most impressive aspect of 'The Heart Is a

Lonely Hunter' is the astonishing humanity that enables a white writer, for the first time in Southern fiction, to handle Negro characters with as much ease and justice as those of her own race."[7]

McCullers followed *Heart* with *Reflections in a Golden Eye* (1941), which appeared in *Harper's Bazaar* and again centered on isolated misfits. Unlike her previous novel, however, this work met with mixed reviews, especially from readers who objected to the "abnormal" characters. Clifton Fadiman, echoing his criticism of McCullers's first novel, once again objected to her humorless use of the grotesque and urged her to "give herself a humorous once-over" and "find something to laugh at in the grotesque and forced hallucinations of which [the novel] is composed."[8] Basil Davenport called the work a "sad disappointment" by one who "seems hardly to comprehend" the "neurasthenic relationships" and "bizarrerie" of her own characters.[9] Fred Marsh again emphasized McCullers's age, writing that her "infant-terrible [sic] insight [was] expressed with quite grown up precision, as yet unmellowed and unhallowed."[10] Marsh reinforced his observations on McCullers's immaturity with suggestions that her publishers had pressured her into a hastily-written followup to her earlier success.

Reflections received some positive reviews, however. James Agee described it as a "mature and finished" masterpiece and "the Southern school at its most Gothic, but also at its best."[11] Writing the introduction to the second edition of *Reflections,* Tennessee Williams criticized reviewers' notions of the Southern Gothic and instead discussed those so-called Gothic qualities in terms of the "modern experience."[12]

Often considered McCullers's best work, *The Member of the Wedding* (1946) received mostly glowing reviews, although Edmund Wilson missed the point of what he called "interminable conversations in the kitchen"[13] and what George Dangerfield described as "three really weird people sitting in an even weirder kitchen."[14] Dangerfield, like other critics who praised McCullers's "universal" and abstract themes, viewed the central concern of the novel as the problem of "human loneliness." He wrote that McCullers explored this problem "savagely, gleefully, [and] tenderly" but without attempting to resolve it. He also noted the symbolic nature of McCullers's characters, who are neither "rounded" nor "quite human" but nevertheless "remind one of faces one *may have* seen, in a dream perhaps, in a tabloid newspaper possibly, or out of a train window" (Dangerfield's italics). In her review, Marguerite Young pursued this symbolic reading of McCullers's characters, contending that the book takes place on a metaphysical level as an argument about human happiness. She singles out McCullers's knack for "continually questioning a great many complacent assumptions as to what is what, for she is too closely a skeptical and analytical writer to suppose that in the accepted platitudes lies the truth."[15] According to Oliver Evans, this tendency to risk the reader's comfort level with unflattering and "uncomfortable" truths accounts for the history of mixed reactions to McCullers's work.[16]

With the novel's success and with the encouragement of Tennessee Williams, McCullers turned *The Member of the Wedding* into a play, which won the New York Drama Critics' Circle Award in 1950 and appeared on Broadway for 501 performances. Although it could not, since it was an adaptation, qualify for a Pulitzer Prize, Brooks Atkinson argued that of all the plays that year, it "came closest to Pulitzer prize specifications."[17] The play—starring Julie Harris (Frankie), Ethel Waters (Berenice), and Brandon de Wilde (John Henry), and with director Harold Clurman—won the Theatre Club, Inc., gold medal and Donaldson awards for best play, best director, and best supporting performance (de Wilde). Its popular success resolved McCullers's financial difficulties, and its critical success earned the novelist respect as a playwright. In his review John Mason Brown praised the cast and direction and connected the work's "plotlessness" and reliance on character and mood to Chekhov. He wrote that the script was the work of an "author who does not stoop to the expected stencils and who sees people with her own eyes rather than through borrowed spectacles."[18] Some critics, however, argued that McCullers lacked "dramatic imagination" and chalked her success up to "luck."[19] Such criticism prompted director Harold Clurman's explanation that the action of the play springs from the characters' "struggle for connection."[20]

McCullers had followed *Reflections* with *The Ballad of the Sad Café* (1943), a novella published in *Harper's Bazaar,* which received very little reviewer attention until 1951, when it was published in an omnibus edition, *"The Ballad of the Sad Café": The Novels and Short Stories of Carson McCullers.* This, along with *The Member of the Wedding,* is frequently considered her finest work. Coleman Rosenberger saw this collection as an "impressive and unified body of work {which} has been produced by Mrs. McCullers at an age when many another writer has hardly started his career."[21] He observed that the work in this volume is tied together by one central theme: "the human tragedy of the failure of communication between man and man, and the sense of loss and separation and loneliness which accompanies that failure." In keeping with this theme, he concluded, McCullers's "freaks" are the expression of the lonely condition of "Everyman." Similarly, in his positive review, William P. Clancy argued that McCullers's grotesques articulate the "metaphysical . . . complexities and frustrations which are so native to man that they can only be recognized, perhaps, in the shock which comes from seeing them dressed in the robes of the grotesque."[22] McCullers's *Ballad* is an "achievement equalled by few other contemporary writers."

Unlike her first foray into playwrighting, *The Square Root of Wonderful* (1957) met with abysmal reviews and closed after only seven weeks on Broadway. Such critical reaction prompted McCullers's vow never again to write for the stage. Originally the short story "Who Has Seen the Wind?" (later published in *The Mortgaged Heart*), this semiautobiographical play went through several producers and directors and was criticized for "stilted dialogue," "wooden action," and "unconvincing characters."[23] Richard Hayes, echoing a familiar refrain in McCullers criticism, saw in it a "bizarre reality" and remarked on its "thematic confusion."[24] His comments seem to grow out of frustration at locating McCullers's position—her failure to impose a defining moral framework on the drama. Wolcott Gibbs, in his unflattering review, called the play a "wan and aimless parody" and spoke of the heroine as a "pinhead" and the "hero and villain [as] a rather stifling moralist and a boozily grandiloquent psychopath, respectively."[25] More than one critic complained that the title was the best part and that the play demonstrated McCullers's unsuitedness for drama.[26] However, critics did admit that it made "surprisingly good reading."[27]

Clock Without Hands (1961), McCullers's final novel, met with mixed reviews but was a popular success, appearing on the *New York Times* bestseller list. Reviewers protested the same old things: strangeness, morbidity, freakishness. Rumer Godden viewed these qualities positively, arguing (as Marguerite Young had and as Oliver Evans would) that McCullers's truths are "not always palatable" and that "[t]ruth . . . can give an uncomfortable bleakness. . . . This book may well be too strange and strong, too frank, for many people."[28] She called McCullers's talent "extraordinary" and "apart, aloof, inevitably lonely."

But most reviewers were disappointed with McCullers's fifth novel and seemed to think that, in the years since *The Member of the Wedding,* she had lost her touch. Although most admired the fine prose style of the novel, they had difficulty coming to grips with its treatment of what they termed a "public" issue, the Supreme Court's decision on integration. Gore Vidal suggested that "the book is odd . . . because what has always been the most private of responses has been rudely startled and bemused by the world outside."[29] Such inability to accept a socially conscious McCullers was perhaps at the center of Catharine Hughes's criticism that Malone is "basically unnecessary to the Clanes; yet he is there."[30] McCullers's attempt to place the dying of J. T. Malone explicitly in a sociohistorical framework met mostly with reviewer confusion and derision. As Donald Emerson wrote, "It is a mistake. . . . The symbolic roles which were to have given *Clock Without Hands* its forceful social reference detract from the effectiveness of the novel on the level of immediate, inward experience where Mrs. McCullers' powers are greatest."[31] Whereas the child-genius, androgynous McCullers's freakish portrayals of human loneliness and the "human condition" were signs of her artistry, her "adult" (and last) attempt to locate these issues directly in a specific social context met with disapproval.

The Mortgaged Heart (1971), a posthumous collection of McCullers's fiction (most not previously published), essays, and poems, edited by her sister Margarita G. Smith, has been valued chiefly for the background it provides about the author. Jeanne Kinney thought it a "valuable appendage to devotees of the author's major works,"[32] but many reviewers have winced at these "embarrassing" and "undistinguished" "apprentice works."[33] Melvin J. Friedman criticized the "worst-foot-forward" approach of the book and described the contents as "prematurely removed from the drawing board."[34] Walter Clemons's "A Memento for Collectors" cited the volume as evidence of a career in "decline from its beginnings."[35] However, the volume establishes in McCullers's early writing the style, characterization, and themes of adolescence and loneliness that readers recognize in her more polished works. Critics have also found significant the section on "Writers and Writing," which includes seven essays McCullers wrote about her artistic credo. In one of these, "The Flowering Dream," McCullers explains her use of "morbidity" or the "abnormal" as a metaphor for human loneliness and the need for love.

Although most reviewers acknowledged McCullers's genius and talent, they tended to agree that she wrote her best work in the 1940s and that, thereafter, for whatever reasons, she produced little to add to her literary reputation. This viewpoint may reflect less on McCullers's later achievements than on critics' inability to come to terms with the maturity of a writer they preferred to consider a tomboyish adolescent. One might also argue that McCullers is a writer's writer. Consistently, well-regarded poets, novelists, and playwrights responded favorably to her work, commenting on her technical genius and artistic vision. This roster of well-known writers, many reprinted here in the "Reviews" and "Tributes" sections, includes Richard Wright, May Sarton, Julian Symons, James Agee, Marguerite Young, Irving Howe, Rumer Godden, Dorothy Parker, Penelope Mortimer, Nadine Gordimer, Muriel Rukeyser, Tennessee Williams, Kay Boyle, and William Trevor.

II. TRENDS IN LITERARY SCHOLARSHIP

> Certainly I have always felt alone. In addition to being lonely, a writer is also amorphous. A writer soon discovers he has no single identity but lives the lives of all the people he creates and his weathers are independent of the actual day around him. I live with the people I create and it has always made my essential loneliness less keen.
> —Carson McCullers, Preface to *The Square Root of Wonderful* [36]

Literary critics began to attend to McCullers's work with the publication of the omnibus edition of *The Ballad of the Sad Café* in 1951, which confirmed the existence of a significant McCullers canon. Until recently, this body of literary criticism was remarkably consistent in drawing upon McCullers's stated themes of love and loneliness, the capacity for art to mediate this loneliness, and the relationship of these themes to their execution through use of what has been variously termed the "grotesque" and Gothic or, less positively, the writer's penchant for the "bizarre," "abnormal," and "morbid."

The task many critics set for themselves was to resolve the tension between a childlike (or at least adolescent), sexually ambiguous Southern "girl" and the strange and discomforting subject matter she chose. In the 1950s and 1960s, scholars resolved the problem of what to do with McCullers through critical strategies that seemed to make her "safe." They framed her oddness in universal and abstract terms, viewing her adolescents, androgyns, and misfits as archetypal symbols for the human condition. Dayton Kohler's "Carson McCullers: Variations on a Theme" established the idea of "unity" of theme—loneliness and longing"—in McCullers's works.[37] According to Kohler, McCullers blends realism and symbolism to craft characters ("grotesques") "whose physical deformities reveal outwardly the twisted, distorted spirits of their inner lives." He suggests that McCullers's work, including *Heart, Reflections,* and *Ballad,* is concerned with the problem of communication for the isolated inhabitants of a modern world. Although it is not allegory, a "systematic and mechanical" approach that "trace[s] an idea," her work *is* one of myth, "haunted by the elusive nature of human truth."

In the 1950s and 1960s several critics followed Kohler's lead in writing about McCullers's theme of isolation. Oliver Evans's 1952 essay argues that this theme evolves throughout her three works and that, ultimately, love is unable to mediate human loneliness.[38] Jane Hart writes sensitively about McCullers's art, finding there the "air of simple, starlike purity and beauty, the truth and humility of one who has learned to love a rock, a tree, a cloud, and finally all mankind."[39] Like Kohler, Hart discusses the relationship of McCullers's theme of loneliness to the grotesque and regards McCullers's Gothic as comprising a "larger vision" than that of Welty or Capote. This larger vision is that "the loneliest of human souls is found in the abnormal and the deformed, the outward and manifest symbol of human separateness." Hart articulates McCullers's now famous theory of love, expressed in *Ballad,* arguing that only the lover gains in her canon, "even if the way is sorrow."

Extending Hart's comments and responding to criticisms that McCullers lacks the "scope, strength, and fury" of Faulkner, Ihab Hassan placed McCullers's use of the Gothic squarely in traditions of Southern literature and the contemporary American novel.[40] He contends that her work is concerned with the "transcendental idea of spiritual loneliness," which is expressed through her Gothic use of the grotesque. The grotesque, Hassan argues, stands "in a necessary and paradoxical relation to the facts of Southern life which emphasizes the power of tradition and pull of community." Several other essays about McCullers's treatment of loneliness appeared around this time, including those by Horace Taylor and John B. Vickery, as did a psychological study by David Madden.[41]

The 1960s saw the publication of several critical assessments of McCullers's career. Oliver Evans's important literary biography appeared in

1965 and included analyses of her major works and critical responses to them.[42] In another essay, Evans posed the question, Why is McCullers so unpopular with the critics? He argues that her work, like Hawthorne's and Melville's, concerns the "labyrinths of the human heart" and that she, like these predecessors, articulates her views in allegorical form.[43] Evans speculates that McCullers's capacity for revealing realistic yet "[un]popular" ideas has led to her problem with the critics.

Another way to explain the discomfort and strangeness of McCullers and her work was to categorize her as a limited or minor writer or even as a "failure." In his overview of McCullers's fiction, Klaus Lubbers argues that her vision of life gains in "order and meaning" as her work progresses.[44] Instead of focusing on loneliness, as earlier scholars had, Lubbers shifts the discussion to "man's problematic and painful existence." McCullers presents life at various "critical points," he observes, including adolescence, death, and loss. Lubbers's assessment of McCullers's career places her in a "Southern triad" with Porter and Welty, but he finds her inferior to Faulkner. This failure, he contends, might be attributed to her "inability" to grasp the burden of tradition and the land or to achieve a certain passion characteristic of Southern writers such as Faulkner and Warren. Given his acknowledgment of a Southern triad of *women* authors, Lubbers's expectation that all Southern writers address the "collective burdens of the fathers" seems curious.

McCullers's "failure" to capture a Southern sense of place is intimately linked, according to Chester E. Eisinger, to her removal from "ideological conflicts in the contemporary world."[45] Eisinger believes that McCullers is cut off not only from the South but from society, morality, religion, and ideas. Similarly, Robert Drake writes that McCullers's "artistic failures . . . deny her a place among the most accomplished and compelling practitioners of twentieth-century American fiction."[46] Drake attributes her "failure," in Hawthornean terms, to a separation of head from heart, a result of her moving away from the South yet continuing to write about it. However, Drake is one of the first critics to address the role race plays in her fiction, calling her African-American characters the "moral and technical center" of her work (an observation that, of course, invokes Faulkner).

With McCullers's death, assessment of her career turned even more emphatically to her place in the Southern tradition. Delma Eugene Presley concurs with Drake that McCullers's portrayals of Southern life are unrealistic; Presley claims that the author failed to understand her heritage and tradition mainly because she was not a member of the upper classes and because she moved away.[47] Although Presley views McCullers's characters as typical of Southern fiction, he echoes Eisinger and earlier commentators in criticizing McCullers's inattention to historical and social contexts. Richard Gray argues that McCullers does not belong to the Southern Renaissance and that she had a mere five-year period of creativity; thus, she is not a major writer but a "very good minor one."[48] Gray diverges from Eisinger's earlier argument, however, in suggesting that Southern history functions as an "absent presence" in her work—that it is more concealed than evaded. McCullers's point, Gray concludes, is that "history, as a common secular resonance and modern substitute for God," is dead.

Richard Cook, on the other hand, ties McCullers's regional "limits" to her restricted thematic and emotional range. He too argues that McCullers's sense of isolation is not connected to contemporary issues. But he believes McCullers's failure to contextualize her work properly lies in her early flight from the South and her attempts to write about it from too great a distance in both time and place.[49]

In the 1970s critics turned from placing the body of McCullers's work within American literary canons to closer and more extended readings of her individual texts. For example, John McNally's article on *The Ballad of the Sad Café* demonstrates the narrator's centrality. McNally argues that the work's vision belongs to the narrator, not to McCullers, as has always been claimed, and that his [sic] so-called digressions measure his search for truth. McNally's essay also explains the epilogue, usually viewed as separate from the narrative proper, as the "positive act of a man of changed perspective."[50] Joseph R. Millichap finds that *The Ballad of the Sad Café* is best read within the context of the ballad tradition. His reading aims to minimize its expressed theory of love, which is after all only the narrator's credo. Millichap contends that by privileging the ballad world of passion, violence, omens, and portents, the reader can better separate the narrator from McCullers and locate the author's viewpoint where it belongs: in the community of the chain gang.[51]

Ray Mathis argues that *Reflections in a Golden Eye* is a critique of modern Christianity that catches its characters in a "universe of materialistic determinism."[52] He claims that McCullers secularizes and mythologizes love even as she frees man from the myths of the past. Mary Etta Scott's study of *Clock Without Hands* also brings philosophy to bear on McCullers's work. She advances the notion that the work expresses an existential truth: Only in facing death does man find meaning.[53]

Robert Phillips revised previous readings of McCullers's "freaks" by analyzing nineteen of her short stories.[54] He argues that, whereas the novels are peopled with freaks, the short stories depict an inner "freaking out," a dissociation from and disunity with society that amount to what McCullers described as spiritual isolation. He suggests that all of her characters are seeking unification of spirit with the environment and that this search is portrayed with much less "sensationalism" in the short stories.

The decade following McCullers's death also saw the publication of important reference materials on McCullers, including Adrian Shapiro's bibliography,[55] which is indispensable for tracking down elusive newspaper and periodical pieces, and Virginia Spencer Carr's meticulous biography, *The Lonely Hunter.* Carr draws on interviews with and letters from McCullers's family, friends, and acquaintances and emphasizes McCullers's childhood in

Georgia, her relationship to New York City literati, her dysfunctional marriages, her literary successes and failures, and her illness and death. The availability of this biographical information spawned literary criticism such as Louis D. Rubin's article, which draws on Carr's "horrifying" account and links McCullers's treatment of grotesque characters and themes of loneliness to her illness, "physical aberration," unconventional marriages, homosexuality, and, finally, to her Southern experience.[56]

Beginning in the 1970s and 1980s, critics have questioned those studies that treat McCullers's work in terms of abstract themes of loneliness and love and those who find "abnormal" her testing of social and sexual boundaries. From feminist, African-American, New Historicist, and poststructuralist perspectives, scholars have concerned themselves with recovering in these literary historical narratives McCullers's use of gendered and racialized characters positioned in specific sociohistorical contexts. Other critics have attempted to place McCullers in dialogue with various American literary traditions besides the Southern Gothic, including women's writing, the Romanticism of Melville and Hawthorne, and modernist alienation.

According to two essays in this volume, McCullers's social and political vision becomes emphatically clear once we take her work out of context. Addressing McCullers's reception in Great Britain, Cicely Palser Havely considers McCullers one of the few women novelists to move beyond the personal vision and "feminine" form that Jane Austen and Charlotte Brontë established.[57] Havely argues that *Clock Without Hands* "achieves a rare and impressive balance between the demands of private feeling and the claims and pressures of the public world." Similarly, Robert Aldridge's essay on the film version of *The Heart Is a Lonely Hunter* focuses on the topical concerns of the novel, which, except for the issue of race, are absent from the otherwise "quiet, principled complement to McCullers' vision."[58]

Gayatri Chakravorty Spivak's "Three Feminist Readings: McCullers, Drabble, Habermas" called for an approach to McCullers's works that goes beyond traditional readings and themes of lost innocence to examine race, class, and sex dynamics. Spivak argues that *The Heart Is a Lonely Hunter* dramatizes the "failure of collectivity" reflected in specific race, class, and gender boundaries with which Mick and Singer struggle.[59] She suggests that such reexamination forces us to confront our own ideologies as they are figured forth in constructions of the "other" in Western literature.

Several feminist critics have recently situated McCullers in various feminine traditions of writing. For example, Linda Huf's study of women's "artist" novels uses *The Heart Is a Lonely Hunter* to illustrate her point that "woman" and "artist" are opposed terms in Western literature.[60] After tracing the gender-biased criticism surrounding both McCullers and her work, Huf demonstrates not only that Mick's creativity and identity must be sacrificed to conventional femininity but also that this "failure," brought on by a sexist culture, is consistently viewed by critics as a "success." In a similar vein, Barbara White argues that *The Member of the Wedding* articulates a young woman's acceptance of feminine limitations.[61]

Louise Westling locates McCullers's treatment of gender within a Southern women's tradition that includes Welty and O'Connor. This tradition grows out of these writers' struggles with limiting constructions of Southern femininity. Focusing on the absence of mothers and on images of androgyny, homosexuality, and transvestism, Westling writes that McCullers's heroines test gender boundaries, which, for McCullers, are always constraining and problematic.[62] Sandra M. Gilbert and Susan Gubar suggest that the female Southern gothic, with its emphasis on sexual conflict and gender confusion, is a direct response to post–World War II attacks on feminism. In McCullers's works "[m]ale willfulness or brutality" and "female freakishness" are emblematic of postwar fears of women's threat to patriarchal hegemony.[63]

Recently, Emily Miller Budick has contextualized McCullers's work in traditions of male and female romance, arguing that her concern is with the "truth of the human heart" and yet is grounded in the "material and maternal."[64] According to Budick, "female romance" links human creativity with family and community, and McCullers achieves this through "multivocalism, authorial decenteredness, and indeterminate open-endedness." Budick believes that McCullers addresses politics and ideology in indirect ways. She argues that *The Heart Is a Lonely Hunter* is "committed to speaking" and, therefore, to understanding and to community. In some sense, Budick responds to readings such as Samuel Coale's, which places McCullers's work in the romance tradition of Hawthorne but describes it as alienated, one that traps individuals yet yearns for the "brotherhood of all men."[65] Budick's essay thus reconsiders the false categorizing that McCullers's work has undergone as a result of her gendered relationship to American traditions.

Ultimately, this recent scholarship questions the relationships among McCullers's works, definitions of American literary traditions, and assumptions about gendered identities and landscapes. Although she has sometimes been considered a "simple" author with only one or two themes, McCullers's critics have consistently struggled with her "uncomfortable truths." The critical history of McCullers scholarship is one of disagreement over the images, traditions, and assumptions that have labelled her. This volume attempts not only to trace that history but to build on McCullers's own statement about her "amorphous" identity through new essays. These new essays extend the work of feminist and New Historicist studies and consider her work from African-American and lesbian perspectives. Perhaps in acknowledging the fluid identities this writer embraces for herself and her characters, we might move toward the necessary discomfort she imagined.

Kent State University

Notes

1. Louis D. Rubin Jr., "Carson McCullers: The Aesthetic of Pain," *Virginia Quarterly Review* 53 (1977): 265–83.

2. Cited in *The Writer's Chapbook, a Compendium of Fact, Opinion, Wit, and Advice from the 20th Century's Preeminent Writers,* ed. George Plimpton (New York: Penguin, 1989), 342.

3. See Virginia Spencer Carr, *The Lonely Hunter: A Biography of Carson McCullers* (Garden City, N.Y.: Doubleday, 1975).

4. Oliver Evans, "The Case of Carson McCullers," *Georgia Review* 18 (1964): 40–45.

5. Rose Feld, "A Remarkable First Novel of Lonely Lives," *New York Times Book Review,* 16 June 1940, 6. See also Ben Ray Redman, "Of Human Loneliness," *The Saturday Review of Literature* 22 (8 June 1940): 6.

6. Louis B. Salomon, "Someone to Talk To," *The Nation,* 13 July 1940, 36.

7. Richard Wright, "Inner Landscape," *New Republic,* 5 August 1940, 195.

8. Clifton Fadiman, Review of *Reflections in a Golden Eye, New Yorker,* 15 February 1941, 80.

9. Basil Davenport, Review of *Reflections in a Golden Eye, The Saturday Review of Literature,* 22 February 1941, 12.

10. Fred Marsh, "At an Army Post," *New York Times Book Review,* 2 March 1941, 6.

11. [James Agee], "Masterpiece at 24," *Time,* 17 February 1941, 96.

12. Tennessee Williams, "Introduction," *Reflections in a Golden Eye* by Carson McCullers, New Classics Series (Norfolk, Conn.: New Directions, 1950), xi–xii.

13. Edmund Wilson, "Two Books that Leave You Blank: Carson McCullers, Siegfried Sassoon," *New Yorker,* 30 March 1946, 87.

14. George Dangerfield, "An Adolescent's Four Days," *The Saturday Review of Literature,* 30 March 1946, 15.

15. Marguerite Young, "Metaphysical Fiction," *Kenyon Review* 9 (Winter 1947): 151–55.

16. See Oliver Evans, "The Case of Carson McCullers."

17. Cited in Virginia Spencer Carr, *Understanding Carson McCullers* (Columbia, S.C.: University of South Carolina Press, 1990), 97.

18. John Mason Brown, "Plot Me No Plots," *Saturday Review,* 28 January 1950, 27–29.

19. Kappo Phelan, "The Stage—'A [sic] Member of the Wedding,' " *The Commonweal,* 27 January 1950, 438.

20. Harold Clurman, "Theatre: From a Member," *New Republic,* 1 January 1950, 28.

21. Coleman Rosenberger, "A Carson McCullers Omnibus," *New York Herald Tribune Book Review,* 10 June 1951, 1.

22. William P. Clancy, Review of *The Ballad of the Sad Café, The Commonweal,* 15 June 1951, 243.

23. Anonymous, "Playwright Tells of Pangs," *Philadelphia Inquirer,* 13 October 1957, B–1, 5, cited in Carr, *Understanding Carson McCullers,* 100.

24. Richard Hayes, "Private Worlds," *The Commonweal,* 13 December 1957, 288–89.

25. Wolcott Gibbs, "The Theater: Music and Words," *New Yorker,* 9 November 1957, 103–05.

26. See A. Alvarez, "Circling the Squares," *The Observer* (London), 15 March 1959, 23; "Coups de Théâtre," *Times Literary Supplement,* 27 February 1959, 110; *Kirkus* 26 (1 May 1958): 348.

27. See Oliver Evans, *The Ballad of Carson McCullers: A Biography* (New York: Coward McCann, 1966), 168. See also *Kirkus* 26 (1 May 1958): 348.

28. Rumer Godden, "Death and Life in a Small Southern Town," *New York Herald Tribune Books,* 17 September 1961, 5.

29.   Gore Vidal, "Carson McCullers's 'Clock without Hands,' " in *Rocking the Boat* (New York: Little, Brown, 1963), 212.

30.   Catharine Hughes, "A World of Outcasts," *The Commonweal,* 13 October 1961, 74.

31.   Donald Emerson, "The Ambiguities of *Clock without Hands*" *Wisconsin Studies in Contemporary Literature* 3 (Fall 1962): 15–28.

32.   Jeanne Kinney, Review of *The Mortgaged Heart, Best Sellers* (University of Scranton), 15 November 1971, 371.

33.   John Alfred Avant, Review of *The Mortgaged Heart, Library Journal,* 1 January 1972, 73.

34.   Melvin J. Friedman, "*The Mortgaged Heart:* The Workshop of Carson McCullers," *Revue des Langues Vivantes* (U.S. Bicentennial Issue 1976): 146, 144.

35.   Walter Clemons, Review of *The Mortgaged Heart, New York Times Book Review,* 7 November 1971, 7, 12.

36.   Carson McCullers, "A Personal Preface," *The Square Root of Wonderful* (Cambridge, Mass.: Riverside, 1958), viii.

37.   Dayton Kohler, "Carson McCullers: Variations on a Theme," *College English* 13 (October 1951): 1–8.

38.   Oliver Evans, "The Theme of Spiritual Isolation in Carson McCullers," in *New World Writing: First Mentor Selection* (New York: New American Library of World Literature, 1952), 333–48.

39.   Jane Hart, "Carson McCullers: Pilgrim of Loneliness," *Georgia Review* 11 (Spring 1957): 53–58.

40.   Ihab Hassan, "Carson McCullers: The Alchemy of Love and Aesthetics of Pain," *Radical Innocence: Studies in the Contemporary Novel* (Princeton: Princeton University Press, 1961), 200.

41.   Horace Taylor, "*The Heart Is a Lonely Hunter:* A Southern Waste Land," in *Studies in American Literature,* ed. Waldo McNeir and Leo B. Levy (Baton Rouge: Louisiana State University Press, 1960), 154–60; John B. Vickery, "Carson McCullers: A Map of Love," *Wisconsin Studies in Contemporary Literature* 1 (Winter 1960): 13–24; David Madden, "The Paradox of the Need for Privacy and the Need for Understanding in Carson McCullers' *The Heart Is a Lonely Hunter,*" *Literature and Psychology* 17.2–3 (1967): 128–40.

42.   Oliver Evans, *Carson McCullers: Her Life and Work* (London: Peter Owen, 1965).

43.   Oliver Evans, "The Case of Carson McCullers," 42, 44.

44.   Klaus Lubbers, "The Necessary Order: A Study of Theme and Structure in Carson McCullers' Fiction," *Jahrbuch für Amerikanstudien* 8 (1963): 187–200.

45.   Chester E. Eisinger, *Fiction of the Forties* (Chicago: University of Chicago Press, 1963), 243.

46.   Robert Drake, "The Lonely Heart of Carson McCullers," *The Christian Century* 85 (10 January 1968): 50–51.

47.   Delma Eugene Presley, "Carson McCullers and the South," *Georgia Review* 28 (Spring 1974): 19–32.

48.   Richard Gray, *The Literature of Memory: Modern Writers of the American South* (Baltimore: Johns Hopkins University Press, 1977), 273.

49.   Richard Cook, *Carson McCullers* (New York: Ungar, 1975), 125.

50.   John McNally, "The Introspective Narrator in *The Ballad of the Sad Café,*" *South Atlantic Bulletin* 38 (November 1973): 40–44.

51.   Joseph R. Millichap, "Carson McCullers' Literary Ballad," *Georgia Review* 27 (Fall 1973): 329–39.

52.   Ray Mathis, "*Reflections in a Golden Eye:* Myth-Making in American Christianity," *Religion in Life* 39 (Winter 1970): 545–58.

53.   Mary Etta Scott, "An Existential Everyman," *West Virginia University Philological Papers* 27 (1979): 82–88.

54.   Robert Phillips, "Freaking Out: The Short Stories of Carson McCullers," *Southwest Review* 63 (1978): 65–73.

55.   Adrian M. Shapiro, Jackson R. Bryer, and Kathleen Field, *Carson McCullers: A Descriptive Listing and Annotated Bibliography of Criticism* (New York: Garland, 1980). See also Robert F. Kiernan, *Katherine Anne Porter and Carson McCullers: A Reference Guide* (Boston: G.K. Hall, 1976); Virginia Spencer Carr and Joseph R. Millichap, "Carson McCullers," in *American Women Writers: Bibliographical Essays,* ed. Maurice Duke, Jackson R. Bryer, and M. Thomas Inge (Westport, Conn.: Greenwood, 1983), 297–319; Virginia Spencer Carr, "Carson McCullers," in *Fifty Southern Writers After 1900: A Bio-Bibliographical Sourcebook,* ed. Robert Bain and Joseph M. Flora (Westport, Conn.: Greenwood, 1986), 301–12.

56.   Louis D. Rubin Jr., "Carson McCullers: The Aesthetic of Pain," 274.

57.   Cicely Palser Havely, "Two Women Novelists: Carson McCullers and Flannery O'Connor," in *The Uses of Fiction,* ed. Douglas Jefferson and Graham Martin (Milton Keynes: Open University Press, 1982), 115–24.

58.   Robert Aldridge, "Two Planetary Systems," in *The Modern American Novel and the Movies,* ed. Gerald Peary and Roger Shatzkin (New York: Ungar, 1978), 119–30.

59.   Gayatri Chakravorty Spivak, "Three Feminist Readings: McCullers, Drabble, Habermas," *Union Seminary Quarterly* 35 (1979–1980): 15–34.

60.   Linda Huf, *Portrait of the Artist as a Young Woman: The Writer as Heroine in American Fiction* (New York: Ungar, 1983), 105–23.

61.   Barbara White, *Growing Up Female: Adolescent Girlhood in American Fiction* (New York: Greenwood, 1985, 89–111.

62.   Louise Westling, *Sacred Groves and Ravaged Gardens: The Fiction of Eudora Welty, Carson McCullers, and Flannery O'Connor* (Athens: University of Georgia Press, 1985), 110–32.

63.   Sandra M. Gilbert and Susan Gubar, *The War of the Words,* vol. 1 of *No Man's Land: The Place of the Woman Writer in the Twentieth Century* (New Haven: Yale University Press, 1988), 100–12.

64.   Emily Miller Budick, *Engendering Romance: Women Writers and the Hawthorne Tradition, 1850–1990* (New Haven: Yale University Press, 1994), 143–61.

65.   Samuel Coale, *In Hawthorne's Shadow: American Romance from Melville to Mailer* (Lexington: University Press of Kentucky, 1985), 84.

REVIEWS
◆

THE HEART IS A LONELY HUNTER

♦

Inner Landscape

RICHARD WRIGHT*

Out of the tradition of Gertrude Stein's experiments in style and the clipped, stout prose of Sherwood Anderson and Ernest Hemingway comes Carson McCullers' *The Heart Is a Lonely Hunter*. With the depression as a murky backdrop, this first novel depicts the bleak landscape of the American consciousness below the Mason-Dixon line. Miss McCullers' picture of loneliness, death, accident, insanity, fear, mob violence and terror is perhaps the most desolate that has so far come from the South. Her quality of despair is unique and individual; and it seems to me more natural and authentic than that of Faulkner. Her groping characters live in a world more completely lost than any Sherwood Anderson ever dreamed of. And she recounts incidents of death and attitudes of stoicism in sentences whose neutrality makes Hemingway's terse prose seem warm and partisan by comparison. Hovering mockingly over her story of loneliness in a small town are primitive religion, adolescent hope, the silence of deaf mutes—and all of these give the violent colors of the life she depicts a sheen of weird tenderness.

It is impossible to read the book and not wonder about the person who wrote it, the literary antecedents of her style and the origins of such a confounding vision of life. The jacket of the book tells us with great reserve that she is twenty-two years old. Because the novel treats of life in the South, we assume that she is Southern born and reared. A recent news story says she is married and now lives in New York. And that is all.

I don't know what the book is about; the nearest I can come to indicating its theme is to refer to the Catholic confessional or the private office of the psychoanalyst. The characters, Negro and white, are "naturals," and are seen from a point of view that endows them with a mythlike quality. The core of the book is the varied relationships of these characters to Singer, a lonely deaf mute. There are Mick Kelly, a sensitive, adolescent white girl; aged Dr. Copeland, the hurt and frustrated Negro; Jake Blount, a nervous and unbal-

*Reprinted from the *New Republic* 103 (5 August 1940): 195.

anced whiskey-head; and Biff Brannon, whose consciousness is one mass of timid bewilderment. All these characters and many more feel that the deaf mute alone understands them; they assail his deaf ears with their troubles and hopes, thereby revealing their intense loneliness and denied capacity for living.

When the deaf mute's friend dies in an insane asylum, he commits suicide, an act which deprives the confessional of its priest. The lives of Miss McCullers' characters are resolved thus: Mick Kelly is doomed to a life of wage slavery in a five-and-ten-cent store; Dr. Copeland is beaten by a mob of whites when he protests against the injustices meted out to his race; Jake Blount stumbles off alone, wistfully, to seek a place in the South where he can take hold of reality through Marxism; and Biff Brannon steels himself to live a life of emptiness.

The naturalistic incidents of which the book is compounded seem to be of no importance; one has the feeling that any string of typical actions would have served the author's purpose as well, for the value of such writing lies not so much in what is said as in the angle of vision from which life is seen. There are times when Miss McCullers deliberately suppresses the naturally dramatic in order to linger over and accentuate the more obscure, oblique and elusive emotions.

To me the most impressive aspect of *The Heart Is a Lonely Hunter* is the astonishing humanity that enables a white writer, for the first time in Southern fiction, to handle Negro characters with as much ease and justice as those of her own race. This cannot be accounted for stylistically or politically; it seems to stem from an attitude toward life which enables Miss McCullers to rise above the pressures of her environment and embrace white and black humanity in one sweep of apprehension and tenderness.

In the conventional sense, this is not so much a novel as a projected mood, a state of mind poetically objectified in words, an attitude externalized in naturalistic detail. Whether you will want to read the book depends upon the extent to which you value the experience of discovering the stale and familiar terms of everyday life bathed in a rich and strange meaning, devoid of pettiness and sentimentality.

Pitiful Hunt For Security:
Tragedy of Unfulfillment Theme of Story
That Will Rank High in American Letters

MAY SARTON*[1]

We have been waiting a long time for a new writer. There have been candid-camera studies of American life, past and present. There have been the usual quota of sensitively recorded novels of personal experience. We have had spontaneous combustion and a good deal of fine etching, wild men who conquered by their vitality and brilliant women who conquered by their style. But we have waited a long time for a new writer, and now one has appeared it is an occasion for hosannahs. Her name is Carson McCullers. She is 22 years old. We have waited a long time for a piece of American literature. Carson McCullers has done all the things other writers have done in pieces and she has done something besides which makes *The Heart Is a Lonely Hunter* literature.

This is the story of a group of people and their lives in a small southern town. It might be almost anywhere. It might be round the corner. Miss McCullers has given us a dozen people who are each absolutely strange and absolutely true so that we know they are real people and we believe everything they do and say, whether it's Mick ordering beer and a chocolate ice-cream soda together on a hot evening, or Dr. Copeland, the Negro doctor, walking out of a family reunion raging over the names of his children, Karl-Marx, Hamilton, Portia, whom he had named with a "real true purpose" but who had not been able to understand their names or the purpose. Whether it's Jake Blount going berserk with savage indignation in a Negro-white fight with razors at the merry-go-round. Whether it's the relationship between Mick and her sore, tough little brother or that between two deaf mutes bound together like the spirit and the flesh, we believe these people and they are our own.

At the end of the book we know them better than our own fathers and mothers and brothers and sisters and we see why they are as they are. The truth about people is always strange, sometimes fantastic, but it is always rec-

---

*Reprinted from the *Boston Evening Transcript,* 8 June 1940, IV:1, by permission of the author.

ognizable. Carson McCullers has given us a group of people in the whole of their humanity and she has given us their relationship to each other, with absolute truth.

DRIVEN BY NEED

But it is not enough to put together a group of people and their relationships. In a letter Tchekov said: "Remember that the writers whom we call eternal or simply good and who intoxicate us have one common and very important characteristic: they get somewhere, and they summon you there and you feel, not with your mind but with your whole being, that they have a certain purpose and, like the ghost of Hamlet's father, do not come and excite the imagination for nothing. The best of them are realistic and paint life as it is but you feel, besides life as it is, also life as it ought to be, and this captivates you."

Every one of these people is driven by an idea, by an inner necessity. Each has a strong need or purpose and each during the course of the book is defeated and we know, because we know all about them, that they were bound to be defeated and there was no hope for them. "There was something not natural about it all, something like an ugly joke," says Biff Brannon to himself and Mick, working for $10 a week in the five and ten with no way of saving for a piano, says: "It was like she was cheated. Only nobody had cheated her. So there was nobody to take it out on. However, just the same she had that feeling. Cheated."

LIVING WORDS

This book is literature. Because it is literature, when one puts it down it is not with a feeling of emptiness and despair (which an outline of the plot might suggest), but with a feeling of having been nourished by the truth. For one knows at the end that it is these cheated people, these with burning intense needs and purposes, who must inherit the earth. They are the reason for the existence of a democracy which is still to be created. This is the way it is, one says to oneself—but not forever.

We have been waiting a long time for a new writer and of this one we must expect a great deal. From the critical point of view there are, it seems to me, just two flaws in the book: one, as the theme is the tragedy inherent in the lives of the people, in the bitter struggle for personal dignity and fulfillment, it was a mistake to allow also the tragedy of accident, the tragedy not inherent in the very stuff of the lives, to take place. There are two incidents, that concerning Bubber and his gun and that final incident between Harry and Mick, of which this might be said. Neither is false. Both are believable but neither is necessary. The beauty of the book is that except for these, every action seems inevitable.

UNFORGETTABLE

The other flaw seems to me the inclusion of Part III. It is natural to wish to tie up all the ends of a book in a neat way. But perhaps Carson McCullers was not aware what momentum she had created in the minds of the readers by the final tragedy. We would go on and think to ourselves all that she has carefully put down in Part III. It would be better to let us do so for ourselves. As it is the book goes on living in an astonishing way in the mind. Something has been added to our life. It is hard to think that we shall have to wait a year or two before we can expect another book from this extraordinary young woman.

Note

1.   May Sarton's appreciative comments about this book might well apply to her own writing. Her next novel will be about Boston. [Ed. of the *Transcript*]

The Lonely Heart

JULIAN SYMONS*

It is within the scope of few novelists at any time to project in their work a wholly personal vision of the world. Most reflect, consciously or unconsciously, the patterns of their age and condition: the truth that they try to set down is one to make a reader exclaim that this was really how people lived in a certain place and time. But there is another kind of truth, imaginative and fabulous, which is seen by another kind of artist. The truths of Trollope or of Turgenev are literal, those of Dickens or Dostoievsky are fabulous visions of the nature of humanity. The most important thing about the work of Miss Carson McCullers is that as an artist she seeks for a fabulous, not a literal, truth. She has a vision of the loneliness of mankind. She approaches this loneliness from many aspects, but always with a poetic vision that takes it off the ground of everyday reality and transforms our common loneliness into something rich and strange.

. . .

The idea that . . . illusions can offer desirable enrichments to human lives is at the core of Miss McCullers's only full-length novel, *The Heart Is a Lonely Hunter,* first published here in 1943, and now reissued. The reissue is very welcome, for it is in this book that her sense of human isolation is most finely put down, and that her compassionate irony obtains its fullest play.

The book is set in a small town in the middle of the deep South. Its central character is a deaf mute named John Singer, who through his very silence and his power of attention to others assumes overwhelming importance in the lives of four confused and frustrated people: a drunken radical agitator who has failed hopelessly in attempts to make other working people feel his own sense of injustice, an atheistic Negro doctor who is bitterly disappointed by the failure of his children to follow his work for Negro emancipation, an adolescent girl who somehow identifies Singer with her passionate love of music, and an impotent restaurant proprietor whose wife has recently died. All of them find some deep satisfaction in visiting the thoughtful, composed and gentle deaf mute. The agitator, Jake Blount, asks him at the end of a long

*Excerpt reprinted from "Human Isolation," *TLS,* 17 July 1953, 460, as revised and reprinted in *Critical Occasions,* by Julian Symons (Hamish Hamilton, 1966), 106–11, by permission of the journal. © Times Supplements Ltd. 1953.

22

political tirade: "When a person *knows* and can't make the others understand, what does he do?" When Singer takes out his silver pencil and writes on a slip of paper, "Are you Democrat or Republican?" Blount feels, in spite of the inadequacy of the reply, that Singer understands him. Doctor Copeland talks at length to Singer, feeling that unlike all other white men he understands "the strong, true purpose" of emancipation. For the poor girl Mick Kelly, desperately attempting to make a violin out of a broken ukulele, the occasions when she listens to the radio in Singer's room are magical, and Singer himself seems like God—"When she thought of what she used to imagine was God she could only see Mister Singer with a long, white sheet around him." To the restaurant proprietor Biff Brannon the mute represents some kind of riddle about the nature of life which he is drawn irresistibly to solve.

Beneath the simple surface of the parable are many complications and ironies. Singer, in whom each of the others finds some fulfillment of the longing for intimacy, is himself utterly alone. For ten years he has lived with another deaf mute, a plump, feeble-minded Greek named Antonapoulos whose interests are limited to a childish greed for food and drink. Antonapoulos, however, begins to lose his mind and commits petty assaults, thefts and public indecencies; he is taken away out of Singer's care to an insane asylum. Singer in his loneliness writes long and passionate letters to his friend. "I am not meant to be alone and without you who understand," he writes; but none of the many letters written is ever sent, for Singer knows that Antonapoulos cannot read. When he is allowed to visit Antonapoulos in the asylum Singer takes with him a moving-picture machine for private use, which he has bought on the installment plan. The Greek is ill with nephritis; he sits propped with pillows, splendid in a scarlet dressing-gown and green silk pyjamas sent him by Singer. He is knitting with ivory needles. He smiles serenely and holds out his plump hand with a turquoise ring (also Singer's gift) on one finger. Singer talks with frantic haste until it is time to go; Antonapoulos nods gravely or drowsily from time to time. "Sitting motionless in his bright, rich garments he seemed like some wise king from a legend."

When Singer pays his next visit to the asylum Antonapoulos is dead. Singer goes home, obtains a pistol, and shoots himself.

There are further ironies in the effects of Singer's death on the four people he has influenced. Doctor Copeland, worn out with illness, submits himself to the loving care of the children who wholly distrust his ideas, and thinks sorrowfully of "this white man who was not insolent or scornful but who was just." Jake Blount, leaving the town in which he has failed, as he failed in all other towns, feels a new surge of energy and a hope that soon the outline of his human journey will take form. Mick Kelly, who has somehow lost the capacity to reach the "inside room" of the mind where she once listened enchanted to music, indulges in a dream about one day being able to buy a piano. And Biff Brannon feels his soul expand for a moment as he sees "a glimpse of human struggle and of valour. Of the endless fluid passage of humanity through endless time. And of those who labour and of those who—one word—love." This vision, however, is momentary:

> For in him he felt a warning, a shaft of terror. . . . He saw that he was look-ing at his own face in the counter glass before him. Sweat glistened on his tem-ples and his face was contorted. One eye was opened wider than the other. The left eye delved narrowly into the past while the right gazed wide and affronted into a future of blackness, error, and ruin. And he was suspended between radi-ance and darkness. Between bitter irony and faith.

*

The compassion of Miss McCullers's writing is apparent here in the depth of her characterization. In her other works the characters sometimes suffer at the expense of her insistence on the loneliness and longings of humanity. Complete and satisfactory as symbols, they are limited as charac-ters. Here, however, Doctor Copeland, Jake Blount and Mick Kelly are fully realized, and the pathos of their fates is much accentuated by the magnifi-cence with which their dreams and hopes are portrayed. This is most emphat-ically evident in the case of Copeland, whose sense of the hopeless suffering of his people fills him with a wild feeling for destruction. He assaults his wife, who leaves him and takes away with her the children, Hamilton, Karl Marx, William and Portia. The passionate plea for his beliefs which is allowed to Copeland on the occasion of a Christmas party is in itself deeply moving: it balances, as no doubt it is meant to balance, the moment of defeat when Copeland feels within himself utter loneliness as he settles down at the table with his books by Shakespeare and Marx and Spinoza, and is solaced by the thought of Singer's face; or the moment of ironic absurdity when Copeland and Blount argue furiously about their wholly impracticable ideas for reform-ing society, Copeland advocating the march of a thousand Negroes on Wash-ington and Blount expressing his belief in the power of a great series of chain letters as a solvent for capitalism.

Yet Blount, although a drunken sponger, is also not entirely ignoble or absurd. The grief that he feels at his final vision of the town which he has, in a sense, betrayed—wretched two-room houses, rotted privies, a few fruitless fig trees, and the children swarming on the filthy earth, the smallest of them naked—has its nobility and its pathos. And the fantasies in which Mick Kelly forgets her slum home while she sits on the roof of a large house that is being built, her dreams of inventing radios the size of a pea that people can carry in their ears and flying machines that can be carried on the back like a knap-sack, have about them a rare and remarkable conviction. Her fantasies bear a close relation to those of Frankie Addams in *The Member of the Wedding,* and the ambivalence of Mick's love for her young brother Bubber is more or less paralleled by the mingled love and indifferent cruelty in Frankie's treatment of her young cousin John Henry West, but Mick Kelly's is upon the whole the more complex and interesting portrait.

On the dust wrapper of *The Heart Is a Lonely Hunter* Mr. Graham Greene joins Miss McCullers's name to those of D. H. Lawrence and William Faulkner as those of three modern writers who possess an original poetic sensibility. He adds that he prefers Miss McCullers's writing to that of Lawrence because she has no message. In a direct Messianic sense this is true, but Miss McCullers has a message nevertheless:

> For the error bred in the bone
> Of each woman and each man
> Craves what it cannot have,
> Not universal love
> But to be loved alone.

Perhaps the message is no more than that, perhaps it has no very general validity. To some it may seem that the emphasis placed on human love, whether universal or singular, is exaggerated and that the "rich, dark sound" that Doctor Copeland found in the words of Spinoza when he read them aloud to himself was humanly more valuable than the peace he found in remembering Singer's smile. But such observations are relevant only to Miss McCullers's philosophy, not to her art. Like other artists of genius with the power to project her vision of reality upon the outer world, she writes upon her own terms. It is her triumph that from her preoccupation with freaks and with human loneliness she makes fictions which touch and illuminate at many points the world to which all art makes, however obliquely, its final reference: the world of literal reality.

REFLECTIONS IN A GOLDEN EYE

◆

Masterpiece at 24

[JAMES AGEE]*

Publishers often complain that the South writes more books than it buys. All over the U.S., static small-town life is the frustration and inspiration of bright young talents. But the South's small towns inspire the most feverish talents of all. Led by William Faulkner and Erskine Caldwell, Southerners write with brilliant intensity, but their subject matter runs to horror—sexual, psychological or economic.

The '20s, when the shrill horn of plenty was heard in the rest of the land, did little to cheer the literary consciousness of the South. In those years Carson McCullers grew up in Columbus, Ga., with a hopeless passion for good music, fine writing, kindly human relationships. Her family was not well off, her opportunities were limited, her observation bitter. At 20 she married a fellow Southerner and started work on her first novel, a long, cloudy story of a deaf-mute. Appearing last year under the publishers' makeshift title of *The Heart Is a Lonely Hunter,* it won great critical acclaim. With the money from her book, Carson McCullers moved to Manhattan in search of kindred spirits.

Obsessed since childhood with a sense of exile, she called on literary exiles, among them British poet Wystan Hugh Auden and his wife Erika Mann. Soon she was invited to join a freakish household of esthetes in Brooklyn Heights. There, sickly, shy and elflike, she presided over a dinner table whose steady boarders were Auden, Anglo-Irish poet Louis MacNeice (now back in England for military service), British composer Benjamin Britten, Wisconsin-raised George Davis (literary editor of *Harper's Bazaar).* The old brownstone became a shabby Mecca for their friends. Russian painter Pavel Tchelitchew decorated its walls, symphonies were composed at its piano, through it trooped painters, writers, musicians and such unclassifiable artists as Gypsy Rose Lee.

*Reprinted from *Time,* 17 February 1941, 96. Copyright 1941 Time Inc. Reprinted by permission. James Agee is identified here for the first time as the author of this review.

Somehow amid the sherry bottles, the inchoate housekeeping, the atonal music and the inspired chitchat, Carson got on with her writing. Then, on doctor's advice, she returned to her family in the South for rest. This week her second novel was published, under a title (this time) of her own choosing: *Reflections in a Golden Eye.* It is not the work of a normal 24-year-old girl.

In its sphere, the novel is a masterpiece. It is as mature and finished as Henry James's *The Turn of the Screw,* though still more specialized. Its story is about life as Carson McCullers sees fit to create it in a Southern Army camp, and is almost desperately psychomedical. Within its 183 pages a child is born (some of whose fingers are grown together), an Army captain suffers from bisexual impotence, a half-witted private rides nude in the woods, a stallion is tortured, a murder is done, a heartbroken wife cuts off her nipples with garden shears.

In almost any hands, such material would yield a rank fruitcake of mere arty melodrama. But Carson McCullers tells her tale with simplicity, insight, and a rare gift of phrase. She makes its tortures seem at least as valid as the dull suburban tragedies from Farrell's or Dreiser's Midwest, commonly called lifelike. *Reflections in a Golden Eye* is the Southern school at its most Gothic, but also at its best. It is as though William Faulkner saw to the bottom of matters which merely excite him, shed his stylistic faults, and wrote it all out with Tolstoyan lucidity.

[Review of] *Reflections in a Golden Eye*

Rose Feld*

When Carson McCullers's first novel, *The Heart Is a Lonely Hunter,* appeared last year it was practically unanimously applauded as a literary "find" by all who gave it a critical reading. It was a strange, dark tale of the almost supernatural influence of a deaf mute over a group of people. That a young woman only a few years past twenty should have written it contributed not a little to the deep impression it made. Those who thought they recognized in her a new star in the literary firmament awaited her next book with a vast amount of interest.

Now it has come, a short novel called *Reflections in a Golden Eye.* It is a more tightly bound tale, more confidently constructed than the first, but the complete answer as to Carson McCullers's ability as a writer is not here. Again she shows a sort of subterranean and ageless instinct for probing the hidden in men's hearts and minds, again a strange grace of movement in exploring dark channels of disturbing moods. But the final impression she leaves with the reader is not of creative perfection, but of his waking up from a nightmare, of relief in knowing that what has passed was neither real nor probable.

Yet, just as one is gripped by the seeming reality and truthfulness of the sequence of events in a nightmare, so is one caught by the strangeness and the dreadful direction of her tale. There are six characters in this tragedy and every one of them is a creature twisted in search of personal peace. There is Major Langdon and his wife, Alison; there is Captain Penderton and his wife, Leonora; there is Private Williams and there is Anacleto, the Langdons' Filipino house-boy. The emotional complications of these six intertwine like snakes writhing in a cauldron. Leonora is the mistress of Maj. Langdon, these two, by the way, being the most nearly normal persons in the book; Anacleto is both slave and equal of Mrs. Langdon; Captain Penderton is a cuckold powerfully drawn to Private Williams; Private Williams is a virgin hypnotized into unbelievable action by Mrs. Penderton. Mrs. McCullers adds a horse to this company, Firebird, who belongs to Mrs. Penderton and, in a way that is not entirely clear, is symbolic of her strength and her husband's weakness.

*Reprinted from *New York Herald Tribune Books*, 16 February 1941, 8.

That the Major and Mrs. Penderton were lovers was known at the Army post. The only ones who suffered in this affair were Mrs. Langdon and Anacleto; Capt. Penderton, involved in his own conflict of self-knowledge, accepted it with bitterness. The first impact of honor in this disturbing tale comes in a revolting incident which grew out of Mrs. Langdon's recognition of her unimportance and impotence. She performs a brutal act of self-violence which is as physically unnerving to the reader as anything that has appeared in print. Mrs. McCullers has been compared to William Faulkner; here, indeed, she seems almost deliberately to be seeking something that could match him at his most morbid. Her success does not, however, add anything to her power as an artist. One is merely impressed with and offended by her arrogant and pitiless fearlessness which, besides giving an unpleasant effect, betrays her youth.

The second impact of horror arises out of Private Williams's witnessing the baiting of Capt. Penderton by his wife. The first incident is superfluous to the story; the second is not, for from this point events drive on to the climax with increasing psychological momentum.

As was said before in this review, the pattern and the sequence of the story possess the quality of reality inherent in a nightmare. There is the fantastic relationship between Mrs. Langdon and the Filipino, real only in the sense that Mrs. McCullers presents it as such; there is the oblique pursuit of Pvt. Williams by the tortured man who thinks he hates him; and, most unreal of all, are the night visits, innocent in a dreadful and terrifying way, of Pvt. Williams to the bedroom of the sleeping Mrs. Penderton.

However one rejects her situations and her characters, one is held by the mood Mrs. McCullers creates. Combined with a perfect technique of plumbing the mentally sick is a grim humor which puts a point on some of her characterizations. Writing of Mrs. Penderton she says, "On the post Leonora Penderton enjoyed a reputation as a good hostess, an excellent sportswoman, and even as a great lady. However, there was something about her that puzzled her friends and acquaintances. They sensed an element in her personality that they could not quite put their fingers on. The truth of the matter was that she was a little feeble-minded."

And again, as in her first book, one is impressed with the maturity of Mrs. McCullers's observations. In explanation of the strange actions of Pvt. Williams, she writes, "The mind is like a richly woven tapestry in which the colors are distilled from the experiences of the senses, and the design drawn from the convolutions of the intellect. The mind of Pvt. Williams was imbued with various colors of strange tones, but it was without delineation, void of form."

Reflections in a Golden Eye is a literary adventure into an emotional underworld and, as such, interesting. But one still hopes that Carson McCullers will use her very real powers to write a book that does not depend completely upon the grotesque and the abnormal for its effect.

Novelist Repeats Success

B. R.*

Praise as heady and extravagant as champagne wine greeted Carson McCullers's first novel, *The Heart Is a Lonely Hunter,* when it appeared about a year ago. Not all of the critics were of the same mind, but among the majority the 23-year-old writer's book was nothing if not "vital" or "magnificent" or "extraordinary."

Her second novel is less than half the length of her first. It is approximately twice as good, although it may not appear so to those who exhausted themselves with praise for *The Heart.*

As spokesman for the publishers, Louis Untermeyer calls *Reflections in a Golden Eye* one of the "most compelling, one of the most uncanny stories ever written in America." This is not an unusual phrase to find on the jacket of a novel. The unusual thing is that it is perfectly true.

From the opening paragraph in which Miss McCullers relates: "There is a fort in the South where a few years ago a murder was committed. The participants of this tragedy were two officers, a soldier, two women, a Filipino and a horse." You are swept away into a world of the author's own remarkable fancy. It is a world in which all of the physical properties are familiar, and yet it is a world viewed to an unreasonable depth and from a disturbing perspective. Miss McCullers is no writer of fantasy; she merely sees from a quite uncommon point of vantage.

The suspense of her story lies less in the rather bizarre narrative that she relates than in the manner of its presentation, her beneath the surface explorations of motives and reactions, her subtle suggestiveness, her extremely deceptive simple style. By and large, Miss McCullers's characters are an implausible lot. But like William Faulkner, who works a somewhat similar vein in this respect, she succeeds in some mysterious way in giving her people not only acceptable reality, but a kind of super-reality.

Readers who follow Private Williams to his secret midnight vigils with Captain Penderton's wife, who accompany the captain on his eerie horseback ride through the forest, who witness the major's wife mutilating herself in a jarring moment of insanity, will report that for pace and suspense and emotional disturbance Miss McCullers has few rivals.

*Reprinted from the *Kansas City Star,* 15 February 1941, 14. Courtesy of the *Kansas City Star.*

THE MEMBER OF THE WEDDING

♦

An Adolescent's Four Days

GEORGE DANGERFIELD*

This is Carson McCullers's third book; and we have now, I should think, sufficient evidence for remarking that, while there are quite a few writers who unfortunately resemble her, she fortunately resembles nobody else. She is unique.

The Member of the Wedding is, more or less, the story of four days in the life of Frankie Addams: how she had become "an unjoined person who hung around in doorways"; how the thought of her brother's approaching wedding gave her a sense of sharing in the world again; how she went out into the town to test this new feeling with rather violent consequences; how she talked around and around the subject of the wedding when she was at home; how the wedding, eventually, was a ghastly failure for her; and how Frankie grew up.

But to write about *The Member of the Wedding* in this way is like writing about a tent pole and forgetting to describe the tent.

But it would be extremely difficult and quite unnecessary to make an adequate précis of this (as the publishers and perhaps the author like to label it) novella. It is not just a study of adolescence. Frankie Addams, it is true, conforms to a possible pattern of behavior. She does nothing which a twelve-year-old girl might not do. Yet the further you read into *The Member of the Wedding* the more you realize, it seems to me, that Frankie is merely the projection of a problem that has nothing much to do with adolescence.

The three chief characters are Frankie herself, her six-and-a-half-year-old cousin John Henry, and the thirty-eight-year-old, one-eyed cook Berenice. At times these three personages behave as if, indeed, one was twelve, one six and a half, and one thirty-eight; but generally they are beings of no special age, discoursing in what appears to be a dream or trance. Their problem is elementary, unanswerable, and common to all age levels. Here is the crux of it:

*Reprinted from the *Saturday Review*, 30 March 1946, 15, by permission of M. L. Dangerfield.

> "I know, but what is it all about? People loose and at the same time caught. Caught and loose. All these people and you don't know what joins them up. There's bound to be some sort of reason and connection. Yet somehow I can't seem to name it. I don't know."
>
> "If you did you would be God," said Berenice. "Didn't you know that?"

In other words, the problem which obsesses them is human loneliness: the basic problem which Virginia Woolf, after years of investigation, could only state in terms of "here is one room, there another." Miss McCullers states it in its most undifferentiated form; places it in this light and in that; looks at it savagely, gleefully, tenderly; seems almost to taste it and to roll it round her tongue; but never attempts to find an answer.

Indeed, what makes this story so unusual is the fact that most of it takes place through the medium of desultory conversations between three really weird people sitting in an even weirder kitchen. Nothing or almost nothing occurs here, and yet every page is filled with a sense of something having happened, happening, and about to happen. This in itself is a considerable technical feat; and, beyond that, there is magic in it.

The words used above—"dream," "trance," "loneliness," "weird," "magic" —are such as are generally applied to work which has severe limitations. I would be the last to deny that Miss McCullers has hers. It must be obvious to everyone who has read her books that her art excludes many important things with which the artist today is rightly preoccupied. It is an exclusive art, not out of choice but out of necessity: not because it does not wish to include but because it cannot.

She is a suggestive rather than an eloquent writer, and often seems to present us less with a meaning than with a hint. And yet the lines of her work are clear and firm. I do not know how this is done; but my ignorance will not deter me from attempting to provide an explanation.

Though she has an acute observation, she does not use it to make rounded people. Her characters invariably remind one of faces one *may have* seen, in a dream perhaps, in a tabloid newspaper possibly, or out of a train window. Their clothes, their gestures, their conversations are selected with an admirable eye and ear to verisimilitude; but the actual inhabitants of these clothes, gestures, and conversations are not themselves quite human. In fact, this book seems more and more to insist that it is, as it were, a monologue furnished with figures.

For Carson McCullers's work has always seemed to me to be a form of self-dramatization. It is true that this can be said of most immature fiction. But Miss McCullers is both a mature and fine writer. She does not dramatize herself in the sense that she is merely autobiographical; but she does dramatize herself in the sense that she seems to invest the various sides of her personality with attributes skilfully collected from the outside world.

From this point of view, *The Member of the Wedding* is a masquerade; but a serious, profound, and poetic masquerade in which the Unconscious (or the Subconscious or whatever you wish to call the subliminal personality) expresses itself, now through the voice of Frankie Addams, now through that of John Henry, now through that of Berenice Sadie Brown. The other characters, who certainly belong to the real world, hover round the edge of this extraordinary monologue, with one foot in it and one out; behaving with none of the awkwardness which you might expect from them in such circumstances, but adding richness to the story and relating it to more normal fiction.

I suppose that I have not yet made it clear that this is, to my mind, a marvelous piece of writing. Not merely does it sustain the interest all the way through, but it does so under circumstances which demand the utmost delicacy and balance from the author.

The book avoids what T. E. Lawrence called "the kindergarten of the imagination" on the one hand; on the other hand, it never becomes a mere sequence of neurotic images. It steers a wonderful middle course between these two morasses. It is a work which reveals a strong, courageous, and independent imagination. There are other writers in the contemporary field who are of more importance than Carson McCullers. Of her it should be sufficient to say, once again, that she is unique.

Metaphysical Fiction

Marguerite Young*

Carson McCullers' *The Member of the Wedding,* astutely and frugally designed, is a deceptive piece of writing, and its candor may betray the unwary reader into accepting it as what it first seems, a study of turbulent adolescence. Indeed, as such a study it has been most often reviewed, often by worldly reviewers who confess their weariness with the problems of a growing childhood, even though such a childhood may be, as in this case, a complexus of unreal, real, and surreal events, in a pattern which is itself as delusive as the dream of a total happiness. Merely by thinking in terms of the individual childhood here presented rather than in terms of the many and carefully erected symbols employed by the author in an argument concerned with man in his relation to various kinds of reality, the reader may miss the importance of this curiously spiritual book. Or he may wonder, especially if he is a parent, why Mrs. McCullers chose as her heroine a child who was more an individual than a type, a child who was herself split into two warring beings though she sought for an eternal harmony. Mrs. McCullers, sometimes depicted as a sensationalist revelling in the grotesque, is more than that because she is first of all the poetic symbolist, a seeker after those luminous meanings which always do transcend the boundaries of the stereotyped, the conventional, and the so-called normal. Here, then, is a fairly clear, explicit writing—explicit even in its use of the anomalous, the paradoxical, the amorphous—the confusions of life. Though its themes are romantic, their working out is classically controlled. There is no wilderness for the reader to get lost in, and if he is lost, it is perhaps because this writing does not weep, gnash, wail, shout, wear its heart on its sleeve. It is rather like a chess game, where every move is a symbol and requires the reader's counter-move. Many modern poems are of this order.

At first level, it is the story of a boy girl Frankie who, during a torrid summer, plans to join her brother's wedding, to get married to the two who are getting married, to belong, to be a member of something, to break down all barriers of atomic individualism, to be somehow intimately involved with all the intimate concerns of the happy human race. If Frankie can only crash in on this wedding of two other people to each other, being the third mem-

*First printed in the *Kenyon Review*—Original Series, Vol. IX, No. 1, Winter 1947. Copyright 1947 by Kenyon College. Reprinted with permission.

ber, loving both, loved by both, even though she is excessive, why, then, there will be the kind of perfect happiness which man has always dreamed of, like a union of all the nations. Good-natured, proverb-haunted Berenice, the Negro cook who has brought up this semi-orphaned child, assures her that her expectations can never be realized in actuality, that if they were realized, they would not be right, for her or the human race. What Frankie is dreaming of is possible only inside her own creative head, is nowhere else, is very far from possible. The purely imaginary goal is still a goal for Frankie, who cannot easily give up. She and Berenice sit discussing these crucial matters in endless, capacious luxury, capacious for them and for the reader, who can ponder as they ponder, think backward and forward. Then there is an audience, John Henry, aged six, who chimes in every once in a while and provides, in the drama, his own special, peculiar insights. He is beautifully described, once as a little blackbird running against the light. In fact, all three characters, all major, are treated with dignity and revealing tenderness, especially Berenice, whose blue glass eye is like Frankie's dream of the impossible wedding, a dream of almost heavenly harmony on earth. Berenice does not precisely dream of turning white, but her blue glass eye is a terrible commentary on the color line and the arbitrary divisions which shut off people from each other. All this book is a discussion of happiness, done as quietly as *Rasselas* by Dr. Johnson, and the conclusion is faintly similar to his. There are minor characters moving back and forth like the minor figures on a chessboard, in this case both cosmic and human. Nobody is ever disparaged. The Negro people are always people, thoughtful, mature, at home with Frankie who wants to belong to the human race, at home with John Henry, who is very soon to leave it and won't have much use for his little walking cane, a gift given to him most ironically on his death bed, given to him by optimistic Frankie, in fact.

By the above paragraph, I see the impossibility of describing the book without describing it in terms of its intricate symbols. Indeed, narrative and allegory are the two-headed flower growing from one stem, and if this is a "Pilgrim's Progress" backward to the cold and unintelligent and unintelligible universe suggested in Matthew Arnold's popular poem, it is still a pilgrim's progress, modernistic, aware of no simple definition of good and evil. One thing is always described in terms of another. The argument, though veiled by diverse imagery, is never lost. The imagery is functional. In fact, if there is any one statement to define Mrs. McCullers' position as a writer, it is not that she is merely the sensationalist but that she is also, like Sterne, the preacher, concerned with theories of knowledge—though the by-play of wit does not entice her away from the main themes. There is no lush undergrowth. Control is never absent. The framework is always visible.

People want to be told what they already believe, and Mrs. McCullers, in this case, is not telling most people what they already believe. Rather, she is continually questioning a great many complacent assumptions as to what is what, for she is too closely skeptical and analytical a writer to suppose that in the accepted platitudes lies truth. She weighs, she measures. Wild idealism does not carry her beyond the boundaries of a rigorous common sense world, partly for the reason that she finds the given world itself a sufficient phantasmagoria of lost events. Her attitude toward human nature is patient, behaviorist, clinical. Her writing, brooding and exploratory though it is, remains for these reasons as formal as a problem in geometry, though the perspectives bewilderingly and constantly shift. She sees life as impressionistic, but she herself is not the impressionist. She is a logician in an illogical realm.

Is there a given pattern in the nature of things, a music of the spheres, or was it all, as Mrs. McCullers implies, accident and chaos and fragment to begin with? Mrs. McCullers, speculative like her characters, dreams of an omniscient pattern but finds that such a pattern is rather more man's project than God's and that its realization may comprise another chaos. Then, too, there is the problem of how to make the inner world and the outer world conjoin, the problem immediately faced by Frankie, an anarchist in an old baseball cap. These three people, Frankie, John Henry, and Berenice, sit around the kitchen table talking most musically while the green summer heat grows more and more oppressive around them. The focal subject is the impossible wedding, the illusory goal, out of which grow other illusory subjects, all related. John Henry draws crazy pictures on the wall. The piano tuner comes to tune the piano (perhaps next door), and the notes become a visible music climbing to the ceiling. And this is almost all that ever happens in the book but enough to keep the sensitive reader appalled to hear meaning after meaning dissolve, while the old problems continue. Is even green a color that can be said to be green to everybody? The metaphysical grows out of the immediate and returns to it, made no less rich because its origin is known. One of the most compelling passages is that in which Berenice tells of her search for happiness, which is exemplified to her in the person of her dead first husband. Berenice has been married three times looking for him, three times unsatisfactorily. She married a man because he had a thumb like that of her dead first husband, another because he wore the coat which her dead first husband had worn and which she had pawned after his death and failed to claim, another because of a physical reason, her loneliness. Berenice says that her ideal world will be a world in which the blacks associate equally and freely with the whites and which will also include her dead first husband—though resurrection is not possible and might not even be feasible. Frankie's ideal world will be one where the wars are restricted to only an island for habitual warriors. It may even be a world made up of flickering cinematic figures. Berenice, Frankie, and John Henry, many-dimensioned, talking about what it means to be human, play in an alien system, all the while at a three-handed bridge game, emblematic of their plight. Some of the cards are, though they do not know it, missing from the beginning, maybe like those cards which God threw down at creation—and maybe that is why nothing ever turns out right, why there are expectation and disappointment. John Henry expresses his desire for an angular vision with which to read through and around the cards, a vision that can bend at will, for John Henry is of a philosophic turn of mind besides being a painter of crazy pictures.

At the end of the book, when the strange trilogy is broken up by death and moving away, it seems, in retrospect, a pattern as illusive and perfect as the wedding of three. It can never be recovered. The enchantment is implied in the writing but is not expressed by Frankie, who has come to the banal point of declaring that she just loves Michelangelo. Uncertainty seems to be her future. Either she will grow up, or she will not grow up.

THE BALLAD OF THE SAD CAFÉ: THE NOVELS AND STORIES OF CARSON McCULLERS

◆

[Review of] *The Ballad of the Sad Café: The Novels and Stories of Carson McCullers*

WILLIAM P. CLANCY*

It is a feeling of intense loneliness, Stephen Spender has written, which gives all great American literature something in common, and this feeling finds expression in its recurrent theme: "the great misunderstood primal energy of creative art, transformed into the inebriate . . . the feeling ox . . . the lost child."

Spender's insight seemed to me a particularly acute one when I first read it. Surely one is haunted by loneliness and longing in Hemingway, in Fitzgerald, in Faulkner. When I was reading the collected novels and stories of Carson McCullers, his observation struck me with new force. Here is a young American talent of the very first order, and one leaves her work with an almost terrifying sense of the tragic aloneness of man. The symbol for this aloneness is always, as Spender has said, the sensitive, the dumb, the suffering, the lost child. In reading the work of Mrs. McCullers we become aware of being in the presence of a great tragic spirit, and we ourselves become possessed of a great pity and fear.

This apprehension of loneliness, this pity and fear, is constant in Carson McCullers' work. The present volume, in addition to the title story, contains her three novels, *The Heart Is a Lonely Hunter, Reflections in a Golden Eye,* and *The Member of the Wedding,* and six of her short stories. Through them all we move from one level of tragedy and terror to another: Miss Amelia, the fearsome and cross-eyed, hopelessly in love with an almost diabolical hunchback; Madame Zilensky, the musician, living vicariously through the pathological lie; the deaf mute, finding his voice only through another mute; the inarticulate soldier, keeping secret vigil by the bed of a woman to whom he can never

*Reprinted from *The Commonweal* 54 (15 June 1951): 243, by permission of the journal. Copyright © Commonweal.

speak; all these and others probe depths of man's misery, depths to which few writers ever gain access.

The art of Carson McCullers has been called "Gothic." Perhaps it is—superficially. Certainly her day-to-day world, her little Southern towns, are haunted by far more masterful horrors than were ever conjured up in the dreary castles of a Horace Walpole. It seems to me, however, that the "Gothic" label misses the essential point. Because Carson McCullers is ultimately the artist functioning at the very loftiest symbolic level, and if one must look for labels I should prefer to call her work "metaphysical." Behind the strange and horrible in her world there are played out the most sombre tragedies of the human spirit; her mutes, her hunchbacks, speak of complexities and frustrations which are so native to man that they can only be recognized, perhaps, in the shock which comes from seeing them dressed in the robes of the grotesque. They pass us on the street every day but we only notice them when they drag a foot as they go by.

At the very opening of the title story, the face of Miss Amelia, the proprietor of the "Sad Café," is described as a face "like the terrible dim faces known in dreams . . . sexless and white, with two gray crossed eyes which are turned inwards so sharply that they seem to be exchanging with each other one long and secret gaze of grief." This description, remarkable for its metaphysical fusion of horror and compassion, might serve as a symbol of Carson McCullers' art. And this fusion, I would say, represents an achievement equalled by few other contemporary American writers.

Books in General

V. S. PRITCHETT*

From a brief indication of the locale and theme of a great many American novels, it has become pretty easy to fill in the rest. The spell of American loquacity comes on one like some interminable talk in a train; it is the spell of the literal mind which breaks down any human situation into the "I said" and "he said" of circumstance and which has submitted life to the mild, friendly chewing of the human jaw. There is a limp democratic charm in this manner of writing: all jaws are equal, all are moving. The liberating quality in a large number of quite ordinary American novels, indeed, seems to spring from the notion that it is enough to talk in our own sagging way through everything. But that idea has long ago lost its novelty. Large areas of very talented American writing is mere repetition work, a hurried laying-down of the macadam of a literature, an expert bustling around to see that all streets are paved, and the talking mind does this more quickly than any other. What we look for is the occasional American genius—the Faulkner, for example—who will build his own original, imaginative or intellectual structures in some small corner of the plan.

Such a genius is Miss Carson McCullers, the most remarkable novelist, I think, to come out of America for a generation. Coverage is ignored by her. She is a regional writer from the South, and behind her lies that classical and melancholy authority, that indifference to shock, which seem more European than American. She knows her own original, fearless and compassionate mind. The short novels and two or three stories now published in *The Ballad of the Sad Café*—the sing-song Poe-like title so filled with the dominant American emotion of nostalgia—make an impact which recalls the impression made by such very different writers as de Maupassant and D. H. Lawrence. What she has, before anything else, is a courageous imagination; that is to say that she is bold enough to consider the terrible in a human nature without loss of nerve, calm, dignity or love. She has the fearless "golden eye" of the title of one of her stories. She is as circumspect as Defoe was in setting down the plain facts of her decaying Southern scene—a boring military camp, the dying little mill town with its closed café and empty

*Reprinted from *The New Statesman and Nation,* 2 August 1952, 137–38, with kind permission of New Statesman and Nation, 1952, and the author.

streets, the back-kitchen life of a widower's daughter—and yet the moment she picks out her people, they are changed from the typical to the extraordinary. Like all writers of original genius, she convinces us that we have missed something which was plain to be seen in the real world. So that if it is a matter of freaks like a gangling, mannish, hard-spitting, hard-hitting old virgin, or the hunchback dwarf she falls in love with, we are made to see that ordinary human love can transform them as it can any other creature; and, reversing the situation, when love gives its twist to a pair of full officers and their wives at a military station, they become as strange, in their way, as the freaks. Like a chorus the mass of ordinary people crowd round these afflicted hearts. It may be objected that the very strangeness of the characters in a story like *The Ballad of the Sad Café* is that of regional gossip and, in fact, turns these characters into minor figures from some American Powys-land. They become the bywords of a local ballad. But the compassion of the author gives them their Homeric moment in a universal tragedy. There is a point at which they become "great." A more exact definition of the range of her genius would be to say that human destiny is watched by her in the heart alone. She is—but in the highest and more sensitive degree—limited to the subject of personality.

On that subject she is a master of peculiar perception and an incomparable story-teller. The *Ballad,* though it concerns oddities, is a most ingenious and surprising work and, as in her other stories, its invention and surprise are found not in plot but in the contemplation of the characters themselves. She winds her way backwards and forwards into her people in a way that is sometimes too dilatory, but at every digression she cannot fail to come upon some new bearing on their fate. The almost intolerable, magnetised suspense of her stories comes from the leisure of telling and her power to catch the fatal changes in people. The little hunchback in the *Ballad* appears first of all as a miserable, weeping abortion at Miss Amelia's store; a meal, a bed, an act of kindness turn him into a hard, proud little fellow; the astonishing love Miss Amelia suddenly thrusts on him—it is described as a sudden hunger of "lonesomeness"—turns him further into a chattering tyrant and dandy. He civilises this terrible virgin who had once thrown a husband out of her room on her bridal night. The dwarf softens her mad quarrels, her cheating and violence; at night she sits up with him because he is afraid of the dark and has a terror of death. But if two strange beings are remade by love, the dwarf strengthened by it, the woman weakened, they are now vulnerable to betrayal. And it is at this moment that Miss McCullers's powers as a storyteller come out, for every trivial detail that has gone before now plays its part in the terrible personal tragedy: the destruction of the heart of Miss Amelia. Miss Amelia fears that when her convict husband comes out he will kill the dwarf; what she does not reckon with is that emulation and slavishness underlie the vanity of the dwarf and that he will idiotically fall for the convict and will betray her. The betrayal occurs in the phenomenal set wrestling-match which takes place between this man-woman and her husband. Here is an example of Miss McCullers's eye for circumstance:

> The fight took place on Ground Hog Day, which is the second of February. The weather was favourable, being neither rainy nor sunny, and with a neutral temperature. There were several signs that this was the appointed day, and by ten o'clock the news spread all over the county. Early in the morning Miss Amelia went out and cut down her punching bag. Marvin Macy sat on the back step with a tin can of hog fat between his knees and carefully greased his arms and his legs. A hawk with a bloody breast flew over the town and circled twice round the property of Miss Amelia. The tables in the café were moved out to the back porch, so that the whole room was cleared for the fight. There was every sign. Both Miss Amelia and Marvin Macy ate four helpings of half-raw roast for dinner, and then lay down in the afternoon to store up strength. Marvin Macy rested in the big room upstairs, while Miss Amelia stretched herself out on the bench in her office. It was plain from her white stiff face what a torment it was for her to be lying still and doing nothing, but she lay there quiet as a corpse with her eyes closed and her hands crossed on her chest.

Turn from this to the opening lines of the portrait of Captain Penderton in *Reflections in a Golden Eye.* Here one meets the irony and tension of D. H. Lawrence, but the irony is classical and the unrest is subdued by a calm, misleading surface in the writing:

> The Captain's restlessness this evening had many causes. His personality differed in some respects from the ordinary. He stood in a somewhat curious relation to the three fundamentals of existence—life itself, sex and death. Sexually the Captain obtained within himself a delicate balance between the male and female elements, with the susceptibilities of both the sexes and the active powers of neither. For a person content to withdraw a bit from life, and able to collect his scattered passions and throw himself whole-heartedly into some impersonal work, some art or even some crack-brained fixed idea such as an attempt to square the circle—for such a person this state of being is bearable enough.

But he had "a sad penchant" for falling in love with his wife's lovers and

> as to his relation with the two other fundaments, his position was simple enough. In his balance between the two great instincts, toward life and toward death, the scale was heavily weighted to one side—to death. Because of this Captain was a coward.

This kind of analysis gives bone structure to a story because it has authority; it is also a valuable point of recuperation in the narrative; and it is unnerving because it discloses the powerful, classical, emotional threats of the unconscious. In her power to show the unconscious breaking surface, Miss McCullers is remarkable. She is a wonderful observer—this is rare in Anglo-

Saxon writers—of the forms of love. In describing things like a neurotic illness, the seductiveness of a silly woman of slightly feeble mind, a pious soldier
suddenly made sinister and exalted by the shock of desire, theory is buried far
out of sight; one sees these things as they are in life but one is covertly made
to understand the force behind them at the same time. Once again, the
atmosphere created from innumerable fine strokes of local detail is momen-
tous, and the winding course of the story adds to its effect. Perhaps, engrossed
by her own skill in the devious line of continuity, Miss McCullers digresses or
pads too much. There is a portrait of a Filipino servant which is a failure
because he too usefully embodies the personal ideal of a moral sensibility that
is perfect aesthetically. He is too precious a distillation of insight and humility
in a story that is, very properly, a satire on the lethargy of life at a military
station.

   Although this is the most ambitious story in the book and the most
powerful, it did not strike me as having the total originality of *The Member of
the Wedding*. This is simply a long study in the character of a motherless girl of
about 13 who is mainly brought up by a Negress in her father's kitchen and
who is shown at the crisis of puberty where the childish personality is struggling to turn into the adult. Stories of adolescence are apt to be fatally
infected by the morbidity, the continued adolescence of their authors. This
one is not. Once again, this story goes on too long; it is filled with too many
instances; but I have never seen anything on this subject done with a comparable insight. The squalor of dirty-faced, aggressive childhood, its physical
awkwardness, its stupidities and jealousies, its ignorance of the world, its
gusts of idealism, its lapses into the infantile are rendered in just detail; and
when I say "rendered" I do not mean merely stated or analysed but, in the
Jamesian sense, dramatised and put into the skin of life. And the terror of life,
the fact that, to an intense imagination, life is terrifying from moment to
moment because we do not know the fierce shadow inside ourselves or other
people, is always conveyed. When the girl is jealous because her brother is
getting married, she throws a butcher's knife across the kitchen as a kind of
dare, to make it stick in the wood. In another mood, and feeling those emotions that drive the young into Youth Movements, badge-wearing groups and
so on, she again picks up the knife "to have something to hold on to."

> "Hold still, Fool," said Berenice. "And lay down that knife."
>   . . ."We will just walk up to people and know them right away. . .We will
> know decorated aviators and New York people and movie stars. We will have
> thousands of friends, thousands and thousands and thousands of friends. We
> will belong to so many clubs that we can't even keep track of all of them. We
> will be members of the whole world. Boyoman! Manoboy!"

A town comes to life in the child's wanderings, a place whose seamy and
sinister meanings are half grasped, half ignored. Running wild about this

place in her condition, the child is walking a tight-rope between normal human kindness and callous, frightful, casual wickedness and she has no fixed notion of either. So again this is a story of terror, but not of morbid terror. The child is not presented as a little sentimentalised victim of seediness, but as a creature forming itself, becoming a member of life, undergoing a completing experience without knowing she is doing so. For the complete are the scarred. Miss McCullers is a writer of the highest class because of her great literary gifts; but underlying these, and not less important, is her sense of the completeness of human experience at any moment. She is a classic, not a convert.

THE MEMBER OF THE WEDDING
(PLAY)

♦

Plot Me No Plots

JOHN MASON BROWN*

On the fifth day of each November bonfires are lighted in London in honor of the discovery of a plot. And Beefeaters, with their lanterns raised, search the basement of the Houses of Parliament as if they still expected to find Guy Fawkes hiding there, with a slow burning match in his hand, ready to set off the powder kegs which would elevate King James I even higher above his subjects.

The story of Guy Fawkes is known to everyone. But between our vague knowledge of his share in this conspiracy and the detailed plan which he and his associates had evolved for carrying it out lies the reason for history's having identified the events with which he is connected, not as the Gunpowder Story, but as the Gunpowder Plot.

Even in the theatre the same distinction can be made. For, strictly speaking, the plotting of a play is not the story upon which that play is founded, or the story that it tells, but the manner in which a particular dramatist, due usually to his times no less than to his personality, has chosen to advance it. It is not those things that happen in a play, but the when, why, and how of their happening.

It is the dramatist's plan of action, his blueprint of events, his mechanical distribution of his fable into acts and scenes. It is the bony structure underlying whatever flesh and blood his characters may boast, the skeleton which makes his play organic and dictates its movements. It is the dramatist's scheme not only for putting his people to the test of deeds or crises but also for arranging, introducing, illustrating, emphasizing, developing, and concluding the basic idea or situation around which he has built his play.

The foregoing paragraphs were written by me several years ago. They appeared in a book called *The Art of Playgoing.* I fall back on them now

*Reprinted from the *Saturday Review,* 28 January 1950, 27–29, by permission of the estate of John Mason Brown.

because Carson McCullers's dramatization of her novel, *The Member of the Wedding,*[1] is an interesting illustration of the differences between plot and story.

Mrs. McCullers's study of the loneliness of an overimaginative young Georgian girl is no ordinary play. It is felt, observed, and phrased with exceptional sensitivity. It deals with the torturing dreams, the hungry egotism, and the heartbreak of childhood in a manner as rare as it is welcome. Quite aside from the magical performances its production includes, it has a magic of its own. The script shines with an unmistakable luster. Plainly it is the work of an artist, of an author who does not stoop to the expected stencils and who sees people with her own eyes rather than through borrowed spectacles.

Common speech becomes uncommon in Mrs. McCullers's usage of it. Her marshaling of words is no less individual than her approach to her characters. She employs the language lovingly to give color and nuance to her unique perceptions. But, though she tells a story, and a very moving one at that, she does so with as little reliance upon plotting as if her aim had been to obey the command of the Citizen in *The Knight of the Burning Pestle* who cried, "Plot me no plots."

A lot happens in *The Member of the Wedding,* that is if you consider its separate incidents and what the average playwright would make of them. Frankie, the young girl who is Mrs. McCullers's central character, dreams of going off with her brother and his bride on their honeymoon. When she learns that they do not want her she runs away from home and comes near to committing suicide with her father's pistol. The little boy who lives next door is stricken with meningitis and dies. And Berenice, the Negro cook at Frankie's dilapidated house, hears first that her no-good foster brother has slashed the throat of a white man with a razor, and then that, after his capture, he has hanged himself in jail.

Though she touches upon these last two tragedies, Mrs. McCullers does not build them up. Instead, she throws them away, treating them with a wasteful casualness. Even when dwelling at length upon Frankie's delusive obsessions about the wedding and the honeymoon, she avoids developing them dramatically in the usual fashion. Character and mood are her substitutes for plot. And admirable and absorbing substitutes they prove to be when she is writing at her best.

Galsworthy's contention was that a human being is the best plot there is. "A bad plot," he said, "is simply a row of stakes with a character impaled on each—characters who would have liked to live but came to untimely grief." Certainly, Mrs. McCullers's characters are not impaled upon such a row of stakes. Three of them, the girl Frankie, the Negro cook, and the young boy, are as vividly drawn as any characters to have come out of the contemporary theatre.

If, in spite of its fascination and distinction, Mrs. McCullers's play ultimately fails to live up to its high promise, the reason is certainly not her choosing to dispense with plotting, as plotting is ordinarily understood.

Healthily, the theatre has grown more and more away from the tawdry contrivances and the delight in artifice for artifice's sake upon which it doted at the century's turn. It has done this in the interest of freedom no less than of truth, done it because both audiences and playwrights have come to realize that the conflicts within individuals possess a greater dramatic value than the prefabricated crises which were once the theatre's mainstay.

The well-made play, with all of its table-thumpings, "plants," big scenes, carpentry, and curtain lines, is nowadays completely out of fashion. Pinero, Jones, and Sardou are very dead indeed. Chekhov's influence is far stronger than that of Ibsen, the master builder. Accordingly, Mrs. McCullers's plotlessness demands no readjustment because it comes as no surprise. It finds her following a tradition most of us like and respect. It is an indication of her probity, a proof that she is writing as an artist.

Considering how fine are the fine things in *The Member of the Wedding,* the pity is that Mrs. McCullers's play lacks inward progression. It is more static than it needs or ought to be. Its virtue is its lack of contrivance, but its shortcoming is its lack of planning. Salty and sensitive as is the delineation of its major characters, they do not develop; they stand still. Some of the scenes in which they appear are written as if they were "sketches." This is particularly true in the last act, the three scenes of which are as unsubstantial as Mrs. McCullers's ten subsidiary characters. Among these even Frankie's widowed father, who could do much to explain the mental instability of his daughter, is a mere wraith. He is as unreal as the three characters who interest Mrs. McCullers are real.

A wise old woman once insisted that she liked bad children best of all. When asked why, her answer was, "They are always sent out of the room." There are quite a few moments when one comes uncomfortably near to wishing the same fate would overtake Frankie. She is a disconcerting young egoist, shrill and excitable, who feeds on dreams and is starved for affection. Her boyishness is aggressive and almost pathological. Her language is as tough as her mind is naive. She is unpopular with children of her own age and unmanageable in her own household. Her only friends are her cousin, the droll little boy who lives next door, and the wise, earthy, much-married, and all-mothering Negro cook who takes care of her.

Towards the evening's end Frankie has apparently passed through her difficult phase. She has begun to care about clothes and to be cared for by her contemporaries. In the person of a young football player she has even found her "Greek god." She remains, however, an egotist. She is unaffected by her cousin's death, and untouched by moving to another neighborhood and having to take her leave of the cook. If the sun has begun to shine for Frankie, the darkness of being alone, forgotten, and without hope is enveloping the cook.

What redeems Frankie from the audience's point of view is the heartstabbing honesty with which her distress, her fancy, and her loneliness are captured both by Mrs. McCullers in her writing and by Julie Harris in her playing. Miss Harris pulls no punches. She does not spare herself or try to prettify Frankie. Her hair is cropped forlornly. The red satin evening dress she buys for her brother's daytime wedding is the sorriest and most saddening costume any actress has had the integrity to wear in years. Miss Harris's is a brilliant performance. It is as sensitive as Mrs. McCullers's insight into people who are strays from the pack. Brandon De Wilde, who plays the bespectacled youngster from next door, is beguilingly free from self-consciousness. He is a manly little individualist, as much at home behind the footlights as if he were actually hanging around someone's kitchen, hoping for a cooky and begging for attention.

As the cook, Ethel Waters demonstrates once again how exceptional are her gifts. No person in our theatre glows with such goodness. Miss Waters's smile is spirit-lifting and cloud-dispelling. Her laugh is one of the most agreeable sounds known to this planet. So is her voice. Her dignity is no less innate than her benevolence. Moreover, she is an actress whose emotional range is wide. If her heart seems to smile in moments of happiness, her face when downcast achieves true tragic grandeur.

Harold Clurman has never done a better job as a director than with *The Member of the Wedding.* He has staged it with beauty, humor, and perception. He has not only assembled an excellent cast but has shown himself to be alert to every shading of an unusual script. The result is an evening as uncommon in its quality as it is radiant in its merits.

Note

1. *The Member of the Wedding,* by Carson McCullers. Directed by Harold Clurman. Settings and costumes by Lester Polakov. Presented by Robert Whitehead, Oliver Rea, and Stanley Martineau. With a cast including Ethel Waters, Julie Harris, Brandon De Wilde, Margaret Barker, Henry Scott, William Hansen, James Holden, Janet De Gore, etc. At the Empire Theatre, New York City. Opened January 5, 1950.

Mood Indigo

Kenneth Tynan*

Carson McCullers's *The Member of the Wedding* (Royal Court) is not so much a play as a tone-poem for three voices in two colours, black and white: and if anyone less gifted than Miss McCullers had written it, I should by now be embarked on a testy indictment of playwrights who presume to fling pots of "mood" in the public's face.

But Miss McCullers bears a charmed style, and wields it like a wand. Like her friend Tennessee Williams, she obtains magical effects of comic innocence by suddenly inserting wild or pedantic words into otherwise simple sentences: her characters are children, solemnly experimenting with grown-up locutions. This is a death-defying feat for a sophisticated writer to attempt: one false move, and she stands revealed as an adult woman dressed up as Shirley Temple. Miss McCullers triumphs, partly because her innate tact rejects the phoney-primitive, and partly because she is writing about the South, which is to America what Ireland is to England and Provence to the French—a playground of the imagination, a retreat from industrialism, a pastoral region set aside, by common consent and common nostalgia, for folklorish extravagance; a romantic limbo fully licensed for the sale of prose poetry at all hours of the day or night. The territory is swampy, and clodhoppers broach it at their peril. Miss McCullers treads it with the aptest lightness.

Her subject is a trio consisting of a jovial, one-eyed coloured servant named Berenice; an owlish seven-year-old named John Henry; and the latter's overgrown tomboy cousin, Frankie—or, as she prefers to be known, "F. Jasmine Addams." At twelve, Frankie belongs nowhere. Her coevals mock at her size, her immediate elders scorn her, her father is preoccupied with running his store, and her mother is dead. With Berenice and John Henry, two other oddlings, she strikes up a precarious camaraderie, which is constantly threatened by her perverse determination to accompany her elder brother and his bride on their forthcoming honeymoon.

For two acts, nothing happens next; and happens happily, for we are content to watch the bright, smog-free, verbal cobwebs with which Miss McCullers fills the stage. Then, overnight, a stormy hell breaks loose. Frus-

*Excerpt reprinted from *The Observer,* 10 February 1957, 11, by permission of the journal.

trated Frankie runs away from home; John Henry goes down with meningitis; and Berenice's closest friend, a hornplaying Negro, is almost lynched. Reality, like lightning, destroys the cobweb world. The shock cures Frankie; as far, that is, as she will ever be cured. She has found friends of her own age, but she will remain—and the point is most compassionately urged—one of nature's gooseberries.

. . .

THE SQUARE ROOT OF WONDERFUL

◆

Private Worlds

RICHARD HAYES*

Mrs. Carson McCullers inhabits a private world full of the shapes of grief; out of it she stares with large, panicked eyes, in whose depths we may yet discern the reflected images of a bizarre reality. It is this oblique authority of the terrible to which I respond in Mrs. McCullers; the surface texture of her work, on the contrary, has always seemed to me monochromatic, dusty and stunned. She is not, I think, an artist at ease with actuality. Her fable of the Southern waif searching for the "we" of "me" had pathetic power chiefly in its dramatization of fantasies: when Mrs. McCullers moved beyond that, she lost security, went prosy and distracted.

There is a comparable instability, though of a more radical penetration, in her new and original play *The Square Root of Wonderful* (at the National)—so coy a title, incidentally, in its blend of mathematical calculation and gush. She inscribes, across the blasted heath of a marriage, rather a cautionary tale of sexual susceptibility and humiliation and the somewhat desperate arrival at what I believe is grandly called psychological maturity. Desperate is indeed the word, for Mrs. McCullers' heroine moves into her new and "adult" alliance with relief rather than choice, just as she renounces an earlier, passionate, compulsive one not out of will or tragic wisdom, but exhaustion. I am not at all certain this is not the actual course of experience, at least in crises of emotional commitment and upheaval, but to render it esthetically is surely to insist on some definition and heightening of tone: if Mrs. McCullers wishes to impose a catastrophic reading on the theme, she has need more heavily to mark and dilate the note of *cost*. If, on the contrary, it is the rueful, bourgeois, social implacability of life catching one up, forcing one to a wry and graceful reason—if it is this she would embody (and I feel it implicit in her material), then Mrs. McCullers must include in her esthetic problem a richer ironic sense of manners and types, of the hard caprice and resilience of

*Excerpt reprinted from *The Commonweal* 67 (13 December 1957): 288–89, by permission of the journal. Copyright © Commonweal.

life, of a world in which pleasure, order, the probable and the possible finally—and not without kindness—call the tune.

This thematic confusion at the center of *The Square Root of Wonderful* radiates to its production, in which, obviously, no one has been willing to take the decisive hand. In that absence—and the presence of an intimidating décor vastly too prosaic for Mrs. McCullers' modulated gouache—the players adopt variously successful modes of what I shall call a mild Gothic realism. Miss Martine Bartlett brings hers off with most telling and perverse uniqueness: her eccentric is created with a shy power, and held at just the right distance for love. Miss Anne Baxter has an interesting, friendly presence as the heroine, yet I felt too assured a knowing in her performance: this role wants more muddle and generous satiric removal in its realization. In sum, there is a formal incoherence about *The Square Root of Wonderful* which disappoints; the play cannot be said to interest on the terms Mrs. McCullers obviously wished it should. Still, it issues from a sensibility which is genuine, however diffuse; it is full, too, of some wreckage of feeling. And it excels in a kind of mad, compulsive logic of wit, which I take to be peculiarly feminine and specifically Southern. It is a play not readily exhausted; always it holds something in reserve.

. . .

CLOCK WITHOUT HANDS

♦

In the Shadow of Death

IRVING HOWE*

The special art of Carson McCullers has always consisted in striking human experience at a tangent. Avoiding "ordinary life" with the caution of a writer for whom the knowledge of her powers is dependent on an awareness of her limitations, Mrs. McCullers has composed novels of tender grotesquerie about the sufferings of lonely deaf mutes, vulnerable adolescents, speechless country boys, gnarled aging women and freakish hunchbacks. Her characteristic style has been mannered, a kind of syncopated angular prose that sometimes achieves the rhythms of a chant; her moral approach has been oblique, as if she hoped to reach the secrets of human endurance by exploring states of psychic deprivation.

"The lover and beloved," Mrs. McCullers has written, "come from different countries"—a conviction that has led her to return, in most of her work, to the central subject of human loss and waste. She has done this not from a morbid preoccupation or improvised metaphysic, but simply because a close study of human loss and waste has seemed to her an avenue for discovering better possibilities. And when these discoveries have come, they have been precious indeed: moments of illumination in her novels where estranged people realize that even a small gesture can renew a human tie or yield a sense of personal value.

Unavoidably the kind of novel Mrs. McCullers has written involves special difficulties. It tends to be extremely fragile in structure and to rely excessively on the vibrations of the author's high-strung nerves. Her work can lapse into the sentimental, as in the otherwise lovely *The Member of the Wedding*; or into the sensationalistic, as in the otherwise powerful *Reflections in a Golden Eye*. At her best, Mrs. McCullers writes with a fierce control. Her first novel, *The Heart Is a Lonely Hunter,* is a poignant evocation of the life of two deaf mutes in a Southern town, cut off from other men yet sharing with them the inescapable human desires and defeats. And *The Ballad of the Sad Café,* in

*Reprinted from *The New York Times Book Review,* 17 September 1961, 5. Copyright © 1961 by The New York Times Company. Reprinted by permission.

which Mrs. McCullers revealed a gift for humor somewhat like that in the tall tale, is one of the finest novels ever written by an American.

Now, after some years of silence, Mrs. McCullers has written a new novel, *Clock Without Hands,* that is more robust, realistic and conventional, yet also less successful, than her earlier books. It opens well, on a Tolstoyan note: "Death is always the same, but each man dies in his own way. For J. T. Malone it began in such a simple, ordinary way that for a time he confused the end of life with the beginning of a new season." Owner of a pharmacy in a sleepy Georgia town, Malone is an American Everyman, decent but dull, his life absorbed in routine, until now, at 40, he discovers he is stricken with leukemia and has only a year to live.

With quiet assurance Mrs. McCullers unfolds the story of Malone, showing how the shock of approaching death forces him into the first glimmers of critical feeling toward his life. However, the awareness that comes from this kind of shock is often too little and too late and for Malone nothing seems left but to shamble through his remaining days. It is as if we were being invited to witness a small-town American version of Tolstoy's great story, "The Death of Ivan Ilyitch," which also portrays the last months of a man who had done no particular good or evil but had simply filled up his share of space and time.

At this point *Clock Without Hands* begins to run erratically. Convinced apparently that her story needs to be snapped into greater dramatic intensity, Mrs. McCullers introduces two weird figures. One is Judge Fox Clane, a sentimental old politician who dreams of reviving Southern glory by a scheme for the redemption of Confederate currency. The other is Sherman Pew, a Negro boy full of grandiose talk, who dreams himself into a romantic past and a heroic future.

The old Judge and the Negro boy meet as employer and secretary-servant, but their delusionary friendship is broken when Sherman refuses to work for the Confederate currency. In a recoil of anger Sherman—somewhat improbably—rents a house in a white neighborhood; and then the riff-raff of the town, incited by the Judge, proceeds to bomb the house and kill the boy. Only Malone, driven by death to a sense of human realities, speaks out against this crime, but without power or success. At the end Mrs. McCullers whips up a dubious dénouement by having the old Judge orate on the town radio, meaning to denounce the Supreme Court but driven by his guilt to recite the Gettysburg Address.

Behind this story Mrs. McCullers clearly had in mind a symbolic scheme: the white Judge and Negro boy seem to represent varieties of the social fantasy choking the South, while Malone embodies the ineradicable truth about human existence. Yet the book is so poorly constructed—one is troubled throughout by a disharmony between the sober realism of the Malone section and the grotesque capers of the section dealing with the Judge and Sherman Pew—that the symbolic scheme fails to carry strength or conviction.

That Malone should have the courage to speak against the mob is possible, but nothing Mrs. McCullers has shown makes it very persuasive. Judge Clane is credible in his public role as Southern reactionary and his private life as hopeless fantasist, but the two sides of him are hard to reconcile, for a man shrewdly realistic enough to be a Southern politician would hardly succumb to anything so fatuous as redeeming Confederate money. And as for Sherman Pew, he is touching as a sad little braggart, but quite implausible as a martyr defying the whites.

What is most disturbing about *Clock Without Hands* is the lethargic flatness of the prose. Such a writer as Mrs. McCullers is never likely to be too strong at realistic portraiture, but in her past work she could carry off almost anything through the virtuosity of her language. The style of her new novel, however, is that of a novelist mechanically going through the motions, and committing to paper not an integrated vision of life but an unadorned and scrappy scenario for a not-yet-written novel. Nothing, to be sure, is more difficult for the critic to establish than the absence of inner conviction and imaginative energy in a novel; yet once all serious intentions have been honored and all technical problems noted, only this conviction, only this energy really matters. And in *Clock Without Hands,* I regret to say, it is not to be found.

Death and Life in a Small Southern Town

RUMER GODDEN*

"And before Martha could return with the water, slowly, gently, without struggle or fear, life was removed from J. T. Malone. His livingness was gone, and to Martha who stood with the full glass of water in her hand, it sounded like a sigh."

As I closed the book on that I gave a sigh myself: perhaps no better tribute could have been paid because it was a sigh of complete fulfillment; for me not a word could be added or taken away from this marvel of a novel by Carson McCullers.

Her talent is extraordinary; the name of her first book *The Heart Is a Lonely Hunter* might be a description of it: the steady life-giving beat that is the core of every book: the pursuit of the quarry she sees and would catch and hold for us, often something so fleeting and ephemeral that most authors would quail at trying to catch it in words—and Mrs. McCullers' words are the coin of every day, plain, frank, slangy, unemotional. Above all her gift is apart, aloof, inevitably lonely: it owes nothing to any other writer and is paradoxical, a sure sign of richness: it is powerful yet humble, dignified yet utterly unpretentious.

One is always afraid when an author one reveres writes another book, and with Mrs. McCullers there has been a long gap: *The Ballad of the Sad Café* was published in 1951: between it and *Clock Without Hands* there has been only *The Square Root of Wonderful*, a play produced on Broadway. Would this new, major novel uphold the standard of the early ones? As soon as I opened it, I knew I should have trusted.

"Death is always the same but each man dies in his own way. For J. T. Malone it began in such a simple way that for a time he confused the end of life with the beginning of a new season." Plainly, kindly, if I can use that word about writing, we are at once in the story of J. T. Malone, the small-town pharmacist who has just learned that he is soon to die. His doctor has told him this, in such a jargon of medical terms that the desperate little man has to sift patiently to find the bitter truth. That sifting is the symbol of his remaining days. The town is Milan—in the South, of course—and its people go on, living their normal lives while J. T. Malone is suddenly suspended: it is

*Reprinted from *New York Herald Tribune Books,* 17 September 1961, 5, by permission of the author.

as if he has been given a new angle from which he suddenly sees himself and his neighbors, in particular his dear friends, the old Judge Fox Clane, once a Congressman, and the Judge's only grandson, Jester. These two are far more important than J. T. Malone's own family, his boy and girl, his wife Martha with her endless capacity for setting his teeth on edge, and the Judge's story is told along with his own, both shaped by the impact on their lives of the blue-eyed Negro boy, Sherman Pew, as sinister as he is disarming. Sherman is the center of the drama, in which they all, "willy-nilly," take part. After years of negation, of wandering, dodging, they are brought sharply up against life and, paradoxically, while the others fade, J. T. Malone, at the point of death, lives more and more intensely.

He is the book's greatest achievement. The old Judge fills the eye; for all his fantastic burblings and ideas he is noble with the pathos of a broken-down stag or lion. Jester, at seventeen rebelling against the old man's worship and finding the passion of first youth "lightly sown but strong," has all the appeal of the nicest kind of boy, while Sherman in his flamboyance and cruelty is oddly touching; but, in the telling of the dying J. T.—"telling" because Mrs. McCullers doesn't "draw" a character, but in the classic way "tells" it, each word revealing more and more—in her telling, this colorless, unattractive, ordinary little man, battling to come privately and respectably to terms with his own death, learning to live his last ironic days, far outshines in nobility the Judge he has looked up to and honored for so long.

"Transcendental"; "master of peculiar penetration"; "an incomparable storyteller." These praises of Carson McCullers do not exaggerate, yet I think she has something more rare: a capacity for telling the unvarnished truth. This sounds simple but it is extraordinarily difficult for a sensitive writer to reach the real truth of what he or she sees; sensitivity glosses with its very depth of feeling; it is the bedevilment of writers, especially women. Everything becomes twopence colored; as Sherman Pew says of himself: "I've had to make up stories because the real, actual was too dull, or too hard to take." Mrs. McCullers never colors anything; one cannot imagine her writing up, exaggerating, even for the sake of her story; this is the "real actual."

Of course truth is not always palatable. There are parts in this book that even now may shock in their matter-of-fact treatment of certain subjects. Truth, too, can give an uncomfortable bleakness, and one can well understand that, of Mrs. McCullers' novels, only *The Member of the Wedding*, a masterpiece, has become universally popular. This new book may well be too strange and strong, too frank, for many people. But like J. T. Malone, it grows richer and quieter as it draws towards its end, until the last hushed scene, where Martha's inept clacklings have become devoted service, gradually dims as if a light were going out.

I had no words when it was finished. I could only sigh.

Clock Without Hands
Belongs in Yesterday's Tower of Ivory

DOROTHY PARKER*

It is a queer thing, maybe even an outrageous thing, to say of Carson McCullers that she, of all writers, would people a book with stock characters. But that is what she has done in her latest novel, *Clock Without Hands*—Lord, what lovely titles she always finds!

The scene of the book is a small town in the Deep South. So faithfully has she cut its figures to the thin-worn pattern that they come out as burlesques. It is true that there are times, indeed whole stretches of time, when the way of certain inhabitants of small towns in the Deep South seems to be pure burlesque—burlesque, unfortunately, without jokes. To speak, and from the heart, as one who has hoisted piles of recent novels, usually first ones, about racial relations in the Deep South, is to be convinced that their authors feel obliged to use the tired old types to drive home their point. But Carson McCullers never needed to drive her point home, and she never, never recognized any *must* to follow where others had gone before. Still here they are in her new book, the old familiar idiots.

There is, in the main place, the old Judge—there is always the old Judge—a former Congressman and a member in his young days of the Klan. He is an enormous man—his like is always impressive on the scales—repeatedly described in the local press as "a fixed star in the galaxy of Southern statesmanship . . . a glory to this state and to the South"; he has saved every clipping. He is a widower. His wife, the traditional fair flower of the South, was called—oh, Mrs. McCullers, Mrs. McCullers!—Miss Missy. (In his employ is a Negro maid named Verily. Now "Verily" is a pretty word, and it is surely possible to assume that Carson McCullers knew a Negro girl so christened. Yet, though this is caviling of the rankest sort, one feels that the name might have been discarded, no matter how reluctantly, in favor of a more usual cognomen; "Verily" is disgustingly reminiscent of those names that white authors of the humorous branch of the trade conjure up to point the comicality of the titles Negroes give their children. Nor are authors the only

*Reprinted from *Esquire,* December 1961, 72–73. Work by Dorothy Parker courtesy of the National Association for the Advancement of Colored People.

whites in on the jest. Once when I was searching for an apartment, in a small town of the South only in that it was in southern California, I fell into the lacquered clutches of a lady real-estate agent, of whom the Hollywoods are full. She had just the thing. It belonged to a movie star so prominent that I can't think of her name, and her colored maid was to be left with the flat. The maid's name was Vanilla. "Think," said the lady agent, her voice a-ripple with fun, "how your guests will laugh!")

I beg your pardon. I am always liable to get way off the course when I think of such things.

The Judge had a son who, on a Christmas day, killed himself; the son's wife died in childbirth. So the child was the undisputed property of the old gentleman, who heaped upon him all the love and the hope that had belonged to his own son. It is his frequent statement that he and the boy are like blood twin brothers. The boy agrees to this fallacy by the use of silence.

The lad, Jester, "the shining boy," is a rather vaguely drawn character, spoiled and arrogant, lonely in the lap of friends, having to think for himself about the treatment accorded by the town to half its population. His thoughts on injustice are passionate in him, so it seems curious that, though he has sat across from the Judge through the long, hot midday for eighteen years, it is not until deep in the book that he speaks out his contempt for the old man's rantings.

For the Judge is grown all muddled in the head, what with his age and his obsession with his almighty plan: his plan for forcing the Federal Government to restore the value of Confederate currency, in restitution to the vanquished states for losses of property and possessions and services of slaves. ("Do you believe for a single instant that the slaves wanted to be free? Many a slave remained faithful to his old master, would not be freed till the day he died.")

The plan is his major theme, but he occasionally bellows his vow to smash the N.A.A.C.P., or in softer voice speaks his admiration for *Gone With the Wind*—"No truer book was ever written"; he could have written it himself.

The boy at last finds a friend, Sherman Pew, a Negro boy whose blue-grey eyes are startling in his dark face. Sherman was a foundling left in a church pew; it is the desire of his life to trace his mother. She was sure to be someone famous, someone extravagantly gifted, for Sherman himself has a golden voice, which could be called, as was Marian Anderson's, one voice in a century. It is a depth to his conviction that Marian Anderson must be his mother—there could not be two such voices in a century. He writes to her, addressing the letter to "Madame Marian Anderson, on the steps of the Lincoln Memorial." But no answer ever comes; he is avenged by stomping her phonograph record to splinters, and referring to her thereafter as "that cheating creep."

Sherman is, I think, the outstanding character of the book, a brilliant teller of whopping lies, insolent, riddled with conceit, yet always conscious of his racial position, taking upon himself all the horrors that have been committed on his people. Always like drumbeats in his head are the words: *do something; do something; do something.*

He does. Through an out-of-town agency, he arranges, not mentioning his color, to rent a house in a white people's zone of his own city; he fills it with elaborate furniture, including a grand piano, bought on credit. And here I find I am in trouble, for it is hard for me to believe that credit for such luxuries as grand pianos would be extended to a Negro lad in a small town in the Deep South.

From then on, *Clock Without Hands* seems to be hurriedly written. Its tragedies are piled almost sloppily one on another. It is known, of course, in the town that a black boy has moved into a white district. A meeting is called by the Judge to decide what steps must be taken. In a small room gathers a group of outraged men; somehow Jester sneaks in and stays to listen, hidden in the shadows. And here, again, I am disturbed, for my overliteral mind will not take in the fact that a tall young man, well-known and dressed according to his high station, can be successfully concealed in the shadows of a little room, back of a store. But so he is, because it says so in the book. He waits long enough to learn that the intruder's house is to be bombed, then goes to plead with Sherman to get out. But Sherman will not leave. The house is bombed: there are two bombs, one a direct hit on the Negro's head, the other setting fire to the house. Jester plans to kill the man who threw the bomb, but can find only compassion for him and throws away his gun.

Which ties up that Jester bit, fairly neatly.

More untidy, I think, is the final picture of the Judge. The ultimate insult has come to his South; the Supreme Court has ruled for the integration of schools. The old man insists on shrieking out against the outrage in a radio speech. But, delirious with fury, he cannot find words fit to fling into the air. His mind—if you insist, which I do not, his poor old mind—can only fumble until it lies on words that he was obliged to learn long ago, when he was a youth in law school, words of the speech that begins "Fourscore and seven years ago our . . ."

I have gone on so long for it is sharply difficult for me to attempt to explain that Carson McCullers has not, to my mind, again written a perfect book. She has been called the best writer in America and even if you flinch from superlatives, you must believe that she is well up close to that. Guesswork I know is the last impudence, yet it seems to me as if she had stayed a long, long time in her own world which is so far apart from this we live in that its noise and terrors could not reach her. Somewhere she sent out her strange, beautiful work. Then, one day, she came back to a world she never made, and found, on her doorstep, a newspaper. She was so shaken by the contents that she felt bounden to write about them.

But the newspaper was nearly ten years old.

Southern Justice

PENELOPE MORTIMER*

Around sixteen years ago Miss McCullers wrote, for her third novel, a minor classic. The first concise and penetrating study of American adolescence, *The Member of the Wedding* was a genuinely creative work—something entirely new (it came five years before *The Catcher in the Rye*), light as air and steel-hard. The penalty of such success is the responsibility it brings. The new Carson McCullers' will mean, to many people, the new *Member of the Wedding*. One may say of other writers that they are almost as good as McCullers. She must, impossibly, be better.

Clock Without Hands is set in a small town in Georgia in the year 1953—the year in which J. T. Malone, the local pharmacist, lived with the knowledge that he was going to die of leukemia. The novel is held, as it were, in this apprehension of death. We leave J. T. Malone for days at a time. We even forget him, distracted by the vitality of other, more positive characters. But when the book is over it is Malone, curiously enough, who lives on in the mind—his indifferent marriage to a wife who scares him by buying Coca Cola shares; his worrying job; his hopeless, plaintive struggle with death, and his final defeat. Not a great character, by any means; but a character who, containing death, moves among others like a Geiger counter, determining the extent of life. The large, central figure of the book is the old Judge, a lifelong friend of Malone, an exorbitant old fool, a one-horse Lear galloping into tragedy with croaking Confederate battle cries. It is easy for Miss McCullers to love; hate comes hard to her. Pity is her *forte*, "solace" her favourite word. It is all the more impressive, therefore, when she brings herself to be cruel, even though one knows it is in order to be kind. The Judge could have been a conventional American Blimp—amusing, tiresome, endearing, you can read them by the yard. It is Miss McCullers' unexpected virulence as much as her art which lifts him out of this category.

The Judge's wife, whom he loved, is dead. His son, after a legal battle with the old man in which, because the defendant was coloured, he was brutally defeated, has shot himself. His grandson, whom he adores, turns violently against him. The old man is last seen, his wits turned by the Supreme Court decision for school integration, screaming the Gettysburg Address into a dead microphone. I mention this scene—the climax of the book—first

*Reprinted from *Time and Tide,* 19 October 1961, 1757, by permission of the author.

because in it Miss McCullers, with an almost visible effort, controls her compassion. She demands the end of reaction, forbids moral blindness, condemns deformity. Personally, I approve of indignation because it is within my means. But for a writer of Miss McCullers' calibre one hopes, perhaps unfairly, for something more. Indignation is the poor man's sense of justice; the rich (it is obvious, I hope, that I use the term symbolically) should be able to afford the real thing.

The Judge's adversaries are the young: Jester, his grandson, and Sherman, a blue-eyed coloured boy. Jester is relatively unsuccessful as a character—perhaps because the skinny, bejeaned American teenager has become such a cliché that even the creator of F. Jasmine cannot revive him; perhaps because Miss McCullers loves him too dearly. Jester, at any rate, is responsible for the only lapses in her otherwise flawless writing: "His hard boy's hands unzipped his fly and touched his genitals for solace." If only it could have been *he* who unzipped it there would be a world of difference—the world possibly, between Salinger, who knows, and Miss McCullers who, in this case, really doesn't.

With Sherman, a basically unsympathetic person, she is far more successful. Sherman is cool. He talks high camp English and is employed by the Judge as an elegant, contemptuous amanuensis ("Oh a super-dooper secretary," Sherman said, his voice soft with enchantment. "I would adore that"). Both the Judge and Jester grow deeply dependent on him. Disgusted, he leaves them and buys a house in the white district of the town—a weary gesture, of self-destruction rather than aggression. The Judge organises a lynch gang and Sherman is killed. Jester plans to kill his murderer. Pocketing a gun, he invites the man for a flight in an aeroplane. The man prattles on about his bad luck in having had triplets, always twins and triplets, never a set of profitable quins. And then, "the grotesque pity of the story made Jester laugh that laughter of despair. And once having laughed and despaired and pitied, he knew he could not use the pistol. For in that instant the seed of compassion, forced by sorrow, had begun to blossom. . . ." And in that instant, too, we abandon the hope of genius and settle for excellence.

No, *Clock Without Hands* is not a masterpiece. It is not, to my mind, comparable with *The Member of the Wedding*. But it is a very, very good novel. Not only does it revive one's respect—irreparably, it seemed, damaged—for the novel as a form, but it excites emotions of pity and joy which normally are too spent to stir. Miss McCullers' talent for comedy is unrivaled and I can think of no one whose writing gives more pleasure or whose powers of stimulation are so strong. If we have to wait 15 years for her next novel, it will be a grave pity, an undeserved deprivation.

THE MORTGAGED HEART

◆

A Private Apprenticeship

NADINE GORDIMER*

This book of previously unpublished or uncollected work by Carson McCullers has been received as an act of familial piety on the part of its editor, her sister Margarita Smith, and a pretext to reminisce about meetings with the writer herself. It deserves better. If Carson McCullers was one of the very few great talents to come out of America since the war—and every critic bobs an obeisance to that—her early writings must be of the deepest interest. As for the personal recollections—Southern, invalid, child-like in spite of or perhaps because of her genius, she was for one reason or another an "experience" to meet. For me, for the first time, a frightening one: it was 1954, she had just recovered from a stroke, she was drinking a lot, and the setting was the old Fifth Avenue Hotel in New York, under mauve lights among cotton wool Easter bunnies. The shock was subjective, entirely; I had never met a famous writer before and in place of glory I found suffering. We met again, over ten years, and those times I found a triumph of survival and an affection and warmth that can come only of joy in life—in spite of everything. I'll put it down, someday, my two cents worth, for her future biographers. But what she was like is of no importance, set against what she wrote.

The most important section of this collection is the juvenilia—bearing in mind that here was a writer who published at 22 a first novel that was as structurally complex as it was fresh, as controlled as it was brilliant, and that stands up to repeated rereadings. Since she was a slow writer, it is reasonable to suppose she must have begun *The Heart Is a Lonely Hunter* not later than the age of 19. What is even more remarkable (and published here) is the outline of the novel, written for a prospective publisher. Any writer will recognize a truly extraordinary accomplishment of another order: the rare ability to stand outside one's own conception and analyse it in terms of its own methodology—and this from a young girl who became what one thinks of as

*Reprinted from *London Magazine,* n.s. 12 (October–November 1972): 134–37, by permission of the author. © Nadine Gordimer 1972. Printed by the permission of Russell & Volkening, Inc., as agents for the author.

the most instinctual and least cerebral of writers. This outline reveals another aspect of her genius (perhaps the key one) by demonstrating the skill with which she concealed the wires of cerebration, carrying the societal ideas of her work, in the living subconscious of her characters, transmuted into totally implicit actions and words. Compare the treatment of the symbolism of the relationship of the deaf mute, Singer, to the five isolated main characters in *The Heart Is a Lonely Hunter* with the creaking ropes and pulleys of "The Problem" symbolized by the solitary black man and white man shut up in a condemned apartment house in Bernard Malamud's *The Tenants!*

Carson McCullers was not an outstanding short story writer despite the poignant accomplishment of the much-anthologized *Wunderkind* and (my own choice, not included in this book) *The Jockey.* The early stories, some never before published and referred to by Margarita Smith as exercises, seem to me precisely that—very important first attempts at themes and means Carson McCullers was going to use in her novels. In them one can follow, fascinated, the private apprenticeship of a writer—without guild, without master, an apprenticeship to oneself, standing by all the while with one eye screwed up in assessment. She had a "teacher" for a time, in a "creative writing" class in New York (teacher's comments are included, for some of the pieces) who clearly recognized what was there and seems understandably embarrassed about having to deal with it within the terms of reference of such classes. But it was a matter of the writer learning to deal with the force within her. It was hit or miss; she grappled with it ably, as in her very first story, *Sucker,* written at 17, and then, trying perhaps to write more like the things she saw published, missed, falling into the weaknesses of *Breath From the Sky* and *The Aliens.* They were weaknesses of which faint traces were to remain, appearing from time to time in her work, and they are—not quite the reverse side of but a sort of occasional sleazy sheen, caught only at certain angles of situation, off the emotional intensity in the work of Southern writers, men as well as women.

Of the later stories, three are what all writers neglect to destroy, and the fourth, *Who Has Seen The Wind,* seems a breathless getting-down, sometimes expanding into the writer's full power, sometimes degenerating into hasty condensation, of what was meant to be a longer work. Which it became, in the form of the play, *The Square Root Of Wonderful.* (A title with that sheen, I'm afraid.) The section on Christmas consists obviously of magazine pieces she couldn't refuse to write because of the money offered; there were times when doctors' bills reduced her to real need. These pieces would have been better omitted, along with the speechifying fragments of the war years. Like most highly individual imaginative writers, she didn't have the poorest hack's knack of turning out conventional sentiments.

In the section on writers and writing she completes, in *The Flowering Dream,* her statement of her credo as a writer, and for this alone Margarita Smith's book justifies publication. These notes throw not the easy flashbulb of tuppenny-ha'penny gossip psychology but the mysterious gleam of the private and individual life-focus on puzzling aspects of her work. Those androgynous characters, the boy-girl Frankies and Micks, the overt homosexuals like wretched little Lily-Mae, and Captain Penderton of *Reflections in a Golden Eye,* and those—how to describe them?—almost polymorphous characters, half human of both sexes, half gentle mythical beast, the hunchback in *The Ballad of the Sad Café* and the deaf mute—are they best explained when she writes: "One cannot explain accusations of morbidity. . . . Nature is not abnormal, only lifelessness is abnormal . . . a deaf and dumb man is a symbol of infirmity, and he loves a person who is incapable of receiving his love . . . a homosexual is also a symbol of handicap and impotence." Or is the preoccupation with the emotionally and socially alienated and the creation of beings who are at once neither man nor woman but both, an attempt, as with Virginia Woolf's *Orlando,* to bring together all that is human and therefore, by Terence's definition, cannot be alien? Is the strange fellowship of these hopeless and unconsummated loves nearest to what is, for this writer, the highest kind of love? She writes: "The old Tristan-Isolde love, the Eros love—is inferior to the love of God, to fellowship, to the love of Agape—the Greek god of the feast, the God of brotherly love—and of man."

Finally, Carson McCullers was a white woman from the black South. Apart from the question of how the background in which she reiterates she felt rooted forever (even to the extent that she was uncertain how to write the speech of non-Southerners) shaped *her,* how, in her work, does the love of man fare in the context of racial fear and contempt? When one thinks back broadly on her novels, it is not what they have to say about black and white that seems to matter at all. She is the high priestess of adolescence: not just the physical adolescence of some of her best characters, but of a kind of second adolescence, an ambivalent state of spiritual possibility, a state of growth outside the optimum of bones and arteries in which she sees the maimed as having a head start. Yet if one returns to her work one sees that the reason why her blacks don't stand out of the page is because they are not "observed" from without, but are simply people presented, apparently, from the same level of knowledge from which she presents whites. It's easy to say she was too fine a writer, etc.; of course, she was, but the shameful "problem" was there, and one of its senseless tragedies is there, acted out, in her first novel, in the person of Doctor Copeland, an astonishingly prophetic portrait of the kind of educated black of the 'thirties to whom present-day black thinkers point as the emasculated man. This seems to me to be a more reliable guide to her attitudes than my wince at her occasional use—in the nonfiction articles collected—of terms like "my yard-men."

In her personal notes on life and work she does not discuss race. But she does speak of her belief in the "innately co-operative" nature of people, and of the "unnatural social tradition making them behave" in ways counter to this. Which would be putting it mildly, apropos the South, if this were to be her last word on the subject. It isn't. What that last word was is to be found in the depth and complexity of her work. Like that of Faulkner (whom as a writer she is so unlike), her refusal to dissociate herself from, to repudiate the white South may seem to us peculiar, given her belief in the love of man. But in her work as in Faulkner's the brutality of white Southerners towards black, and the degradation of black and white through this has—I'm afraid—been brought to life more devastatingly than by any black writer so far.

The Mortgaged Heart:
The Workshop of Carson McCullers

MELVIN J. FRIEDMAN*

C arson McCullers remarked in "The Flowering Dream: Notes on Writing," one of the pieces included in *The Mortgaged Heart:* "Always details provoke more ideas than any generality could furnish. When Christ was pierced in His *left* side, it is more moving and evocative than if He were just pierced." (p. 276) This statement goes a long way in explaining her concerns as a fiction writer. It places her in the company of Eudora Welty, Katherine Anne Porter, and Flannery O'Connor—a literary gathering suggested by Lawrence Graver in the final paragraph of his Minnesota pamphlet on Carson McCullers. Flannery O'Connor seems especially to the point. We can recall a statement she made in *Mystery and Manners* (the collection of "occasional prose" edited by Sally and Robert Fitzgerald) which echoes the McCullers judgment: "It's always necessary to remember that the fiction writer is much less *immediately* concerned with grand ideas and bristling emotions than he is with putting list slippers on clerks." (p. 70) She said this after examining a sentence from *Madame Bovary* and marvelling at its economy and powers of suggestiveness. She perhaps saw a special kinship between Flaubert's controlled methods of composition, realized through his famous *style indirect libre,* and her own "habit of art" (an expression she was particularly fond of). Carson McCullers was also drawn to Flaubert. She commented rather eloquently in a later passage in "The Flowering Dream": "*Madame Bovary* seems to be written with divine economy. It is one of the most painfully written novels, and one of the most painfully considered, of any age . . . In its lucidity and faultless grace, it seems to have flown straight from Flaubert's pen without an interruption in thought." (p. 278)

An interesting publishing coincidence brought the two Georgia fiction writers in close juxtaposition: in the fall of 1971, Farrar, Straus and Giroux brought out *The Complete Stories of Flannery O'Connor*[1] and Houghton Mifflin published Margarita G. Smith's edition of her sister Carson McCullers' uncollected writings, *The Mortgaged Heart.* The surface resemblances—both writers

*Reprinted from *Revue des Langues Vivantes,* U.S. Bicentennial Issue (1976): 143–55, by permission of the author.

born in Georgia, products of creative writing courses, victims of crippling illnesses which cut short their lives—suggested to reviewers that the two volumes belonged on the same shelf. The differences between these two posthumous collections, however, clearly outweigh the similarities. There seems to
be much more of Flaubert's "divine economy" in evidence in the O'Connor
collection than in the McCullers volume. All thirty-one of *The Complete
Stories*—even those six which were originally part of her Iowa master's thesis—seem splendidly finished. Many of the stories (or "exercises," as Margarita Smith prefers to call some of them) in *The Mortgaged Heart* appear to
have been prematurely removed from the drawing board. The O'Connor stories need no props or critical underpinnings, although the collection is clearly
enriched by a discreet introduction by Robert Giroux. The tentative and miscellaneous nature of *The Mortgaged Heart* depends crucially on the introduc-
tory directives and frequent apologies of Margarita Smith. It is a patchwork
quilt of short pieces, fiction and nonfiction, stitched together with some editorial finesse by Carson McCullers' sister.

The only fair way to judge the relative merits of the two collections
would be to compare the six stories which comprised Flannery O'Connor's
master's thesis with the early stories which Carson McCullers wrote for Sylvia
Chatfield Bates's class at New York University. The O'Connor stories, quite
simply, are finished pieces and point with assurance to her best work in the
shorter form, like "Revelation," "Everything That Rises Must Converge," and
"Judgement Day." Her earliest story, "The Geranium," in fact proves to be a
first draft of her last story, "Judgement Day" (which gives *The Complete Stories*
an intriguing symmetry nowhere in evidence in *The Mortgaged Heart*); the
characters are renamed, the situation is altered, the vision is deepened, but, in
the end, the O'Connor of 1946 has curiously much of the wisdom, finesse,
and narrative control of the O'Connor of 1964. Flannery O'Connor seems not
to have passed through the painful apprenticeship of a Carson McCullers.

One can see Flannery O'Connor's six stories moving toward her first
published book, *Wise Blood.* In fact, the first ten of *The Complete Stories,* all
written before the publication of *Wise Blood,* directly or indirectly make us
ready for this novel. There is a much more startling and radical leap from
Carson McCullers' early stories to *The Heart Is a Lonely Hunter.* Some of them,
like "Court in the West Eighties," "The Aliens," and especially the fairly
lengthy "Untitled Piece," anticipate situations and characters developed in
Mrs. McCullers' first novel but there are few hints in these early pieces to jus-
tify Tennessee Williams' strong statement (quoted in the introduction to *The
Mortgaged Heart*): "The great generation of writers that emerged in the twenties, poets such as Eliot, Crane, Cummings and Wallace Stevens, prose-writers
such as Faulkner, Hemingway, Fitzgerald and Katharine [*sic*] Anne Porter,
has not been succeeded or supplemented by any new figures of corresponding
stature with the sole exception of this prodigious young talent that first
appeared in 1940 with the publication of her first novel, *The Heart Is a Lonely*

Hunter." It could be argued, of course, that Carson McCullers' talents were always best realized in her novels and novellas while Flannery O'Connor's strength was the short story. Yet the astonishing distance separating apprenticeship story from first novel in the one instance and the proximity of the two in the second must have another explanation. The answer is probably to be found in the nature of the two writers and in their compositional habits. Everything is worth preserving in *The Complete Stories of Flannery O'Connor* while a large part of *The Mortgaged Heart* is salvageable only when we recall that it was written by Carson McCullers. Flannery O'Connor apparently never wrote any fugitive pieces; there was clearly no emptying of waste baskets or raiding of cobwebbed attics to fill out the pages of her *Complete Stories.*

One worries also about the miscellaneous nature of *The Mortgaged Heart.* Was it advisable to enclose within the same covers an outline for a novel, fiction, essays, and poetry? The solution arrived at by Flannery O'Connor's literary executors was to collect her critical pronouncements and prose divagations, which often required a good deal of editorial arrangement, in one volume and leave the stories for another. Thus we end up with a slim volume with little print on the page, *Mystery and Manners,* and an impressive tome of 550 pages offering all the stories Flannery O'Connor ever wrote in their order of composition. We are accurately reminded at every turn by this arrangement of the slightness of Flannery O'Connor's critical gift and of the enormity of her talent as a writer of short stories. This is as it should be. *The Mortgaged Heart,* unfortunately, does not function so valuably as a literary barometer. It exerts a numbing effect and fails to make distinctions. The stories and essays have a way of running together as if there were no generic difference between them. The best of McCullers—and that is very good indeed—is to be found in her two novels and three novellas. There is very little left to sustain *The Mortgaged Heart,* which illumines mostly the darker corners of the writer's workshop.

With this said, one should consider the collection in some detail. The three main divisions of the book, "short stories," "essays and articles," and "poetry," are preceded by editorial notes which offer useful biographical props and explain the principles of selection: "to show in part the growth of a writer." The growing-up process involves change and that is rarely in evidence. The numbing sameness of the language, authorial voice, techniques, and literary strategies—despite the fact that *The Mortgaged Heart* covers most of the years of Carson McCullers' life as a writer—alerts us rather cruelly to the vast distances separating her remarkable longer fiction (*The Heart Is a Lonely Hunter* through *The Member of the Wedding*) from her intermittent efforts in the shorter form. Even then, unexplainably, her best short stories, like "A Tree, a Rock, a Cloud" and "The Sojourner," are left out of Margarita Smith's gathering.

This worst-foot-forward approach seems to offer a kind of negative principle of selection for *The Mortgaged Heart.* Things are included, we are told, largely for their unavailability: "So this book is to give some idea of the early work of a writer and to illustrate, within the range of material chosen from her least-known work, the development of that talent." (p. xiv) (Actually some of her later work is included; in fact, four of the stories are referred to as "later stories" and several of the essays were written quite late in her career.) One wonders about the purpose served by such a collection. Margarita Smith herself is beset by uncertainty: "I am plagued with doubt because I wonder why Carson did not collect some of this material while she was living since money was always a problem." (p. xiv)

The early stories and "exercises" do supply a measure of "foreshadowing." The first story in *The Mortgaged Heart*, "Sucker"—as Oliver Evans already remarked in his excellent *The Ballad of Carson McCullers*—anticipates elements in the later work. One occurrence is almost exactly duplicated in *The Heart Is a Lonely Hunter*. Just as the nickname Bubber gave way to George in the novel so we are told in the next-to-the-last paragraph of the story: "I don't even want to call him Sucker any more and unless I forget I call him by his real name, Richard." (p. 18) The circumstances of the name-change are more than passingly similar.

"Court in the West Eighties," the next story in the collection, shifts scene to New York City and reveals a somewhat different narrative focus although it is written, like "Sucker," in the first-person. The storyteller here is more an observer than a participant. She settles her attention on a red-haired man, with a "calm drowsy face," who lives across the court from her. Margarita Smith suggests in her editor's note that the redhead may have anticipated Singer in *The Heart Is a Lonely Hunter;* indeed he stands toward the narrator in much the way Singer existed in the imaginations of Mick Kelly, Jake Blount, and Dr. Copeland. Here is the storyteller trying to account for her fascination: "It is not easy to explain about this faith I had in him. I don't know what I could have expected him to do, but the feeling was there just the same." (p. 26) She says again in the final paragraph of the story: "But no matter how peculiar it sounds I still have this feeling that there is something in him that could change a lot of situations and straighten them out." (p. 29)

There is a sense of anonymity about virtually everything in "Court in the West Eighties"; the characters are identified as the man with the red hair, the cellist, the young couple, a friend of mine. Everything seems quite conjectural, including the final words: " . . . in a sense it is true." (p. 29) This unwillingness to name, to identify with precision carries over into the novels and novellas. The opening sentence of *The Heart Is a Lonely Hunter* could scarcely be less revealing: "In the town there were two mutes, and they were always together." The last two sentences of the opening paragraph of *Reflections in a Golden Eye* proceed in the same intentionally vague manner: "There is a fort in the South where a few years ago a murder was committed. The participants of this tragedy were: two officers, a soldier, two women, a Filipino, and a horse." "The town itself is dreary" are the opening words of *The*

Ballad of the Sad Café. Cities and towns are usually not named in the novels and novellas (*Clock Without Hands* is an exception) and their settings seem more parabolic than real. "Court in the West Eighties," despite the mention of New York City, seems to gain its sense of place more from the imagination of its narrator than from any series of believable urban circumstances.

The unnamed, rather haunting figure of the cellist reappears in the next story, "Poldi." This piece is much closer to what Robbe-Grillet was later to speak of as an "instantané." (Sylvia Chatfield Bates, in her comment following it, accurately describes it as a " 'picture' story.") The temperament of the musician is on display here as it is in other selections in *The Mortgaged Heart.* We know from Oliver Evans how Carson McCullers came north to study at Juilliard and how a curious twist of fate thwarted her efforts in that direction. We get a sense of mockery in "Poldi" which we don't get in the longer works—like *The Heart Is a Lonely Hunter*—in which musical concerns are introduced. Poldi can appear quite ridiculous when she says: " 'I believe my playing has deepened much in the last month . . . Life does that to me—it happens every time something like this comes up. Not that it's ever been like this before. It's only after you've suffered that you can play.' " (p. 33)

The fragility-of-childhood theme figures prominently in the next two stories, "Breath from the Sky" and "The Orphanage." The second is little more than a sketch and does not seem very different from several of the pieces grouped under "essays and articles" later in the collection. There is indeed some fine expository prose here, including a brief series of near-poetic turns on a subject central to all of Carson McCullers' work: "The memories of childhood have a strange shuttling quality, and areas of darkness ring the spaces of light. The memories of childhood are like clear candles in an acre of night, illuminating fixed scenes from the surrounding darkness." (p. 50) This deserves a place next to the famous passage about the lover and the beloved in *The Ballad of the Sad Café* and the *we of me* passage in *The Member of the Wedding.*

One can only agree with Sylvia Chatfield Bates's estimation of the next story, "Instant of the Hour After": "I like this the least of anything you have done . . ." (p. 62) The kind of in-joke, sophisticated conversation, with the occasional literary allusions, is not what Carson McCullers does best. She manages somewhat better with it in the later story, "Who Has Seen the Wind?", probably because she fleshes out her material and gives it some narrative thrust. Yet the best of her early work is concerned with children and adolescents (or with ingenuous older men like the redhead in "Court in the West Eighties"). These types, in fact, predominate in most of the remaining stories in *The Mortgaged Heart.*

"Like That" returns to the matter and method of "Sucker." The colloquially-tuned voice of the adolescent manages the narration. The disappointments which come from growing up are as central to this story as they were to the earlier one. The final sentence of the story establishes the fear and uncertainty so essential to McCullers characters like Mick Kelly and Frankie Addams: "I don't want to grow up—if it's like that." (p. 73)

"Wunderkind" is clearly not among Carson McCullers' "least-known work" as it has long been available in a collection called *The Ballad of the Sad Café and Other Stories;* it is apparently reprinted here for sentimental reasons: " . . . it marks the beginning of her [Carson McCullers'] professional career." (p. 4) It continues some of the musical preoccupations of "Poldi." Adolescence and its torments are again of central importance. The former prodigy fails on her crucial day—the day the story is mainly concerned with although much of its substance is gained through flashback—to play even the most elementary piece of music. Failed talent and frustration are revealed through the staccato syntax and movement of next-to-the-final paragraph: "Her coat. The mittens and galoshes. The school books and the satchel he had given her on her birthday. All from the silent room that was hers. Quickly—before he would have to speak." (p. 86)

The principal character in "The Aliens" is also a musician. (There are all kinds of musical references which reinforce the poetic base of the story and give it a kind of melodic texture.) But his being a Jew, with a strong sense of the Diaspora, is more important. His bus ride south, accompanied part of the way by a young southerner, carries with it strong symbolic properties. The allegorist in Carson McCullers is very much in evidence, especially in a sentence like this: "The journey of this fugitive—for the Jew had fled from his home in Munich two years before—more nearly resembled a state of mind than a period of travelling computable by maps and timetables." (p. 91) One of the music teachers in "Wunderkind" was identified, in a passing reference, as a Jew, but this fact held no special consequences for the story.

"The Aliens" seems to uncover a tendency to make the Jew a metaphor for suffering and alienation in Carson McCullers' work. It should be recalled that Singer was taken for a Jew by Dr. Copeland in *The Heart Is a Lonely Hunter.* Singer's original name, we know from "The Flowering Dream," was Harry Minowitz (with its distinctly Jewish ring); when Singer finally emerged in the finished novel, the name Harry Minowitz was given to the Jewish boy who had the fleeting adolescent sexual relationship with Mick Kelly. Finally, it should be noted that Jake Blount accused Biff Brannon of looking "like a Jew in Germany." The response by Biff was that he was "an eighth part Jew." The Jew's special kind of poetry and his enviable remoteness give him a favored position in most of Carson McCullers' fiction. The dying J. T. Malone in *Clock Without Hands* resents Jews, but in a quite irrational way.

"Untitled Piece," the next selection in *The Mortgaged Heart,* indicates how close Carson McCullers was to writing *The Heart Is a Lonely Hunter.* Margarita Smith may be right in suggesting that it could have been the beginning of a novel *manqué* or abandoned. In any case, it offers a view of a family very like Mick Kelly's, although the vantage point is very different from *The Heart Is a Lonely Hunter.* The story gains its frame from the son Andrew's returning to his home town in Georgia after a three-year absence. Much of it proceeds through flashback. One of the central symbols is the glider he and his sister Sara had been working on many years before: " . . . and perhaps he kept remembering it because the things he had felt at that time were so much like the expectancy this journey now brought." (p. 99) Music is also a vital concern of this story; it shapes the situation as well as the imagery. At one point we are told: "Music to them [Andrew and Sara] was something like the glider should have been." (p. 106) Two Jews figure prominently: Aunt Esther who takes Sara off with her to Detroit; and Harry Minowitz who is an older and less attractive version of the character in *The Heart Is a Lonely Hunter.*

There is no mistaking the proximity of this "exercise" to Carson McCullers' first novel, especially to the Mick Kelly sections. The next step on the way to the novel is the "Author's Outline of 'The Mute' " which appeared for the first time as the appendix to Oliver Evans' book on Carson McCullers. These blueprints for the novel offer an intriguing view of her workshop. It is the same kind of glimpse of the creative process as we get from something like Gide's *Journal of "The Counterfeiters."* The comparison is especially apt when we see how preoccupied both novelists were with the possibilities of musical analogies and references in fiction. Here is Gide in the opening paragraph of his *Journal:* "I am like a musician striving, in the manner of César Franck, to juxtapose and overlap an andante theme and an allegro theme." Here is Carson McCullers in the final section of her outline: "This book is planned according to a definite and balanced design. The form is contrapuntal throughout. Like a voice in a fugue each one of the main characters is an entirety in himself . . ." (p. 148)

This "outline" is one of the more valuable items in *The Mortgaged Heart.* It is placed at the end of the section which Margarita Smith calls the "Early Stories." In a sense it ends Carson McCullers' apprenticeship with all its self-consciousness and youthful indulgences. It exposes the rawness of her nerves and the innocence of her compositional habits. We rarely get such an unedited view of the sensibility of the writer. We certainly do not get this close to Gide in his *Journal of "The Counterfeiters."*

The four "later stories" still do not seem to be vintage McCullers. Most critics of her work seem to prefer the novellas to the novels and both in turn to the short stories. Ihab Hassan, in *Radical Innocence,* speaks of "the deficiencies of Carson McCullers in the short form." Dale Edmonds, in his pamphlet on her in the "Southern Writers Series" (published by the Steck-Vaughn Company in Austin, Texas), is more charitable: "Of the dozen stories (not including portions of novels) Carson McCullers published over a span of nearly thirty years, at least half may be classified as good, and perhaps three of these may be considered distinguished." (pp. 32–33) He singles out for special mention "Correspondence," which is the first of these "later stories" included in *The Mortgaged Heart.* This piece is made up of four letters sent by an American teenage girl, Henky Evans, to a prospective pen-pal in Brazil. The letters are never answered. Mr. Edmonds places it in the mainstream of the *œuvre:* "Another of Mrs. McCullers' gawky adolescent girls on the outside yearning to become part of a 'we,' Henky is characterized extremely well by her letters." (p. 33)

"Art and Mr. Mahoney" is little more than a blown-up anecdote. "The Haunted Boy," however, deserves serious attention. It has something in common with another McCullers story, not included in *The Mortgaged Heart,* "A Domestic Dilemma." In each case a psychologically disturbed mother and wife is the center of attention. We see "A Domestic Dilemma" through the eyes of the husband who despairs of his wife's excessive drinking. "The Haunted Boy" offers the vantage point of the teenage son who fears that his mother has had another nervous breakdown. The "terror of the afternoon"— while the son imagines that all kinds of horrible things have happened to his mother—is relieved by her unexpected appearance following a harmless shopping expedition. The sense of relief pervades the last sentence of the story: "Although he felt he would never cry again—or at least not until he was sixteen—in the brightness of his tears glistened the safe, lighted kitchen, now that he was no longer a haunted boy, now that he was glad somehow, and not afraid." (p. 177)

"Who Has Seen the Wind?" is less characteristic of Carson McCullers' manner than almost any other story included in *The Mortgaged Heart.* It seems, however, well placed in the collection, coming as it does at the end of the short story section. Indeed it offers a natural bridge from the stories to the essays. It contains some interesting literary theorizing and some judgments of other writers, especially Proust; it perhaps belongs side by side essays like "The Vision Shared" and "The Flowering Dream: Notes on Writing."

"Who Has Seen the Wind?" concerns the author of a successful first novel and a failed second novel who seems unable to manage a third. His marriage has fallen to pieces; even his cocktail-party behavior has taken on certain unpleasant eccentricities. At the end of the story he searches irrationally and distractedly for his wife who has left him.

We are told several times in the long opening paragraph about the blank page which faces the author, Ken Harris. Carson McCullers seems to be speaking here about the problems the writer encounters when confronted with "le vide papier que la blancheur défend" (Mallarmé's famous image). Ken Harris is spared temporarily by a six P.M. cocktail party at which he manages to introduce Proust in the opening conversation. (He incorrectly speaks of "that last party of the Duc de Guermantes"; the final party he refers to occurred at the home of the Prince and Princesse de Guermantes—the kind of mistake allowable when discussing almost any other writer but Proust who was so careful in the distinctions he made among the nobility. One suspects that this lapse may have been intentional on Carson McCullers' part as a way of indicating Ken Harris' carelessness in his literary judgments.) Other writers like Joyce, Thomas Wolfe, and Thoreau are also mentioned in the text.

One noticed the same kind of literary name-dropping in "Instant of the Hour After." But it is not, certainly, a characteristic of her work.

The "Essays and Articles" section of *The Mortgaged Heart* is divided into three parts: "The War Years," "Christmas," and "Writers and Writing." We are told in Margarita Smith's editor's note that most of Carson McCullers' nonfiction is included here. Words like love, communication, loneliness, and spiritual isolation seem to appear with the same regularity in her essays as they do in her fiction. Despite the seeming unliterary nature of the first two parts of "Essays and Articles," they are filled with references to writers and their works.

Probably the most interesting piece included under "The War Years" is "Brooklyn Is My Neighbourhood." When reading it one is reminded very much of Truman Capote's "A House on the Heights" with its spirited beginning: "I live in Brooklyn. By choice." In fact, Capote refers in his essay to the house on Middagh Street which Carson McCullers at one time shared with W. H. Auden, Richard Wright, Benjamin Britten, Paul Bowles, Gypsy Rose Lee, and other celebrities. Carson McCullers' piece is not as exaggeratedly poetic as Capote's (Capote could rarely withstand the alliterative temptation and gave way to excesses like "greenless grime-gray," "plenipotentiaries from the pearl-floored palace of Poseidon," or "pimpled purple birthmark bandit-masked") but it has the same remarkable sense of place. She sees in Brooklyn great dignity, restraint, respectability, and a sense of tradition. Just as Brooklyn fails in her eyes to be exciting, brilliant, and flashy, so does her manner in this essay eschew these very qualities and opt for understatement.

Christmas, we are told, was Carson McCullers' favorite holiday and so we should not be surprised to find three essays devoted to it. As we read her in this section of *The Mortgaged Heart,* we are probably again reminded of Capote, this time of his "A Christmas Memory." (The connection between the two writers, by the way, has been amply explored by both Mark Schorer in his "McCullers and Capote: Basic Patterns" and Frank Baldanza in his "Plato in Dixie.") Her last piece concerned with Christmas, "A Hospital Christmas Eve," is an especially compelling statement. The setting is a hospital ward. Carson McCullers focuses attention on her roommate: "We talked for a while, and I read to her the most living piece of literature, except for the Bible, that I know. James Joyce's 'The Dead.' " (p. 245) Then she quotes the famous last paragraph of the Joyce story with its alliteration of the "f" and "s" sounds. When Margarita Smith reminds us that this was the last thing Carson McCullers wrote before she died, the experience takes on another dimension.

The "Writers and Writing" section contains several personal statements about craft, a convincing essay on the relationship of modern Southern literature to 19th century Russian realism, and two pieces on Isak Dinesen. The second sentence in "The Vision Shared" makes her position very clear: "The ingenuities of aesthetics have never been my problems." (p. 262) She further enforces this notion on the following page: " . . . my creative life has done nothing to equip me for formal aesthetic evaluations." Despite Baudelaire's celebrated statement that every creative writer contains a critic, many poets, novelists, and playwrights have refused to take critical or aesthetic stands. Flannery O'Connor, for example, is unyielding on this subject in *Mystery and Manners:* "I think that if there is any value in hearing writers talk, it will be in hearing what they can witness to and not what they can theorize about." (p. 36) She speaks of herself as being "an author congenitally innocent of theory." (p. 114)

Carson McCullers' literary judgments are in numerous other ways very close to those of Flannery O'Connor. "The Flowering Dream: Notes on Writing" has much in common with several of the composite pieces in *Mystery and Manners.* A passage like this could easily have been written by Flannery O'Connor: "As a writer, I've always worked very hard. But as a writer, I've also known that hard work is not enough. In the process of hard work, there must come an illumination, a divine spark that puts the work into focus and balance." (p. 280) Although Flannery O'Connor, to my knowledge, never commented in her fiction or essays on Isak Dinesen, one can imagine her joining with Carson McCullers in her praise of the Danish writer's "radiance" and the "tightrope grace of [her] sentences."

The slightest part of *The Mortgaged Heart* is the last one—which is turned over to her poetry. We are told by Margarita Smith that she did not write poems until she was established as a fiction writer. The verse included here makes the point tellingly that her poetic habits were at best an unfortunate addendum to her other literary talents.

One must wonder, then, how much *The Mortgaged Heart* will advance Carson McCullers' reputation. The miscellaneous nature of the collection can only be unsettling. The notion of including all the difficult-to-come-by uncollected work of a writer seems not to be a substitute for quality. When John Hawkes brought out *Lunar Landscapes* in 1969, he was careful to limit himself to his stories and novellas—although he might indeed have rounded out the collection with his early poetry and his critical essays. Hawkes' short stories are considerably weaker than his novellas but they do not suffer especially when brought in close juxtaposition with them; in fact, *Lunar Landscapes* gains a kind of balance from the way in which the six stories circle the fringes of the three longer pieces and support and footnote certain of their themes. One leaves with the feeling that the Hawkes collection is very much of a piece, something which cannot be said about *The Mortgaged Heart.*

There is the uncomfortable feeling of late that Carson McCullers' position in Southern literature is suffering some sort of decline. An example of what I have in mind was recently expressed in an essay by Robert Drake, "Cultivating My Antique Garden," *Modern Age,* Spring 1972. (Drake is a Southern short story writer who teaches English at the University of Tennessee; he is also the author of an able pamphlet on Flannery O'Connor.) He says, in the course of overviewing the Southern literary scene: " . . . despite

Mrs. McCullers' genuine triumphs, she ultimately betrayed her own gift and began willing herself to venture away from her true country into foreign lands, even to write up the news of the day, which is always fatal for the truth-telling novelist." (p. 190) *The Mortgaged Heart,* alas, is not likely to change Drake's mind.

A long and compelling analysis of the McCullers collection appeared after the completion of this essay: David Madden—another Southern writer and a very gifted one—has his say in "Transfixed Among the Self-Inflicted Ruins: Carson McCullers's *The Mortgaged Heart*" (*Southern Literary Journal,* Fall 1972). His conclusions are not very different from mine. His opening sentence puts the matter forcefully: "By assembling *The Mortgaged Heart,* Carson McCullers's younger sister, Margarita G. Smith, former fiction editor of *Mademoiselle,* has given the world a long look at the mediocre side of the author of *The Member of the Wedding.*"[2]

Notes

1. See my "Flannery O'Connor: The Canon Completed, The Commentary Continuing," *The Southern Literary Journal,* Spring 1973, 116–123.

2. See also the following recent books on Carson McCullers: Virginia Spencer Carr's definitive biography, *The Lonely Hunter: A Biography of Carson McCullers* (Garden City, N.Y.: Doubleday, 1975), and Richard M. Cook's *Carson McCullers* (New York: Frederick Ungar, 1975).

TRIBUTES

◆

The Watchers

MURIEL RUKEYSER*

for Carson and Reeves

She said to me, He lay there sleeping
Upon my bed cast down
With all the bitterness dissolved at last,
An innocent peace within a sleeping head;
He could not find his infant war, nor turn
To that particular zoo, his family of the dead.
I saw her smile of power against his deep
Heart, his waking heart,
Her enmity, her sexual dread.

He said to me, She slept and dreaming
Brought round her face
Closer to me in silence than in fire,
But smiled, but smiled, entering her dark life
Whose hours I never knew, wherein she smiles.
Wherein she dim descending breathes upon
My daylight and the color of waking goes.
Deep in his face, the wanderer
Bringing the gifts of legend and the wars,
Conspiracy of opposing images.

In the long room of dream I saw them sleep,
Turned to each other, clear,
With an obliterated look—
Love, god of foreheads, touching then
Their bending foreheads while the voice of sleep
Wept and sang and sang again
In a chanting of fountains,
A chattering of watches,
Love, sang my sleep, the wavelight on the stone.

*Reprinted from *Waterlily Fire: Poems 1935–1965* (Macmillan, 1962), 159–60. ©1962, 1978 Muriel Rukeyser, by permission of William L. Rukeyser.

I weep to go beyond this throne and the waterlight,
To kiss their eyelids for the last time and pass
From the delicate confidence of their sly throats,
The conversation of their flesh of dreams.
And though I weep in my dream,
When I wake I will not weep.

The Author

TENNESSEE WILLIAMS*

Ever since a novelist told me that the theatre was an art manqué, meaning something less than an art, and I got so mad that I nearly drove my car through the lowered gates of an Italian railroad crossing and smack into the *Rapido* from Naples to Rome, I have thought it best to limit my personal encounter with other writers almost as strictly as collisions should be limited between two speeding vehicles in any country. And yet somehow I have managed to make many close and deeply satisfying friendships with other writers, such as Paul and Jane Bowles, Gore Vidal, Truman Capote, Donald Windham, William Inge, Alberto Moravia, and, perhaps most of all, with Carson McCullers, despite the long periods in which we lived in very separate parts of the world. Let's face the fact that the almost constantly irritated sensibilities of writers make it difficult for them to get along together as well as they should. This is especially true between novelists and playwrights. Novelists have the idea that playwrights are the pecuniary favorites of fortune, and they have some justification in this suspicion. Novelists and poets seem to be expected to live on air and subsidies, usually meager, while it is embarrassingly true that playwrights are recipients of comparatively large royalties, have Diners' Club cards, eat at Sardi's, and can travel first class. And so, on the surface, which is always misleading, they appear to be the favorites of fortune, and it is quite understandable and forgivable that their poet and novelist friends are tempted to goad them about the impurities of their medium.

Yet when this invidious attitude is dispelled, it can be agreeable for them to get together. The playwright must put aside his envy of the poet's or novelist's connection with a purer medium, and the novelist or the poet must have the good sense and sensibility to see that the material advantages of the playwright are incidental.

Carson McCullers and I have never had this embarrassment between us, although she is more consistently a writer of fiction than a playwright. From the moment of our first meeting, Carson, with her phenomenal understanding of another vulnerable being, felt nothing for me but that affectionate

*Reprinted from the *Saturday Review,* 23 September 1961, 14–15, by permission of the Lady St Just, trustee under the will of Tennessee Williams.

compassion that I needed so much and that she can give so freely, more freely than anyone else I know in the world of letters.

On the island of Nantucket, the summer of 1946, we worked at opposite ends of a table, she on a dramatization of *The Member of the Wedding* and I on *Summer and Smoke,* and for the first time I found it completely comfortable to work in the same room with another writer. We read each other our day's work over our after-dinner drinks, and she gave me the heart to continue a play that I feared was hopeless.

When I told her that I thought my creative powers were exhausted, she said to me, wisely and truly, an artist always feels that dread, that terror, when he has completed a work to which his heart has been so totally committed that the finishing of it seems to have finished him too, that what he lives for is gone like yesteryear's snow.

At the end of that summer's work I became very ill, and only a few months later so did she, with a mysterious paralysis of her right arm. I have such a fierce resistance to physical illness that I continually push it back; Carson's strength is enormous but primarily exists in her spirit. From 1947 to the present year she has been, as many interested in American writing know, a gallant invalid. She has lived with that paralysis of the right arm and with an excruciating series of operations to correct it, yet all the while she has never surrendered to it. During those fourteen years she has kept on working steadily and with all the creative and personal distinction that makes her an inspiring figure to us relative weaklings. She has completed two plays of the most impressive quality, and at the same time she has given us stories and poems of the purest distinction.

And all this time, these fourteen years, she has also been working on her fifth novel, *Clock Without Hands.*

Before I went abroad last spring, she told me that she felt she couldn't complete it, that she had paid out all her strength. Then I reminded her of what she had told me, those fourteen years ago, that at the end, or near it, of a work to which the artist's heart is totally committed, he always feels that dread, that terror which is greater than the fear of death.

When I returned from abroad, two and a half months later, an advance copy of the completed novel was waiting for me in Key West.

If I hadn't known before that Carson is a worker of miracles, this work would surely have convinced me of it, for without any sign of the dreadful circumstances under which she accomplished it, this work was once again a thing set on paper as indelibly as if it had been carved onto stone. Here was all the stature, nobility of spirit, and profound understanding of the lonely, searching heart that make her, in my opinion, the greatest living writer of our country, if not of the world.

I Wish I Had Written
The Ballad of the Sad Café by Carson McCullers

KAY BOYLE*

Aside from the first quick unconsidered emotion which moved me as I read for the first time "The Ballad of the Sad Café," there are several quite definable reasons why I still wish, two and a half years later, that I had been its author. One or two of them I would like to set down here.

I believe the better part of envy to be admiration, and in this story of Carson McCullers I admire the bold objective approach—graced with reverence and with humility as it is; I admire the ruthless and fearless self-imposed experience of severing herself from all that would have made the content of this story applicable to and identifiable with self. I speak first of this because it denotes a sense of proportion which we demand of architects and painters, of plumbers and carpenters, but not of women writers. I pay homage to it because the work of many women writers of our century has been hopelessly invalided by the shape and dress of that tender, fragile, insufferable, and recognizable figure of feminine ego which is pivot for their books. In "The Ballad of the Sad Café," Carson McCullers accepted the responsibility of being artisan as well as sensitive artist. I believe that the deliberation of thought which brings one, while still young, to the knowledge that sensitive artistry is not enough, is undoubtedly the greatest endowment a writer can have.

Second, there is this reason why I wish I had written "The Ballad of the Sad Café." Its specifications are far more profound than time of year, than geographical place, than century—although time of year, and place, and even the hour of the day and night are technically there. Each line of it has been written not for a wide public or for a small group of critics, but as though in the presence of the very simplest and therefore the very greatest human emotions. It is as if love, and anger, and grief were there as audience, and it was their approval or their censure which brought the action and the speech of despair, and patience, and loyalty to remarkable articulation.

We come, then, to the language of this story. It proceeds with beauty and with balance to evoke not only the exact image of what was seen, but the exact measure of its truth.

*Reprinted from *I Wish I'd Written That: Selections Chosen by Favorite American Authors,* ed. Eugene J. Woods (McGraw-Hill, 1946), 300–01. Reprinted by permission of the author and the Watkins/Loomis Agency.

I should like to have written:

"It was toward midnight on a soft quiet evening in April. The sky was the color of a blue swamp iris, the moon clear and bright. . . . Down by the creek the square brick factory was yellow with light and there was the faint, steady hum of the looms. It was such a night when it is good to hear from faraway, across the dark fields, the slow song of a Negro on his way to make love."

Tennessee and Carson:
Notes on a Concept for a Play

DAVID MADDEN*

Tennessee: "From the moment of our first meeting, Carson, with her phenomenal understanding of another vulnerable being, felt nothing for me but that affectionate compassion that I needed so much and that she can give so freely, more freely than anyone I know in the world of letters."

Donald Spoto, Tennessee Williams' biographer, says: "And so began one of the most affecting and strange relationships in American literary history."

Carson: "As soon as I was installed, Tennessee asked me, 'Why don't you make a play out of *Member*?' I was challenged in one malicious part of myself because *The New Yorker* in reviewing the novel said that I had many of the components of great writing, but the chief thing I lacked was a sense of drama. Clifton Fadiman attacked the book because it 'was not dramatic.' "

Carson McCullers' biographer, Virginia Carr, says that with Tennessee, she had what "proved to be one of the most enduring friendships and *loves* she was ever to experience with a fellow artist."

One morning, in the spring of 1980, Peggy Bach and I were driving down to New Orleans, that city of possibilities, talking about her plans to choreograph a medley of scenes from *The Glass Menagerie, A Streetcar Named Desire,* and *Summer and Smoke,* focusing on Laura, Blanche, and Alma. I told Peggy that I had just been reading the chapter in Virginia Carr's biography of Carson McCullers where she tells about the weeks young Carson and Tennessee spent together at Nantucket writing their plays, *The Member of the Wedding* and *Summer and Smoke,* across from each other at the same dining room table. By the time we were walking in the French Quarter, Peggy and I had envisioned an evening of the theater of Carson McCullers and Tennessee Williams in which two actors would portray Carson and Tennessee in Nantucket and also recite key speeches from those two plays, as a kind of reader's theater production. Peggy and I had discussed several possible ways of presenting the concept, which we call *Tennessee and Carson*. After six years, we have gotten back to work on the play.

*Reprinted from *Pembroke Magazine* 20 (1988): 96–103, by permission of the journal and the author.

In 1980, I wrote to Tennessee Williams' agent, asking permission to quote from *Summer and Smoke.* After the agent had described the play to Tennessee (whom I had known since 1957), he reported that Tennessee would like to collaborate with us on writing the play. But Tennessee and I were deeply into other works and agreed to put off getting to work. We waited too long.

So Peggy Bach and I will write the play about Carson McCullers and Tennessee Williams.

We have very little down on paper at this point, so I want to describe the possibilities we are exploring.

I first became aware of Tennessee Williams in 1949 when my first play "Call Herman in to Supper" was performed in the round at the University of Tennessee in Knoxville, Tennessee, my home town, and people told me I ought to get rid of the Williams influence. I was 16 and had never read or seen any of Williams' plays.

I saw *Summer and Smoke* at the Circle in the Square, the revival with Geraldine Page, sometime after its opening April 24, 1952 (it ran to April 1953). *Summer and Smoke* is not my favorite Williams play. For me, *A Streetcar Named Desire* is one of the greatest plays ever written. I think Eugene O'Neill is our American Aeschylus, Arthur Miller is our American Sophocles, and Tennessee Williams is our American Euripides. My play and novel *Cassandra Singing* is similar to *Orpheus Descending,* although I saw that play after I had written my play.

I met Tennessee in 1957, when he came to my hometown Knoxville, Tennessee, for the funeral of his father. I saw him only once more. The evening I handed the corrected galleys for my first novel *The Beautiful Greed* to Random House, I ran into him as he was walking down Fifth Avenue with Gore Vidal.

I first heard of Carson McCullers when I saw the old Penguin paperback of *The Heart Is a Lonely Hunter,* designed by Robert Jonas, and read the opening line: "In the town there were two mutes and they were always together." The character of Mick and the structure of *The Heart Is a Lonely Hunter* influenced my novel *Cassandra Singing. The Heart Is a Lonely Hunter* is on *my* list of the ten great American novels.

I saw *The Member of the Wedding* in 1950 when I was 17. My first Broadway Play. I read the novel much later. I had read only part of *The Heart.* The character Frankie and Julie Harris' portrayal of her influenced my creation of Cassie in *Cassandra Singing,* play, novel, moviescript, radio script. I met Julie Harris at the stage door of the Empire Theater and told her, "Someday *I* will write a play for you." *Cassandra Singing* was that play. I never met Carson McCullers, but we corresponded in 1959 about my desire to adapt *The Heart Is a Lonely Hunter* to the stage. She decided to adapt it herself.

The time is June-July 1946, but, like *The Glass Menagerie, Tennessee and Carson* is "a memory play" and so will move from 1946 back and forth in time. "Time," said Carson, "the endless idiot, runs *screaming* around the world."

The place is the island of Nantucket *and,* simultaneously, the consciousness of Tennessee and Carson. "The mind is its own place and can make a heaven of hell, a hell of heaven." We get a sense of Tennessee's childhood in Columbus, Mississippi, and of Carson's in Columbia, Georgia, about 200 miles apart, *almost* on a line, as Tennessee and Carson sit opposite each other at the dining room table. We get some sense of Carson in the future, in Nyack, New York on the Hudson, and of Tennessee in Rome, New Orleans, and Key West.

My imagination and Peggy Bach's are free to move in time and space. "What is more intimate," said Carson, "than one's own imagination?" "The Imagination is truer than reality." "The Imagination combines memory with insight, combines reality with the dream."

We are trying to get in focus a theatrical image: Tennessee and Carson, at the table, with a set that will give the audience an image of our concept of the Tennessee and Carson experience that summer. (In fiction, I call this the charged image. I think of Katherine Anne Porter's "Flowering Judas." Porter focuses on Braggioni and Laura sitting at a table.)

We are imagining *possible* styles for this theatrical image: realistic or stylized? We will stylize the set, idealize Tennessee and Carson and the events, and conceptualize the meaning of it all.

One possible theatrical image is this: Tennessee and Carson at the table center, a projected image behind Tennessee of the sketch of the set of *Summer and Smoke,* a projected image behind Carson of the sketch for *The Member of the Wedding.* Perhaps we see one broken window downstage center to suggest the storm before Carson came?

A motif from *Summer and Smoke*'s set that expresses an aspect of Nantucket is the sky. A motif from *The Member of the Wedding* set is the table itself.

I always *see* Tennessee and Carson sitting at a small *kitchen* table, not the long dining room table, because the theatrical image of *The Member of the Wedding* with the kitchen table as focus was, 40 years ago, so powerful and is so memorable.

We see two typewriters; perhaps there will be a moment when Tennessee and Carson seem to do a duet on the typewriters and realize it, and laugh. We see a piano and a Victrola. We see two bicycles. We see fresh cut flowers.

There will be no curtain. There will be no intermission. The play will last 90 minutes.

We will use the music Paul Bowles wrote for *Summer and Smoke* and the flute music for *The Member of the Wedding* and perhaps the music from the musical version. We may use some of the incidental music from *The Member of the Wedding,* such as Honey's blues horn, and Berenice's songs: "I Sing Because I'm Happy" and "His Eye Is on the Sparrow." Carson could sing these for Tennessee. We may do an odd counterpoint between Carson's typewriter in Nantucket and the sound, in the play, of the piano tuner, tuning the piano, playing scales and arpeggios.

We may have Tennessee read to the audience the letter he wrote to Carson praising her novel *The Member of the Wedding.* We haven't found it yet. The novel afflicted him with a terrible nostalgia at a time when he thought he was dying. He wanted to meet Carson before he died. He arranged for her to join him and his lover at Nantucket.

We will have Tennessee and Carson deliver what Tennessee called "arias," relatively long speeches, such as this one, as Tennessee is waiting for Carson to come on the ferry to Nantucket:

"My God, what am I going to do with this perfect stranger for a whole week? And what if I don't die as I promised I would? . . . Almost immediately after Carson and the sun appeared on the island, I relinquished the romantic notion that I was a dying artist. My various psychosomatic symptoms were forgotten. There was warmth and light in the house, the odor of good cooking and the nearly-forgotten sight of clean dishes and silver. Also there was some coherent talk for a change. Long evening conversations over hot rum and tea, the reading of poetry aloud, bicycle rides and wanderings along moonlit dunes, and one night there was a marvelous display of the Aurora Borealis, great quivering sheets of white radiance sweeping over the island and the ghostly white fishermen's houses and fences. That night and that mysterious phenomenon will always be associated in my mind with the discovery of our friendship, or rather, more precisely, with the *spirit* of this new-found friend, who seemed as curiously and beautifully unworldly as that night itself."

We imagine Tennessee, 35, very short, plump, mustached, smoking a cigarette in a holder, and Carson, 29, very tall, skinny, with bad, crooked teeth, wearing a straw hat (says Carr), a ball cap (says Tennessee).

One of the major decisions Ms. Bach and I must make is whether to bring other characters into the play: Tennessee's violent, jealous lover, Pancho; Reeves, Carson's jealous, suicidal husband (who committed suicide in 1953, seven years later). Other people Tennessee and Carson met there included Oliver Smith, set designer; Jerry Robbins, choreographer; and Rita Gam, "one of the most beautiful women Pancho and Carson had ever known." Carson was terribly in love—or infatuated—with several women at Nantucket. She made no effort to get over these infatuations.

Tennessee: "Instead, she would go out and buy a fifth of Johnny Walker, then sit drinking at the foot of the stairs, perched on a step or in a straight-back chair nearby in which she sat to 'punish' herself. There she would remain for most of the night, or until the bottle was empty. When I got ready to retire for the night, I would step around her, pat her fondly good night, remind her to put the cats in or out, wherever they needed to be, and go up the stairs to bed. Sometimes she sat fantasizing for half the night about a romance that went on only in her head. Finally Carson began to keep company with a baroness. Then there was no more mooning over her unrequited lover." As Berenice would say, "Bawl, Misery!" Should we let Tennessee and Carson talk over the trick they played on the Baroness's chow dogs after they killed one of the kittens a cat had given birth to on Carson's bed?

Should we tell how Carson went with Tennessee to visit Katherine Cornell to discuss whether she would play Alma in *Summer and Smoke*?

"As soon as they arrived, Carson rushed up to her hostess and announced 'rather indecorously,' said Williams, that she 'needed a sanitary napkin and would Miss Cornell please get her one.'

"'My dear, I'm through with all that,' the actress replied. Nevertheless, Miss Cornell 'marched off with Carson and somehow took care of things. . . . You know, somehow I never thought of Carson doing things like that'" (Carr).

Ms. Bach and I have considered letting the theatrical image of Tennessee and Carson working at the table be the audience's *only* orientation for 1946, so that the two actors never talk *to* each other as Tennessee and Carson of that time; they speak directly to the audience only, about past, present, and future.

We have almost decided to make this a two-character play. Even so, Tennessee can talk *as if* to his lover, and Carson can talk *as if* to her husband. They can talk *as if* to other characters.

But this question remains: Should the two actors who play Tennessee and Carson also speak the arias, long speeches of Alma and Frankie that we want to present? We think so. We think we want only to watch and hear Tennessee and Carson, two actors. We want to show Tennessee and Carson *doing* these things: They read Hart Crane to each other. Tennessee tells Carson he stole the copy of *Crane's* poems from the St. Louis library (I stole Thomas Wolfe's stories from a drugstore rack). Carson also reads Russian writers to Tennessee. Carson plays piano and sings and they sing together. They play old records on a Victrola. Carson cooks; they have candlelight dinners; but she gets tired of that. Tennessee: "We ate a lot of soup together." Maybe we see them coming in from riding bicycles, maybe coming in from swimming. Of course, we see them smoking as they work.

Carson had not seen *The Glass Menagerie*, but she had read it. Carson: "Tennessee, how did you first think of *The Glass Menagerie*?" Tennessee: "I once saw a glass curtain at the house of one of my grandfather's parishioners." Carson had seen six plays in her life, only two of which were on Broadway. Carson: "In our old Georgia home we used to have two sitting rooms, a back one and front one, with folding doors between. These were the family living rooms and the theatre of my shows. The front sitting room was the auditorium, the back sitting room the stage. The sliding doors the curtain." Janice to Frankie: "Jarvis told me how you used to write plays and act in them out here in the arbor."

Perhaps Carson delights Tennessee by reciting from memory a passage from *The Glass Menagerie:* "To begin with, I turn back time. The play is memory. Being a memory play, it is dimly lighted, it is sentimental, it is not realistic. In memory everything seems to happen to music." Carson: "I knew that *The Member of the Wedding,* like *The Glass Menagerie,* had to be a mood play—a mood of nostalgia."

They are *very* articulate, almost, at times, as in a Noel Coward play.

We want to show in the theater two creative consciousnesses simultaneously. Tennessee and Carson, isolated and communing simultaneously. Tennessee and Carson, flesh and spirit simultaneously. The theme of *The Member of the Wedding* is expressed by Carson: "Spiritual isolation is the basis of most of my themes." The theme of *Summer and Smoke,* as in many of Tennessee's plays, is the conflict of flesh and spirit as embodied in two characters, each of whom is deficient in things of the flesh or in things of the spirit.

Which lines, if any, for either play *seem* to have come out of their writing together at the same table? Is there any aspect of Tennessee in Carson's play? Is there any aspect of Carson in Tennessee's play? What elements in the play *Member of the Wedding* are not derived from the novel, but perhaps from Carson's and Tennessee's working and playing together?

Before Tennessee died in 1983, Ms. Bach and I considered presenting the play from his perspective, so that he would step away from the table and talk to the audience about Carson *then* and Carson in the future. Now that both are dead, Tennessee and Carson will *share* perspectives on past, present, and future. Tennessee and Carson, fluidly, go in and out of past-present-future (their dynamics are timeless), and in and out of their own plays, alone and together. Tennessee speaks of Carson when she's there at the table as if she isn't—from the future also. Carson speaks of Tennessee when he's there at the table, as if he isn't—from the future also.

In some of the arias, Tennessee and Carson will talk to the audience about the writing time they shared at the table. Tennessee: "When I told her that I thought my creative powers were exhausted, she said to me, wisely and truly, an artist always feels that dread, that terror, when he has completed a work to which his heart has been so totally committed that the finishing of it seems to have finished him too, that what he lives for is gone like yesterday's snow." Tennessee: "For the first time I found it completely comfortable to work in the same room with another writer."

Carson: "Writing is like a flowering dream. Ideas grow, budding silently, and there are a thousand illuminations coming day by day as the work progresses." Carson: "It was a wonderful summer of sea and sun and friendship, and after that year was over, I never again experienced the happiness of good health."

We like to imagine Tennessee giving Carson technical advice, while Carson tells him "weird anecdotes for novels and stories she will write." Tennessee: "In no sense of the word was I Carson's mentor. If she wanted to ask me something or read some lines aloud for my reaction, she would. But that was rare. Carson accepted almost no advice about how to adapt *The Member of the Wedding.* I did not suggest lines to her more than once or twice, and then she would usually have her own ideas and say, 'Tenn, honey, thank you, but I know all I need to know.'"

As they are writing, Tennessee learns that Laurette Taylor, who played Amanda in *The Glass Menagerie,* was dying. He talks to Carson about his deep love of Laurette in such a way that the audience anticipates his reaction to Carson's own long illness and death. Tennessee will tell the audience about the death of Laurette Taylor in December 1946.

In some of the arias, Tennessee and Carson talk to each other, or to us, of their past lives. Carson talks of her parents, her brother Lamar, her sister Margarita, Reeves, and Gypsy Rose Lee. Tennessee talks of his grandfather, his mother, Edwina, Rose, his demented sister, his brother Dakin. Carson tells the story of how her money that she had saved to study piano at Juilliard was stolen in the subway. Carson tells of renting a room, unknowingly, in a whorehouse. Tennessee tells her two or three of his past experiences—in the shoe factory perhaps, in New Orleans perhaps.

Tennessee: "I was going on with the writing then of *Summer and Smoke,* but the play was a tough nut to crack. Miss Alma Winemiller may very well be the best female portrait I have drawn in a play. She simply seemed to exist somewhere in my being, and it was no effort to put her on paper. However, the boy she was in love with all her youth, Johnny Buchanan, never seemed real to me but always a cardboard figure, and I knew it, and it distressed me but I kept at the play for a couple of months; I wrote several drafts of it. Then one evening, when I thought it completed, I read it aloud to a young man who was friendly to me. He kept yawning as I read, and so I read badly, and when I finished, he made this devastating remark: 'How could the author of *The Glass Menagerie* write such a bad play as this.'" Tennessee dedicated *Summer and Smoke* to Carson McCullers.

Carson tells the audience that as she continued work on the play version of *The Member of the Wedding* back in Nyack, "I was paralyzed, and my outward situation was miserable indeed, but when I finished that script, I wrote to a friend of mine, 'Oh, how wonderful to be a writer, I have never been so happy.'" *The Member of the Wedding* is dedicated to Reeves. She may also tell the audience about the ordeal of writing *The Square Root of Wonderful* and, with Edward Albee, *The Ballad of the Sad Café.*

For Tennessee, does Carson substitute for Rose? Tennessee gave Carson Rose's ring; she became a surrogate sister. Tennessee called Carson "sisterwoman" in later years. Carson: "Kiss me, Miss Rose!" Rose: "No, thank you. I have halitosis." For Carson, does Tennessee substitute for Reeves? Do Carson and Reeves parallel Carson and Tennessee?

Aria: Carson expresses jealousy of Tennessee's fame. Carson: We became "transfixed among the self-inflicted ruins," "agony immobilized."

When he was alive, Ms. Bach and I imagined how poignant it would be to listen to Tennessee tell about Carson's sickness and death as she sits there very young and healthy writing her play. Now that Tennessee himself is dead, we want the audience to listen to each tell about the other.

Tennessee: "After that summer Carson and I remained friends, and over the years the memories accumulate. I think of three important times in my life when Carson was there, all of them exits in which Carson and I took part: three of the longest, the most agonizing exits that I can remember.

"One was from the birthday party given for Dylan Thomas by my publishers, who were also his. When I was introduced to him, all that he said by way of acknowledgment was this put-down: 'How does it feel to make all that Hollywood money?'

"In retrospect it was thoroughly understandable and excusable, but then it stung me badly. Carson he simply ignored. After a few moments, she said, 'Tenn, honey, take me out of here!'—This was after her stroke, and as I led her out of the birthday celebration, she trembled in my supporting arm and the exit seemed to be everlasting.

"Another exit was more painful.

"Carson had made the mistake of attending the opening night party of her play, *The Square Root of Wonderful,* and the greater mistake of remaining there till the reviews came out.

"They were simply awful.

"Carson again said to me, 'Tenn, help me out of here.' And it was an even longer and more agonizing exit.

"The third exit we made together was also from an opening night party: the opening in New York in 1948 of the Margo Jones production of *Summer and Smoke.* On this occasion it was I who said to Carson: 'Let's get out of here.' It was also a long and agonizing exit, everyone staring at us, the notices out. . . . And those notices were not very good. I was living then in a Tony Smith-designed apartment on East Fifty-Eighth Street. When I woke in the morning, it was to a record of Mozart. Carson had already arrived in the apartment and put the record on to comfort my waking moments.

"Well, I was not in the mood for comfort or for pity, which is really not comforting, much . . . so I told Frank Merlo (. . . I lived with him for a long, long time) to cut the Mozart off and to see Carson to a cab before I got out of bed.

"I wanted to get back to work: alone, and right away."

Tennessee: "Carson's last days were horrific. . . . Finally, she could only use one finger. She sat at her typewriter every day and wrote, and everytime she hit a key she felt pain. But she wrote until she could not write anymore. Carson was heroic."

Tennessee was in Key West when he heard that Carson had died September 29, 1967, in a hospital in Nyack, New York.

Aria: Carson tells us how Tennessee died, alone, as he had feared, in his suite in the Elysee in New York, on the night of February 24, 1983, 16 years after her own death. He was found with the cap of a bottle of barbiturates lodged in his throat. As Frankie says when she learns that John Henry is sick: "The world is certainly a sudden place."

Tennessee thinks he's dying of a heart condition. Later he realized he had been identifying too intensely with Alma, who had heart palpitations. John: It's best not to ask for too much. Alma: I disagree with you. I say, ask for all, but be prepared to get nothing! No, I haven't been well. I've thought many times of something you told me last summer, that I have a doppelgänger. I looked that up and I found that it means another person inside me. Another self, and I don't know whether to thank you or not for making me conscious of it!—I haven't been well. . . . For a while I thought I was dying, that was the change that was coming. . . . But now the Gulf wind has blown that feeling away like a cloud of smoke, and I know now I'm not dying, that it isn't going to turn out to be that simple. Oh, I suppose I am sick, one of those weak, and divided people who slip like shadows among you solid strong ones. But sometimes, out of necessity, we shadowy people take on strength of our own. I have that now. You needn't try to deceive me. You needn't try to comfort me. I haven't come here but on equal terms. You said, let's talk truthfully. Well, let's do! Unsparingly, truthfully, even shamelessly, then! It's no longer a secret that I love you. . . . I've lived next door to you all the days of my life, a weak and divided person. . . . And that is my story! Now I wish *you* would tell *me*—why didn't it happen between us?"

Carson: "I become the characters I write about . . . Nothing human is alien to me." That summer was like Carson-Frankie (whose name means "the free"); she was healthy for the last time. Frankie: "Just now I realized something. The trouble with me is that for a long time I have been just an 'I' person. All other people can say 'we.' When Berenice says 'we' she means her lodge and church and colored people. Soldiers can say 'we' and mean the army. All people belong to a 'we' except me. Not to belong to a 'we' makes you too lonesome. Until this afternoon I didn't have a 'we,' but now after seeing Janice and Jarvis I suddenly realize something. . . . I know that the bride and my brother are the 'we' of me. So I'm going with them, joining the wedding. This coming Sunday when my brother and the bride leave this town, I'm going with the two of them to Winter Hill. And after that to whatever place that they will ever go. (Pause) I love the two of them so much and we belong together. I love the two of them so much because they are the *we* of me."

Her Own Enduring Heart

WILLIAM TREVOR*

I once listed Carson McCullers' *The Heart Is a Lonely Hunter* as one of my ten favourite novels. Among the others were *Bovary, Middlemarch, Delta Wedding,* and *The Good Soldier.* My list could easily have been different: Scott Fitzgerald brought in for *The Great Gatsby,* Evelyn Waugh for *Decline and Fall,* Anthony Powell for *A Dance to the Music of Time.* But Carson McCullers will always have a place on that longest train journey or the most remote desert island—wherever it is that favourite books belong.

A good novel is a single world. The pleasure of reading is when that world draws you to its heart, when there's a magic you cannot understand and you're happy to leave it at that. Many pass such worlds by: there is a consciousness that reacts not at all to stories or their telling, that fails to hear a tone of voice, that sees nothing of a face, that feels nothing of imaginary passion. And those who do not pass by make lists of their own, quite different from mine, which is just as it should be: storytelling is a personal art.

I read Carson McCullers again and again. I take the memories of her world with me wherever I go: Antonapoulos, Frankie and John Henry, Miss Amelia, Marvin Macy, Sucker, Mister Bilderbach. I value her perceptions, the casting of her spell, what she says and how she says it, her own enduring heart.

*This essay was written for this volume and is published here for the first time by permission of the author.

ESSAYS

♦

Carson McCullers and the South

DELMA EUGENE PRESLEY*

Writers of Southern fiction generally have had trouble living in the South. William Faulkner's adoption of his native Oxford, Mississippi, is exceptional. As Louis Rubin has said, the South is a "faraway country" for most of its writers. Thomas Wolfe and James Agee, not Faulkner, probably reflect the common experience of the creative Southerner: he goes away, usually to a northern city, and in exile recovers imaginatively his own region. It is this act of recovery which identifies most Southern writers, regardless of their places of residence.

The case of Carson McCullers is perplexing. There are ways in which she was unlike either Faulkner or Wolfe and Agee. After living her formative years in Columbus, Georgia, she moved to New York. The move northward was permanent. Throughout her career she wrote about Small Town, Georgia, utilizing her knowledge of regional dialect and place names. However, McCullers did not transmute Columbus into a universe of the imagination. Her fictional Southern town is different in kind from Faulkner's Jefferson or Wolfe's Altamount or Agee's Knoxville. What she recovered of her childhood through her creation was a deeply embedded ambivalence about the land of her youth, about her own past. The fact that she was a Southerner was a great burden she struggled to displace very early in her career. Significantly, out of the struggle emerged some literature of the first order. But once she abandoned the landscape of her agony, she wrote works which lack distinction. Her early success and her ultimate failure, I maintain, can be attributed in large measure to this pattern of struggle in her relationship to the South.

I

Lula Carson Smith, born February 19, 1917, was the first of three children born to Lamar and Marguerite Smith of Columbus, Georgia. Her biographer, Oliver Evans, notes striking parallels between young Carson and the adoles-

*Reprinted from *The Georgia Review* 28 (1974): 19–32. Reprinted by permission of *The Georgia Review* and the author.

cent characters of *The Heart Is a Lonely Hunter* and *The Member of the Wedding:* "Certainly the resemblances between Lula Carson Smith and Mick Kelly are too obvious to be ignored: both are tall for their age, both are tomboys, and the fathers of both are small-town jewellers. The resemblances between Lula Carson Smith and Frankie Addams are stronger still" (*The Ballad of Carson McCullers,* 1966). However, there is an important difference between the author and Mick Kelly. The fictional character is frustrated and walks the downward path toward disillusionment when the novel ends; she is about to be suffocated in the muggy atmosphere of that eternally lifeless Southern town. Mick Kelly's destiny as a clerk in Woolworth's is the author's projection of her future in the South, had she not escaped.

To live in Columbus as those around her lived would have been a painful defeat for Lula Carson Smith. Always she felt the first step toward a fulfilling life was northward in direction. And she was anxious to begin the journey. In her early teens, both she and her mother believed she would have a piano debut in Carnegie Hall. Indeed, Lula Carson tried very hard to become a prodigy. Her piano teachers, while confident of her talent, felt she was so eager for recognition that she prematurely attempted the difficult, flashy pieces, without first mastering the simpler, discipline-building ones.

When she turned fifteen, it was becoming obvious, even to her relatives, that she lacked the single-minded devotion required of a concert pianist. At the same time, approaching the end of her high school career, she made the decision to seek fame as a writer. Success in her academic subjects, however, she did not consider prerequisite to her proposed literary career. Roberta Lawrence, who taught her English in the junior and senior years, has written:

> She made a mediocre academic record—about as many C's as B's, no A's. . . . She had an aloof, unconcerned attitude toward grades. . . . I remember only one of her themes. It was creative—something about a Bach fugue—brief and fragmentary. Shortly after this theme had been turned in, I encountered Carson's mother on the bus as I was going home in the afternoon and she asked me why I didn't give Carson better grades, adding that she was brilliant and very talented as a writer. I remember telling her that I would be more than glad to give Carson a better grade if she would produce for me some of this work of which she was capable. (Talk to Book Club of Milledgeville, Georgia, September 9, 1969)

She was seventeen when she left Columbus for New York City, where she held part-time jobs and studied writing—in the spring of 1935 at Columbia with Helen Rose Hull and in 1936 at NYU with Sylvia Chatsfield Bates and again at Columbia that summer with Whit Burnett. Stung by the first real criticism of her work, she was discouraged, but she did not abandon easily her desire to become a writer. When Miss Bates arranged to publish in *Story* magazine a short story, "Wunderkind," about a young girl's failure to please her piano teacher, Carson felt vindicated. She was in fact an author. She had demonstrated how wrong all those people in Columbus had been. Polk's Columbus *City Directory* for 1937, published only a few months after "Wunderkind" appeared in *Story,* contains the following personal listing on page 435: "Smith Carson writer r1519 Stark av."

When she married Reeves McCullers in September, 1937, she planned to move with him to Paris as soon as they saved enough money. A friend asked: "Why Paris?" Carson replied: "That's where writers live, of course." A native of Jesup, Georgia, Reeves had adolescent frustrations there equal to Carson's in Columbus. When he was sixteen, his parents' recent separation deeply disturbed him and probably robbed him of a nomination to West Point for which he had prepared diligently at Fort Benning. Like Carson, whose vision of the South was shattered by adolescent experiences, he longed to live far removed from his unpleasant past. He too wished to prove himself a writer. After coming within a breath of landing a job with the *Charlotte Observer,* he wrote his good friend Vincent Adams:

> Of all the places to get cornered and trapped this is about the worst, but I suppose I'll have to stay on here a little while longer as nothing better has turned up and newspaper work in this section is lighter than ever, and someone will have to die or stay drunk for a month for me get a decent job on one. The town itself is only a barren little island like thousands of others in America . . . and for diversion or any pleasantry one's resources are the only basis, and there's nothing to match with them. I still study and read a bit and have foolishly high hopes about my particular star, but things get a little thicker each day. (Letter of August 29, 1937)[1]

Like Carson, Reeves looked on his years in the South as an unpleasant, if necessary, prologue to the good life. And writing, for both of them, was the fulcrum they would use to accomplish their elevation. About two months after his letter describing his "high hopes," he wrote Vincent again, this time as a married man:

> Around the last of September Carson and I were married in Columbus at her home. It had about reached the point of then or never and everything was taken into consideration before the license was purchased. Since then we have been living a rather happy life here in Charlotte and at present are still en rapport. Sometimes the sledding is rather tough but the landlady usually smiles at us and we have great fun.

The town had not changed, he said, but their future expectations made the experience there bearable:

> The rest of the town is dull dead and dying and we seldom go out, and week days are spent in hard work and study. By spring Carson will have sold a novel and I will get gas money on a book of essays and we will be up to see you. . . .

Life serves me pretty well at present but the key to the situation is not to be too damned serious about it. I am very happy here and am on the way to being the person I want to be. (Letter of November 8, 1937)

Reeves's teachers and friends in Jesup considered him a disciplined young man whose goals and accomplishments were noteworthy—his county's first Eagle scout, one of the best English students in his high school, and so on. He was serious about his school work, and he seemed to learn from the criticism of his teachers. An important difference between Reeves and Carson was his belief that he was a "future" writer. Carson genuinely felt she had arrived, and her published story (not to mention the *City Directory* listing) was proof. He kept reading, studying, and preparing, while he supported Carson in North Carolina for three years. Carson, on the other hand, neglected reading and learned by writing and rewriting.

In the winter of 1938, Reeves wrote Vincent: "Carson is hard at work on a novel which to my unprofessional eyes reads damn good. She learns steadily from herself and her writing improves." *The Heart Is a Lonely Hunter* was accepted officially by Houghton Mifflin in 1939. Elevation now was inevitable, and Carson especially was eager to move up. Reeves wrote Vincent: "I have to keep Carson tied by a leg to the bedpost at times to keep her from going mad as she hates the South so." Within a few months the couple moved from North Carolina to Greenwich Village—not Paris, but a pretty good American imitation, especially in 1940.

II

When her first novel received substantial notices and reviews, some of them ecstatic with praise, she performed for the public as she long had planned—sensationally. The press hounded this twenty-three year old "phenom," seeking and receiving fascinating copy. She revealed to reporters that her book really was a subtle parable about fascism—a subject of no little interest to the literate world of 1940. Gore Vidal would proclaim Carson McCullers "the young writer" of the decade. By the end of 1940, having recently divorced Reeves, she was living with what she called an "assortment of geniuses" in a Brooklyn brownstone.

An early non-fiction piece she fed the voracious press in 1941 is called "Brooklyn Is My Neighbourhood." It is an especially revealing insight into the transition she was making from the South to New York. She makes an effort to understand the heritage of her "real neighborhood," Brooklyn. "Comparing the Brooklyn that I know with Manhattan is like comparing a comfortable and complacent duenna to her more brilliant and neurotic sister." Her new home, she says, has a "sense of quietness and permanence that seem to belong to the nineteenth century. . . . There is a feeling for tradition." After speaking of those "liberal intellectuals" associated with Brooklyn's past—Walt Whitman, Henry Ward Beecher, Whittier, and Talleyrand—she sketches a menagerie of colorful rogues, including the proprietor of a junkshop, Miss Kate.

Mrs. McCullers quotes the owner of a competing antique shop: "Miss Kate is a good woman . . . but she dislikes washing herself. So she bathes once a year, when it is summer. I expect she's just about the dirtiest woman in Brooklyn." Mrs. McCullers continues: "His voice as he said this was not at all malicious; rather, there was in it a quality of wondering pride. That is one of the things I love most about Brooklyn. Everyone is not expected to be exactly like everyone else." (Reprinted in *The Mortgaged Heart,* 1971)

In Brooklyn, the young Mrs. McCullers found what, in the simple logic of *The Heart Is a Lonely Hunter,* could have saved Mick Kelly: a place where she could relish being different, a sympathetic community in which she could find uncritical acceptance. Although her stay in Brooklyn was of relatively short duration, she always maintained the experience was one of the most significant in her life. The last interview she granted before her death in 1967 was to Rex Reed. His article begins with a description of her life in the legendary brownstone in Brooklyn, apparently faithful to Mrs. McCullers' account:

> With the late *Harper's Bazaar* editor George Davis she established the only important literary salon in America . . . where the boarders included Christopher Isherwood, Richard Wright, Thomas Mann's son Golo, Oliver Smith, Jane and Paul Bowles and Gypsy Rose Lee. Gypsy provided the cook, W. H. Auden kept house and they all chipped in on the groceries. Their friends who came and went at all hours of the night were people like Anais Nin, Leonard Bernstein, Salvador Dali and his wife Gala, Marc Blitzstein, and Aaron Copeland. (*Do You Sleep in the Nude?,* 1969)

It was not really the place, Brooklyn, which meant so much to her, but those fascinatingly brilliant people. She liked nothing more than to be around others who currently were popular. Carson's sister, Margarita Smith, writing in her introduction to the posthumous collection of McCullers' works, *The Mortgaged Heart,* recalls:

> She had recognition from sources that pleased her and she enjoyed fame from the time she was twenty-three when *The Heart Is a Lonely Hunter* was published. There were standing ovations for the magical Broadway production of *The Member of the Wedding.* There were invitations to presidential inaugurations and teas with Edith Sitwell and Marilyn Monroe, and her long and constant

friendship with Tennessee Williams. Stage-struck like Frankie, she enjoyed having her picture taken with John Huston when she visited him at his castle in Ireland.

Carson McCullers returned to Columbus several times after her colorful life in New York had been chronicled by the hometown newspapers. Roberta Lawrence has written about Carson's visits in Columbus:

> After Carson had had the outstanding success as a writer, she came fairly often to visit in Columbus. By this time she had changed her manner of dress— which had been conservative in high school days. Years before other people went about in slacks, we would see her so clothed down at Kirven's, the department store where in those days one knew whoever was in there. She adopted an arty looking hair style—long, straight stringy bob with long, stringy bangs. It seemed as if she were definitely dressing to attract attention by her appearance.

Of course she was baiting the provincials—a temptation she could not resist, at least until she had made her point. Eventually her emotional war with Columbus ended, and she did feel very much the victor. No longer was she simply Lamar Smith's tall daughter. The tables were turned. Perhaps her last skirmish with her hometown was in 1958 when she promptly declined the local library's request for one of her manuscripts. Her reason was that Columbus' "separate but equal" policies discriminated against the blacks—a position she had espoused years earlier in a letter to the newspaper:

> I understand there has been some altercation about allowing all citizens, both white and Negro, the use of the new Columbus Public Library. I do not understand the concrete issues involved but I understand too well the abstract ones. Always it has been an intolerable shame to me to know that Negroes are not accorded the same intellectual privileges as white citizens. As an author, represented in the library, I feel it is my duty to speak not only for myself but for the august dead who are represented on the shelves and to whom I owe an incalculable debt. I think of Tolstoy, Chekov, Abraham Lincoln, and Thomas Paine.
>
> I would like to go on record and like to say that we owe to these (the molders of the conscience of our civilization) the freedom of all citizens regardless of race, to benefit by their wisdom, which is our greatest inheritance. (Columbus *Ledger,* March 8, 1948)

The personal contact she had with the town after 1940 was limited largely to interviews with reporters from the Columbus newspapers. Most of the columns romantically rehearse the success story: how the hometown jeweler's daughter became a celebrated writer and public figure. The underlying and unwritten theme of these columns was unsubtle and patronizing: if most Columbusites could not appreciate her novels, at least they should admire her triumphs in the world of letters.

III

Carson McCullers' relationship to the land of her youth reminds us that she engaged in something other than a lover's quarrel with the South. A quarrel between lovers implies that both parties have mutual understanding, mutual respect, as it were. Not so in this case. She felt that Columbus was, as Reeves had described Charlotte, "a barren little island like thousands of others in America . . . dull dead and dying." She accepted without humor H. L. Mencken's tirades against the South as "The Sahara of the Bozart." And she wanted nothing to do with the land of yokels and reactionaries. Occasionally she poked fun at backwoodsmen-come-to-town, as in "The Ballad of the Sad Café." But the clearest examples of how Carson McCullers appropriated her perception of the South are the novels, particularly *The Heart Is a Lonely Hunter* and, to a lesser degree, *The Member of the Wedding.*

The central characters in these two novels, Mick Kelly and Frankie Addams, are adolescent girls. Both live in small towns in southwest Georgia. Both have dreams of living in faraway places, and in the novels their dreams never materialize. At the end of each novel, the juvenile heroine verbalizes a deep sense of betrayal. After Mick realizes she will be a dime store clerk—not a musician, not a world traveller—she meditates on the nature of her frustration:

That was a funny thing. It was like she was shut out from the inside room. Sometimes a quick little tune would come and go—but she never went into the inside room with music like she used to do. It was like she was too tense. Or maybe it was like the store took all her energy and time. Woolworth's wasn't the same as school. When she used to come home from school she felt good and was ready to start working on the music. But now she was always tired. At home she just ate supper and slept and then ate breakfast and went off to the store again. A song she had started in her private notebook two months before was still not finished. And she wanted to stay in the inside room but she didn't know how. It was like the inside room was locked somewhere away from her. A very hard thing to understand. . . . It was like she was cheated. Only nobody had cheated her. So there was nobody to take it out on. However, just the same she had that feeling. Cheated.

The theme of unavoidable entrapment surfaces at the climax of *The Member of the Wedding,* when Frankie Addams recognizes she has been left out of the wedding party: "Her cheap heart hurt, and she pressed her crossed arms over it and rocked a little. 'It was a framed game. The cards were stacked. It was a frame-up all around.'"

For both Mick and Frankie, leaving home would have been a means of escaping the inevitable trap. Indeed, Frankie attempts to run away, but "the Law" catches her. While waiting for her father who will take her back home, Frankie broods: "The world was now so far away that Frances could no longer think of it. She did not see the earth as in the old days, cracked and loose and turning a thousand miles an hour; the earth was enormous and still and flat. Between herself and all the places there was a space like an enormous canyon she could not hope to bridge or cross." These adolescents discover excruciating pain—the result of their having been placed on an arid spiritual desert where youthful dreams and tender sentiments evaporate with the dawning of adulthood. At best, they can hope for momentary release—Mick can escape temporarily by visiting Biff's café, and Frankie undoubtedly will make new friends—but their ultimate isolation is as certain as the new day's oppressive sunshine.

Mick and Frankie are Mrs. McCullers' metaphors for the human condition. The point is underlined in *The Member of the Wedding*, by McCullers' Dilsey, Berenice: "We all of us somehow caught. We born this way or that way and we don't know why. But we caught anyhow. I born Berenice. You born Frankie. John Henry born John Henry. And maybe we wants to widen and bust free. But no matter what we do we still caught. Me is me and you is you and he is he. We each one of us somehow caught all by ourself." As the author works out *The Member of the Wedding*, these philosophical speculations are not, despite the sound of the words, an existential confession. Despair is not so much a sobering truth as it is a whining lament that, somehow, things have a way of going sour.

Of all her works, *The Heart Is a Lonely Hunter* is the most artful instance of how she appropriated her perception of life in the South. In this novel she transmuted her own feelings of frustration into a shrunken cosmos in which even the most fundamental moral efforts, the most basic attempts at communication, are fruitless. In this extraordinary first novel, Mrs. McCullers elaborated her bleak metaphors and cast doubt on man's ethical potential. There is the labor organizer, Jake Blount, Mrs. McCullers' fictional representation of Fred Beal, an organizer for the National Textile Union, whose futile efforts to unionize mill workers around Charlotte in 1929 were hotly debated even in 1937—the year she moved to that city with Reeves and began writing her novel. Blount flounders hopelessly because the "lint heads" he wants to help are not interested in improving their lot. Furthermore, Blount's idealism is thwarted by his own intemperance. Also in the novel is the prototype of the struggler for racial identity. The idealism of Dr. Benedict Mady Copeland, the black doctor, is neither appreciated nor understood by his fellow blacks. Even his own wife and children prefer being natural "niggers" rather than unnatural "Negroes." Dr. Copeland, like the labor worker Blount, is at heart self-destructive. These two idealists, Blount and Copeland, reveal their souls to Singer, the silent "listener," but they are victims of a cruel joke. The mute puts into perspective their somber plight: he does not understand a single word they say. Singer is like a dead god; those who trust in him, who believe in the redemptive potential of communication, deceive themselves. What they think is genuine dialogue is but an empty illusion.

We should not forget that *The Heart Is a Lonely Hunter* is the only novel Mrs. McCullers wrote while she lived in the South. As she moved away from her native soil, in time and in space, she carried with her the fascination for adolescent problems, but she left behind the morally serious subjects she explored at length in her first novel. *Reflections in a Golden Eye,* an adaptation of Reeves' unpublished manuscript entitled "Army Post," was published in *Harper's Bazaar* just four months after the appearance of her first novel; this brief novel is a playful montage of colorful language and lifeless characters. "The Ballad of the Sad Café" (*Harper's Bazaar,* 1943) is a nearly perfect allegory of human loneliness, even though she does not distinguish between her characters' stupidity and their wisdom. As we have seen, *The Member of the Wedding* (1946) again reflects Mrs. McCullers' preoccupation with adolescent frustrations, although the novel lacks the broad ethical landscape of her first book.

IV

After 1946, she embarked on a slow voyage in the shallow waters of uncritical public acclaim. It was to be an undistinguished tour of life's harbors—a journey which ended only at her death some twenty years later. If Mrs. McCullers were judged solely on the literary qualities of what she wrote after *The Member of the Wedding,* serious readers scarcely would remember her. Buttressed by the loyal support of Tennessee Williams, she attempted a play in 1957, "The Square Root of Wonderful"—a trite and incoherent attempt of the author to deal with the psychological strain she suffered after the alleged suicide of Reeves in 1953 and the death of her mother in 1955. Understandably, the play folded immediately after it opened; as more than one critic pointed out, the best part of the play is its title. In 1961 came *Clock Without Hands.* Public relations efforts of the publisher successfully brought the novel to the attention of book reviewers. Pre-release materials emphasized Mrs. McCullers' inspiring struggle against failing health. Supportive literary friends of the author did their best to embellish it in their reviews, but, as Irving Howe pointed out in a review, the novel is hollow:

> What is more disturbing about *Clock Without Hands* is the lethargic flatness of the prose. Such a writer as Mrs. McCullers is never likely to be too strong at realistic portraiture, but in her past work she could carry off almost anything through the virtuosity of her language. The style of her new novel, however, is that of a novelist going through the motions, and committing to paper not an integrated vision of life but an unadorned and scrappy scenario for a not-yet-written novel.

More damning than her technical failure, Howe claimed, was her failure of artistic nerve: "Nothing, to be sure, is more difficult for the critic to establish than the absence of inner conviction and imaginative energy in a novel; yet once all serious intentions have been honored and all technical problems noted, only this conviction, only this energy matters. And in *Clock Without Hands,* I regret to say, it is not to be found."

In terms of the subject of this essay, *Clock Without Hands* is a poignant example of the consequences of Mrs. McCullers' perception of her native region. This novel, she said, concerned "the South regenerate," and "the South finding its conscience at 11:59." Again she treats the theme of the adolescent's quest for identity in Sherman Pew, a black boy who is murdered when he tries to "blockbust," and in Jester Clane, a white, conscience-ridden grandson of the notorious segregationist, Judge Clane. While Sherman and Jester go through the motions of inner struggle, the town's druggist, J. T. Malone, faces the larger problem posed by his impending death. The ending of the novel asserts hope for man when enemies dare look into the eyes of each other.

No one can deny that these characters and their situations are the stuff of serious fiction. However, *Clock Without Hands* does not qualify as serious fiction. The characters' manifold, at times inconsequential, ambiguities rob their destinies of potential meaning. For example, when Jester Clane refuses to kill the Klansman Sammy Lank, he does so out of moral weakness which may be related to his previous homosexual attraction to the black victim of Lank. If *Clock Without Hands* is supposed to be about Southerners finding a moral sense, Mrs. McCullers fails to make the point. Her Southerners are either too foolish, like the Judge, or too mixed-up in general, like Sherman and Jester, to appropriate a moral sense should they find one. The only cogent character in the novel, J. T. Malone, is slowly dying of leukemia. He faces death with a sobriety which approaches Kierkegaardian intensity at times. He is the Ivan Ilyich of Milan, Georgia. But his struggle appears trivial in the midst of the shallow, melodramatic episodes involving Sherman, Jester, and the Judge. In *Clock Without Hands* Mrs. McCullers attempted to go back home, but the South as she described it never existed, and it does not exist in this fiction.

V

Granville Hicks has written that Mrs. McCullers went downhill after her first novel. With the exception of the brilliant story, "The Ballad of the Sad Café," I would agree. Why the decline? Because her subsequent works depend almost entirely upon the imaginative use of language, and neglect the solid foundation of place. Too many of her characters are like those created by her friend, Tennessee Williams—poetic but shallow. She continued to write about the South even though she did not live there—physically or spiritually. She said Brooklyn was her "real neighborhood," but, as if obligated by birth, she continued to write about unreal people in that fictional town somewhere south of Atlanta and west of Milledgeville. Carson McCullers could not recover the South in her fiction, because she left it before she really understood it. The only novel which approaches a serious exploration of the moral dimension of her characters, *The Heart Is a Lonely Hunter,* she wrote while living in North Carolina. This novel does rest upon a solid foundation of place. Furthermore, it elaborates a correlation between the emotional estrangement of the adolescent Mick and the anomie of those around her—the only instance of a successful correlation of this sort in her works.

Writing as an established and acclaimed writer, Carson McCullers occasionally reflected publicly on her struggle with the South. In some sketches published in *Esquire,* she wrote: "People ask me why I don't go back to the South more often. But the South is a very emotional experience for me, fraught with all the memories of my childhood. When I go back South I always get into arguments, so that a visit to Columbus is a stirring up of love and antagonism" (Reprinted in *The Mortgaged Heart).* If her early years in the South contributed anything to her craft, it must have been, as she said, in terms of language: "I love the voices of Negroes—like brown rivers." Flannery O'Connor, another Georgian who was McCullers' contemporary, could talk about how the "Christ haunted" South made possible the literature of the grotesque, but Carson McCullers attributed the vision of grotesque fiction to the "cheapness of human life in the South."

It is clear that Carson McCullers did not assimilate much of the intellectual and cultural heritage of the South. Her chief difficulties as a writer stemmed from her disregard of her own past. Ironically, this disregard lies at the heart of the fundamental problem she spent her life writing about—the perennially-thwarted search for identity. The early novels and stories were written by a pessimistic young woman who, like her adolescent protagonists, longed to transcend the environment of her frustrated childhood. The last novel came from a less sober, more optimistic McCullers who claimed there was something worth saving in her South. But in *Clock Without Hands* she was unable to identify exactly what she had in mind. If her early familiarity with the South bred contempt, then her exile's unfamiliarity with it bred something worse than contempt—vacuity.

In a larger sense, this discussion about Carson McCullers and the South concerns the matter of cultural symbols which continue to motivate many modern, upwardly-mobile Southern intellectuals. Carson McCullers, let us remember, experienced the South quite differently from writers like Donald Davidson, Allen Tate, John Crowe Ransom, William Faulkner, Walker Percy, and a host of others whose parents and/or grandparents were aristocrats of the Southern mind. She did not inherit a sense of tradition, and the record she left indicates she did not attempt to embrace any tradition. She built her life on the hope that, somehow, Paris or New York would reach down and rescue her from the frustration and stagnation she felt and feared in the South. Unlike many whose lives have been galvanized by this kind of hope, she had the rare misfortune of seeing the hope fulfilled when she was very young— too young, indeed, to know that the fulfillment would be self-defeating.

One cannot know what might have happened to Carson McCullers had she remained in the land of her birth, or had she attempted to absorb the heritage, say, William Faulkner absorbed. Possibly she would have wrestled with the demon of self-destruction not a few landlocked Southern intellectuals have experienced. Out of the agony might have emerged creation of a different kind, or perhaps only suffering and defeat would have emerged. One can only wonder about such matters. The most succinct speculation about this problem came from the author herself in an interview in 1963 with a journalist from the *Charlotte Observer*. The journalist asked why the author never returned to the South. Carson McCullers' quick answer perhaps revealed more than she or her interviewer realized at the time. "No roots," she replied. "No roots."

Note

1.   I express deep appreciation to Mr. Adams who has allowed me to make use of his collection of correspondence from Reeves McCullers.

Carson McCullers: The Aesthetic of Pain

LOUIS D. RUBIN JR.*

I

I think it is not without importance that the all-night restaurant in Carson McCullers' first novel, *The Heart Is a Lonely Hunter,* is called The New York Cafe. In the small-sized southern city in the late 1930s, when the story takes place, there is little doing at night and none of the people involved in the story are either very contented or very hopeful; the New York Cafe is the only place for them to go, and its forlorn hospitality is indicative of what is barren and joyless about the lives of those who go there. From Columbus, Georgia, to New York City is a long way.

Biff Brannon's restaurant is presumably called the New York Cafe because of the ironic contrast between what it is and what its name signifies. The name is an attempt at sophistication, at the glamour of the big city, at a greater than provincial importance; New York is the metropolis, where important things happen and ambitions come true and talent is rewarded and all is exciting, rich, romantic. Set in the backwaters of civilization (as Carson McCullers' imagination saw it, anyway), the pathetic name given the all-night restaurant mocks the romantic dream with its commonplace actuality. The habitués are there because they live in a small city in southwestern Georgia instead of New York, or even Atlanta. It is like the blue hotel in Stephen Crane's story of that name, set out on the Nebraska prairie and painted a surrealistic blue to signify the exaggerations of its pretension amid the lonely, terribly barren, and empty expanses of a late nineteenth-century West only recently changed from being uninhabited prairie and now only the dreary backwash of a crude provincial life. Just so, the inappropriateness of the name New York Cafe is meant by the author to convey a sense of cultural starvation, the provincial dreariness of the kind of city where the side-

*Reprinted from the *Virginia Quarterly Review* 53 (1977): 265–83, as revised and reprinted in *A Gallery of Southerners,* by Louis D. Rubin Jr. (Baton Rouge: Louisiana State University Press, 1982), 135–51. Used with permission.

walks, as they used to say, are rolled up each night at ten o'clock. As well call it the Café de Paris.

Is that what Columbus, Georgia, was like? I suppose it depends upon the viewpoint, and Carson McCullers' viewpoint at the time she was writing *The Heart Is a Lonely Hunter* was not exactly that of the Nashville Agrarians, or even of William Faulkner or Eudora Welty. Frankie Addams' view of Columbus and her own, she once remarked, were identical. From Virginia Carr's fascinating and I think horrifying biography, *The Lonely Hunter,* we know that during those years, the late 1930s, Carson and Reeves McCullers wanted above all to get to New York City. Carson had had a taste of it as an apprentice writer, and though living on short rations she had no doubt whatever that it was the place for her. There were to be found the writers and artists and teachers and publishers, the people who understood, as she thought, what was really worthwhile in life. New York was the place of art, of culture, of fulfillment, where the dreams of the lonely provincial could come true. She wrote *The Heart Is a Lonely Hunter* for numerous reasons, and an important one was so that it might make her famous and enable her to move to New York and escape the dreariness of the provinces forever. Which it did—though it cannot be said that ultimately she found what she was looking for there, either.

In this respect, as in several others, she is reminiscent of another southern author, Thomas Wolfe. In the novel published as *You Can't Go Home Again,* Wolfe explains how it was that the townsfolk of Libya Hill got involved in a frantic real estate boom in the 1920s, resulting in disgrace and disaster when the Depression came on.

> As he stood upon the hill and looked out on the scene that spread below him in the gathering darkness, with its pattern of lights to mark the streets and the creeping pin-pricks of the thronging traffic, he remembered the barren night-time streets of the town he had known so well in his boyhood. Their dreary and unpeopled desolation had burned its acid print upon his memory. Bare and deserted by ten o'clock at night, those streets had been an aching monotony, a weariness of hard lights and empty pavements, a frozen torpor broken only occasionally by the footfalls of some prowler—some desperate, famished, lonely man who hoped past hope and past belief for some haven of comfort, warmth, and love there in the wilderness, for the sudden opening of a magic door into some secret, rich, and more abundant life. There had been many such, but they had never found what they were searching for. They had been dying in the darkness—without a goal, a certain purpose, or a door.
>
> And that, it seemed to George, was the way the thing had come. That was the way it had happened. Yes, it was there—on many a night long past and wearily accomplished, in ten thousand little towns and in ten million barren streets where all the passion, hope, and hunger of the famished men beat like a great pulse through the fields of darkness—it was there and nowhere else that all this madness had been brewed.

Like Carson Smith McCullers, Thomas Wolfe was raised in a small southern city, of lower middle class origins and status, and yearned to get away. Eugene Gant looked out northward and eastward over the mountains toward the shining city of his dreams; Frankie Addams and Mick Kelly, unlike their creator, are less precise about exactly where they wish to go, but they are sure they want to get out of their imprisoned circumstances. In neither McCullers nor Wolfe is the hold of the southern community upon characters very real. Neither is very much involved in the kind of historical tradition or community identification that writers such as Faulkner and Welty use for the stuff of their fiction.

A major difference between McCullers' South and Wolfe's is that there is no sense of Wolfe himself feeling trapped in it. He is going to leave. Carson McCullers' people are there to stay, and their yearning for something better and finer and more fulfilling has a kind of painful *angst* about it. Their yearning for the metropolis, as has often been said, is like that of Chekhov's provincial Russians for Moscow: for a place of impossible fulfillment that is too far off in time and space to represent anything more than a forlorn hope.

II

The Heart Is a Lonely Hunter burst upon the national literary scene in 1940; thirty-seven years later and it is still going strong. *Reflections in a Golden Eye* followed the year after; of all Mrs. McCullers' fiction it is probably the most bizarre, the least pleasant. It is a *tour de force,* a sustained exercise in pure pain, without respite or humor. In 1943 she published *The Ballad of the Sad Café,* one of the most intense short novels of the twentieth century, in many ways the essence of her art. In 1946 came *The Member of the Wedding,* the most enjoyable—if that is a word to be used with *any* of her work—of all her books, and also, so far as living in the everyday world that most of us must inhabit is involved, the most "normal." In those books, produced over a period of less than a decade and while the author was still in her twenties, we have a very impressive body of fiction indeed.

That was all. Nothing that she wrote in the remaining two decades of her life adds much to her achievement. *Clock Without Hands* was an artistic disaster; only her most devoted admirers could say much for it. Whatever it was she had in the way of a gift, she had lost it. When she died in 1967, I doubt that anyone felt that she was leaving good books unwritten.

We are dealing, therefore, with certain works of fiction written and published during a period of intense and often brilliant creativity, by a young writer, a *wunderkind* as it were, one who did not develop or extend her range afterward. I think it is important to remember that. Whatever the faces and tensions that were central to her life and art, and which ultimately destroyed both, they attained, during this period, an equilibrium that made her fiction possible.

A writer, too, whom I have found can exert a very powerful influence on young people, in particular other young writers. I have taught courses in creative writing for some years, and so do not undervalue the considerable influence she can have on a certain kind of young writer. All in all, it is a benign and valuable influence, for if the young writer is any good the more obvious imitative elements are soon thrown off, while what remains is the sense of the possibility of self-expression. What she has to teach the young writer is the realization, which seems obvious but is not, that the qualities of youthful artistic sensibility, of being "different" and unwilling or unable to conform to the expected patterns of conventional adolescence, are not merely uselessly burdensome and painful, but can be transformed into the insight and awareness of art. The impetus to self-fulfillment involved in that realization can be enormously creative.

Mrs. McCullers' fiction, in particular *The Member of the Wedding,* can speak to the adolescent reader in very intense fashion, for what it conveys is the frustration and pain of being more than a child and yet not an adult, with the agony of self-awareness and sense of isolation thereby involved. There is the shock of recognition—something of the same kind of reassurance through identification that books such as *Look Homeward, Angel* or *The Catcher in the Rye* have been known to provide. It is fashionable, of course, to outgrow such identification—and also inevitable, if the young writer is to develop his or her own talent—and what it means is that much of the criticism that has been written about Carson McCullers' work is either pedestrian or else unsympathetic, because the kind of perspective that makes the act of criticism meaningful is something that is possible only when the reader gets beyond the intense, uncritical emotional response that characterizes the youthful impact of a novel such as *The Member of the Wedding.*

Please understand: I am not saying that only persons without critical discernment can enjoy Carson McCullers' fiction; clearly that is not so at all. What I am contending, however, is that the way in which her work can speak to the young reader is not susceptible to very much critical analysis, because it comes at a stage at which the reader's response is based upon intense emotional assent and identification rather than a mere selective discrimination. When the reader subsequently comes to acquire that intellectual discrimination, he can no longer muster the emotional assent in the intense way that was possible when he first read Carson McCullers. Mrs. McCullers' fiction, in other words, taught him that his feelings were worthwhile and could be given artistic dignity, enabling him to recognize what he must have felt. But having learned that, the reader, if he is to develop his critical talents, goes on to other writers and becomes interested in exploring the quality and nature of his response to works of literature as well as exposing himself to the naïve intensity, and so needs to investigate that response in terms of fiction that yields more to careful discrimination.

In short, Carson McCullers is in certain important ways a writer for young readers, and one has to be young to receive what she offers. She speaks not to the intelligence so much as to the untutored emotions, and with such tremendous intensity that one must either accept it or reject it. There is almost no middle ground. She does not let you think about it, choosing this and suspending judgment on that as you go along; it is all of a piece, and if you like the experience of fiction to be intricate and subtle, she is probably not for you.

The McCullers fiction, I believe, has at its center a fundamental premise: which is that solitude—loneliness—is a human constant, and cannot possibly be alleviated for very long at a time. But there is no philosophical acceptance of that condition, and none of the joy in it that one finds in, say, Thomas Wolfe or even Hemingway. The solitude is inevitable, and it is always painful. Thus life is a matter of living in pain, and art is the portraying of anguish. Occasionally, a character of hers knows happiness, but never for very long. Thus in *The Ballad of the Sad Café* there is a time when Miss Amelia believes she has the love of Cousin Lymon, and so permits her cafe to be a place of joy, but it cannot last. Marvin Macy shows up; Cousin Lymon has been waiting for someone like him; Miss Amelia's happiness disintegrates; you might as well go listen to the chain gang, the narrator tells us.

Mrs. McCullers explains it by her remarks on love, which she says involves the lover and the beloved, who come from two different countries. There is no way that such love can be shared, for one of the two must love and the other be loved; no reciprocal relationship, whereby one both loves and is loved in turn, is possible.

Obviously love in this definition involves possession. The lover, she says, "is forever trying to strip bare his beloved. The lover craves every possible relation with the beloved, even if this experience can cause him only pain." For this reason, she points out, it is much more desirable, and most people wish, to be the lover rather than the beloved, since the "beloved fears and hates the lover" who is trying to possess him. It is something like Frost's "Fire and Ice": love can be destructive because it wishes to consume the beloved, or because in reaction it produces the glacial impenetrability of freezing disdain. But Frost was making a different moral entirely. He was speaking against love that involves only possessiveness, or self-protective hate that refuses to open itself to human warmth. Carson McCullers not only declares that it *must* be that way, but that the very nature of being loved, which is to say, wanted and needed by another, is intolerable.

Such of course is the scheme of *The Heart Is a Lonely Hunter*. "In the town there were two mutes, and they were always together." Singer is the lover, Antonapoulos the beloved. Antonapoulos accepts Singer because it is convenient and comfortable for him to do so, but then he loses his intelligence and also his need for what Singer can provide, since as a vegetable he requires nothing outside himself. So Singer is left, bereft, loveless. As long as he could retain the illusion that Antonapoulos had a place for him in his affections, he could cope; Antonapoulos' very inchoateness and lack of awareness were an advantage, since they permitted Singer to believe in the fiction that his love understood and returned.

Singer's self-deception in turn makes possible the self-deception of all the others—Biff, Dr. Copeland, Jake, Mick Kelly. So long as Singer will sit and listen to them speak their troubles, they can, for a time at least, function. Singer understands them only imperfectly; he depends upon lipreading. The fact that he cannot answer back, cannot carry on a dialogue, is what makes him so satisfactory, for in that way the others are enabled to believe that he understands, sympathizes, and accepts all that they say and feel. In this respect, Singer fills the role of the beloved; he allows himself to be loved, because he is insulated from the demands and the possessiveness of love by virtue of his deafness. If he were not deaf, and thus solitary in a world of talkers, he could never tolerate the others, of course, and this not because he is selfish or mean—he is neither—but because he is a human being. Thus Singer serves the others as the object of their love (which obviously is self-love), while Antonapoulos fills a similar role for him, and the self-deception works—until Antonapoulos dies, whereupon the occasion for Singer's love collapses and he shoots himself, and the others are left stranded. The artistry is in the pain—Mrs. McCullers has never let us participate in the deception; we have witnessed it at all points for the ruse that it is, and when the arrangements collapse we perceive only the inevitable outcome of what we have seen developing all along. Again, you might as well go listen to the chain gang—which is pretty much what as readers we have been engaged in doing.

III

The Heart Is a Lonely Hunter was and is a remarkable book—that a 23-year-old woman could write with so much mastery and so much perception about so diverse a range of characters was odd indeed. The talent that was able to observe the variety of experience that went into those characterizations was something close to genius. The capacity for observation, for perceiving and detailing the concerns of the various people, was stunning in its virtuosity. What I find most remarkable, reading the novel over again and in light of those that followed and also from what I have learned from Mrs. Carr's biography, is that a writer whose imagination is so subjective, whose art is so suffused with emotional coloration and is based upon the capacity to convey the endless sameness of human suffering, could at the same time see and record and catalogue so much, with such clear specificity and concrete objectivity of detail. For one whose view of the human condition is so thoroughly pessimistic to be able to combine that with the kind of knowledge of people and things outside of her that surely stems from a considerable fascination in observing the varieties of experience seems odd, to say the least.

The question that it poses is this: what is the relationship between the obvious fascination with which Mrs. McCullers viewed various kinds of human life and the terrible loneliness and anguish that she felt was hers and everyone's lot? By all logic one would think that the conviction of loneliness and separateness should involve a closing down of the blinds, so to speak, a withdrawal from what she would say is the impossible attempt ever to reach out to include others. Or conversely, that so rare a talent for observing and understanding and feeling compassion for others would produce something other than the anguished conviction of emptiness and solitude. One thinks of Eudora Welty, whose marvelous gift for observation and insight into many kinds of people goes along with a real joy in the life-giving mystery of human personality.

With Carson McCullers, it did not work that way, however, and perhaps one avenue toward understanding the apparent contradiction is to think about what Mrs. McCullers has Biff Brannon say about his fondness for freaks:

> What he had said to Alice was true—he did like freaks. He had a special friendly feeling for sick people and cripples. Whenever somebody with a harelip or T.B. came into the place he would set him up to beer. Or if the customer were a hunchback or a bad cripple, then it would be whiskey on the house. There was one fellow who had had his peter and his left leg blown off in a boiler explosion, and whenever he came to town there was a free pint waiting for him. And if Singer were a drinking kind of man he could get liquor at half price any time he wanted it.

Mrs. Carr begins her biography with an incident, which I assume was told her by Mrs. McCullers' childhood friend Helen Jackson, that demonstrates Carson McCullers' lifelong interest in the freak shows at the Chattahoochee Valley Fair. She remarks rightly that "deeply compassionate, the youngster was becoming increasingly aware that one's physical aberration was but an exaggerated symbol of what she considered everyman's 'caught' condition of spiritual isolation and sense of aloneness in spite of his intense desire and effort to relate to others." This is quite true. The physically grotesque is a way of exaggerating the everyday by making it all-important and inescapable. But perhaps there is more to it than that, even. I recall a remark of Flannery O'Connor's when asked why so many southern novelists tended to describe grotesques. The South, she said, was the last section of the country where you could still recognize a freak when you saw him.

What Miss O'Connor was suggesting, I suppose, with her customary wit and hyperbole, was that the southern experience was still very much an affair of the complex patterns of community life, with the comings and goings of individuals taking place within a clearly recognized set of expectations and assumptions. In that kind of established social context, individual behavior ran along expected forms, so that there were certain agreed-upon limits and standards of human conduct. Anything truly deviant, genuinely aberrant, would therefore stand out, since there was something against which it could be measured and identified. I'm sure Flannery would have been the first to insist (after laughing at any such pompous interpretation of her remark) that it was no stifling conformity that was produced, but a kind of set of agreed-upon manners and formalities that made social experience convenient and tolerable, with a minimum of abrasiveness and considerable respect for privacy. She would also, I believe, insist that the implicit but firmly defined set of social forms went along with a set of similarly defined moral assumptions and values, so that moral freakishness— *i.e.,* deviation from what is agreed upon and expected—was also and equally recognizable.

This is the context, I think, within which so much of Flannery O'Connor's fiction operates, and Carson McCullers', too. The difference is in the use of the freakishness—*i.e.,* of the characters and the conduct that deviates from the accustomed and comfortable. Miss O'Connor uses her Hazel Moteses and Misfits and Francis Marion Tarwaters and the like to comment upon the moral and spiritual evasions and shortcomings of the supposedly "normal" community; they appear freakish because in their exaggeration they dramatize moral ultimates, and refuse to abide by the comfortable evasions of a too complacent, too secular society. Their apparent grotesqueness is actually spiritual consistency: the true freakishness is the secular materialism of the everyday, which Miss O'Connor felt was spiritually grotesque. Thus, in *Wise Blood,* when Hazel Motes takes to wrapping barbed wire about his chest to mortify himself for his sins, his landlady tells him that people have quit doing that a long time ago, whereupon Hazel replies that people haven't quit doing it so long as he is still doing it.

By contrast, Carson McCullers focuses upon her maimed, misfitting, wounded people not as a commentary upon the complacent "normality" of the community which would term them freakish, but as exemplars of the wretchedness of the human condition. It isn't that freaks are commentaries or criticisms on normality; they *are* normality. Their physical grotesquery merely makes visible and identifiable their isolation and anguish; "normal" people do not confront these on quite such immediate and inescapable terms, perhaps, but they are really no better off, no happier. Everybody that is human is on the chain gang; on some the stripes and chains are merely more readily visible.

IV

The particular vision of Carson McCullers, the capacity for recognizing and portraying and sympathetically identifying with pain and loneliness, could arise only out of a social situation in which the patterns and forms and expectations of conduct and attitude are very firmly and formidably present, so that the inability or failure to function within those patterns seems crucial. If everything is permitted and expected, then there is no need to feel pain or frustration because one's own behavior and inclinations are different from those of others. But if there is a strong set of expectations, and one is unable to fulfill them and yet be oneself, then one searches out for kindred sufferers, in order to feel less lonely through assurance of their pain as well. Thus the portrait gallery of Carson McCullers' "freaks"—*i.e.,* of those who must accept being set apart. And the conviction that this is the way the world goes, and no genuine human sharing is possible.

The appetite of Mrs. McCullers for viewing and identifying the details of human life, and the accuracy with which she was able to create so many sharply delineated people, then, was not exactly a joy in the richness and variety of experience, so much as a hunger for possession. It wasn't enough to see and identify; she had to demonstrate that, despite the varied surfaces and individually realized characterizations, they were really all alike, and what lay at the core of each was suffering and pain deriving from loneliness. One is reminded of a writer that Mrs. McCullers very much admired: Marcel Proust—significantly, a homosexual, as Mrs. McCullers was a lesbian. In that brilliant and profound panorama of men and women who appear in the seven volumes of the *Recherche du Temps Perdu,* each individual struggles to possess and to use others. Charles Swann, Gilberte, Saint Loup, the Baron Charlus, Morel, Bloch, the Duc and Duchesse de Guermantes, Albertine Simonet, above all, the narrator himself, who calls himself Marcel—at the core of each one is the unsatisfied desire to possess, to use, to pleasure oneself through or upon (never with) others, and it is all doomed, for life in human time is meaningless, since everything changes and nothing remains. Only the art that derives from personal, involuntary memory can achieve meaning; art is *not* life, but its subjective recreation in the possessive imagination of the artist.

Something like this, I imagine, is what the writing of fiction was for Carson McCullers; art was a way of possessing. It was the creative act of taking what she saw and molding it, transforming it beyond identifiable shape into the form of art, so that it represented her kind of world. And I am tempted to say that, in the tension between the observed authority of the recalcitrant materials she drew upon and the powerful, possessive will to shape them to her desired meaning, the artistic equilibrium came that made her best work possible. Her first book, *The Heart Is a Lonely Hunter,* produced the most convincing and richest of all her characters, Dr. Benedict Mady Copeland, the black physician, and this is because, more so than with any of the others, there was a kind of palpable and inescapable social integrity in the material itself. With the other characters in the novel (and all have their individual integrities), the pain and loneliness were personal, subjective; with Dr. Copeland, there was added a specific and very formidable social deprivation. We may not quite believe in Jake Blount's outrage over the victimization of the proletariat—not that the victimization does not exist, but that Jake's outrage seems motivated less by social injustice than by his own thwarted desire for violence. The social consciousness seems to be something of an excuse for Jake to use for his own personal needs. Biff Brannon's loneliness is believable, but it seems insufficiently anchored. As for Mick Kelly, ancestor as she is of Frankie Addams, it is adolescence, not the eternal misery of the human condition, that gives her loneliness its authority, and when the author seeks to insure its permanence through family economics and misfortune, it seems somehow gratuitous, excessive; I can't really see her job in the five-and-ten as any kind of permanent entrapment. But Dr. Copeland is an educated, talented black man in the segregated society of southwest Georgia; any chagrin, mortification, rage he feels requires no dependence upon personal, subjective sensibility. Thus the kind of sensibility with which Mrs. McCullers invests him—the loneliness and anguish—blends so completely with the social outrage that the one gives body to the other. Each time I reread *The Heart Is a Lonely Hunter*, I am the more impressed with the characterization of Dr. Copeland. He is masterful, one of the reasons I share David Madden's feeling that the first novel is the best of all her full-length works.

I say this despite my admiration for so much of *The Member of the Wedding*. Frankie Addams is the most appealing of Mrs. McCullers' people; I like her better than Mick Kelley because she is less strident—less written, I think, to a thesis. She is what Mick Kelly would perhaps have been, had there been room for her to have a whole book of her own. In *The Heart Is a Lonely Hunter*, the "Mozart" motif always seemed a bit incongruous and sentimental to me, as if it were somewhat forced upon the characterization. Frankie Addams has the same sensibility without the extraneous element, as I see it, and her struggles with preadolescence are entirely convincing and wondrously done—up to a certain point. That point is reached when, two-thirds of the way through, Frankie's sensibility moves beyond that inherent in her situation and becomes something bizarre and genuinely distorted—when the piano tuner goes to work and Frankie and Berenice have some kind of surrealistic, mystic vision of pain and misery. After that point, I cease to believe fully in the meaning Mrs. McCullers is (as it now seems) forcing upon Frankie. That's not Frankie as we have known her, and she never recovers. The novel, in other words, goes beyond the pain of preadolescent awkwardness and becomes truly aberrant; it drops off the deep end into distortion for the sake of distortion. The death of John Henry, for example: he seems to be killed off gratuitously, in order to provide more misery. And in the epilogue, when Frankie enters full adolescence, becomes Frances, and is made into a "normal" teen-ager, it seems too arbitrary, too pat. That isn't Frankie, either.

It is interesting, and particularly in light of the revelations in Mrs. Carr's biography of Carson McCullers' adult sexual ambivalence, that her two important artist figures, Mick and Frankie, cannot go beyond the point of incipient sexual awakening and yet remain consistent with their characterizations. These young girls, both with masculine names, remain fixed in preadolescence; when they have to become women, as they must, they are, as characters, all but destroyed. Mick seduces Harry Minowitz; her initiation accomplished, she wants nothing whatever to do with him, and gladly lets him run away. Frankie, more innocent, smashes the vase over the head of the soldier, dreams of escaping into a world of snow and wintry calm, then becomes Frances and is Frankie no more. I think of those photographs in Mrs. Carr's biography, of Carson at Yaddo looking like a boyish preadolescent girl, and of what she did to poor Reeves McCullers.

V

The psychology of the artist is a complex matter, and I have no intention of trying to work it out as it involves Carson McCullers. I shall suggest only this. Those seven years, from the time she wrote *The Heart Is a Lonely Hunter* up through *The Member of the Wedding,* must have represented, in Mrs. McCullers' career, a period during which the confusion, chaos, and contradiction that characterized most of her adult life could be made into art because the issues that were involved still seemed capable of solution. She could, in other words, embody the contradictions in language; they could evolve into a counterpoint, which she as an artist could see as significant. The quarrel within herself was genuine, and she could make poetry out of it. But the time came when she capitulated, ceased as a writer to struggle against the confusion of her life by attempting to give it order and form through language, as she had been doing, and let the subjective, ultimately destructive element have full sway. This is the impression I get from Mrs. Carr's biography. The creative tension was relaxed. The personal suffering continued, but no longer could she approach it with the assumption that the suffering represented a deprivation, a frustrated yearning for a more beautiful and happier situation *outside* herself which was, at least theoretically, attainable in this world. Instead, the pain became itself the objective; there was nothing more to be discovered through and with it. Now she knew physical pain as never before; her life revolved around it. It seems clear that, in some strange but powerful way, the mental anguish becomes physical, and is henceforth made permanent and acceptable. In Marcel Proust's explanation, "the life of the writer does not end" with the work of art he makes out of it, and "the same temperament which caused him to undergo certain sufferings which have been incorporated in his work will continue to exist after the work is completed. . . . Viewed as an omen of misfortune the work should be regarded solely as an unhappy love which is the forerunner of others and will end in the poet's life resembling his work, so that he will scarcely have any more need to write, such a faithful forecast of what is to come will he be able to find in what he has already written."

I was struck by the way in which, as evidenced in Mrs. Carr's biography, Proust's dictum was borne out in Mrs. McCullers' life. She herself noted, with more than a little satisfaction, that everything that happened to her characters either had been or would eventually be experienced by her in her own life. David Madden has stressed the intensity of this imaginative relationship between her art and her own life: "One might say that all her work is autobiographical in the sense that whatever she read and whatever she conjured up in her imagination *really happened* to her." This is something more, I believe, than what is usually signified by autobiography: *i.e.,* than Flaubert's famous remark that he was Emma Bovary. Instead of her characters representing aspects of Carson McCullers' sensibility, they seem to have *become* her sensibility. Not only was the gap between life and art erased; the fantasy, and the suffering it embodied, were allowed to become the reality. Whatever anchor to everyday life had existed before, in the form of her childhood identity, her early experience, the necessity of having to fit into and live in a world beyond and outside her emotional needs, ceased to hold. The pain, the suffering, the yearning, no longer a commentary upon experience, were now the experience itself. Were the crippling illnesses that increasingly ravaged her psychosomatic in origin? Her friends suspected as much; perhaps she too knew it, as Mrs. Carr notes. She was caught up in her pain, and did not struggle to escape it because the pain was, as she saw it, her art and her identity.

Again the profound insight of Marcel Proust into the nature of suffering and sexual abnormality is instructive: "When life walls us in, our intelligence cuts an opening, for, though there can be no remedy for an unrequited love, one can win release from suffering, even if only by drawing from it the lessons it has to teach. The intelligence does not recognize in life any closed situations without an outlet." But this, Carson McCullers was unable to do; she is each of her suffering characters, in turn, but the next, ultimate step, which enabled Proust to create his great apologia, she was ultimately unable to take. She could not draw from the pain and loneliness the truths that, in Proust's words, "take the place of sorrows," since "when the latter are transformed into ideas, they at once lose part of their noxious effect on the heart and from the very first moment the transformation itself radiates joy." For Carson McCullers this never happened. "She was never an intellectual," a onetime friend said of her; "she only felt." If so, she had reached a stage at which the perception of pain was not enough, if she was to go beyond the early fiction. But that was all she knew. There was, for her, no Recapture of Lost Time, but only *Clock Without Hands.*

Like certain other of her contemporaries, Carson McCullers, it seems to me, constructed her art out of the South, but not out of its history, its common myths, its public values and the failure to cherish them. What is southern in her books are the rhythms, the sense of brooding loneliness in a place saturated with time. Compare *The Heart Is a Lonely Hunter* or *The Member of the Wedding* with, say, *Winesburg, Ohio,* and the relationship with the region is obvious. Sherwood Anderson's grotesques are more simple; a few clear, masterful sentences and we get their essential quality. Carson McCullers must show her misfits, whether spiritual or physical, in an extended context; there is plenty of time for everything. The southern quality is unmistakable, in the unhurried fascination with surfaces, the preoccupation with the setting in which the characterization reveals itself. Character is not for McCullers, any more than for Eudora Welty or William Faulkner or Thomas Wolfe, an idea, but a state of awareness. To repeat, there is plenty of time. And when the violence comes, as it so often does, it erupts in a place and a context, and it jars, queerly or terribly or both, the established and accustomed patterns. Before and after, there is lots of waiting, lots of time to think about everything.

Robert Penn Warren, in his novel *Flood,* has a southerner explain to a friend from the North that the key to the southern experience is lonesomeness. "It is angry lonesomeness. Angry lonesomeness makes Southerners say the word *South* like an idiot Tibetan monk turning a broken-down prayer wheel on which he has forgotten to hang any prayers." No southerner, he continues, "believes that there is any South. He just believes that if he keeps on saying the word he will lose some of the angry lonesomeness." Warren was writing fiction, not an essay on the South, but if we discount the metaphysical hyperbole that is proper for the particular characterization, the remark makes sense. What is involved, I think, is the same contrast between the formidable community patterns and social context mentioned earlier and the solitude of the private individual confronting these. Southern literature is filled with depictions of characters who, set for one reason or other on the outside, contemplate the intense coming and going of a community life from a private distance. The Reverend Hightower, Jack Burden, Eugene Gant, most of Eudora Welty's people—this is an essential element in southern fiction, and in no other southern author's work is it more essential than in the fiction of Carson McCullers.

Surely this situation lies at the heart of her relationship with the South, and nowhere is it given more pathetic rendering than by her. This is what one takes away, most of all, from Carson McCullers' people in their time and place: the way that it feels to be lonely.

That is why her people do and say what they do. That is the source of the pain. That is why the New York Cafe keeps open all the time: "the only store on all the street with an open door and lights inside." And that is why her best work may survive.

The Case of Carson McCullers

OLIVER EVANS*

I

Few living American writers have been the subject of as much controversy as Carson McCullers. The battle began in 1940, with the publication of her first book, *The Heart Is a Lonely Hunter,* and is still going strong: Edward Albee's recent dramatization of *The Ballad of the Sad Café* has brought the case of Mrs. McCullers once more into public prominence.

For a first novel, *The Heart Is a Lonely Hunter* was widely praised, though it must be admitted that much of the praise was owing to the fact that it *was* a first novel and that its author was only twenty-two. And the praise even then was by no means unqualified. Robert Littell, in *The Yale Review,* called it "a queer sad book that sticks in the mind," and prescribed that the author study *Huckleberry Finn* and Chekhov—presumably to take some of the queerness, if not the sadness, out of her work. Lewis Gannett commented: "A strange and uneven book, at times almost miraculous in its concise intensity, at times baffling." And Clifton Fadiman, then doyen of the *New Yorker*'s book reviewers, complained: "She writes without humor, and reveals no special gift for story telling. She might be a flop at handling ordinary human beings." He went on to add, however, that he was willing to place "a small bet" on her future.

Reflections in a Golden Eye, the following year, fared even worse; the critics labeled it Southern Gothic (the label has stuck) and accused the author of taking an unwholesome interest in grotesque characters and situations. Mr. Littell, who has trouble with things sticking in his mind, noted this time: "Strong traces of the talent are still here, and make the inversions and mutilations and nastiness stick in one's mind like burrs." And Mr. Fadiman, relieved that there were no takers for his bet, expressed disappointment with the book's "grotesque and forced hallucinations" and deplored Mrs. McCullers' "too obvious desire to create people and situations that are strange and star-

*Reprinted from *The Georgia Review* 18 (1964): 40–45. Reprinted by permission of *The Georgia Review.*

tling." Even *The Member of the Wedding* (1946), which has nothing more unwholesome for its subject than the growing pains of adolescence, struck Edmund Wilson as an "utterly pointless" story. (In justice to Mr. Wilson, however, it should be pointed out that, as though a bit uneasy about this verdict, he added: "I hope that I am not being stupid about this book.")

Curiously enough, Mrs. McCullers' next novel, *The Ballad of the Sad Café* (1951), was not denounced as much as its three main characters (an ex-convict, a man-like giantess, and a dwarf who is also hunch-backed, homosexual, and tubercular) would have led one to expect: it is as if the very grotesqueness of the situation, and the extreme degree to which it is stylized, enabled reviewers to "catch on" at last. One of them (W. P. Clancy in *Commonweal*) certainly did: "It seems to me that the Gothic label misses the essential point. Because Carson McCullers is ultimately the artist functioning at the very loftiest symbolic level, and if one must look for labels I should prefer to call her work 'metaphysical.'" This book was followed by a play, *The Square Root of Wonderful,* which, though the production had been a failure on Broadway, was nevertheless courteously received by the book reviewers.

One would have thought the long battle almost won; yet now, twenty-four years after *The Heart Is a Lonely Hunter,* it is being fought once more, and over very much the same fundamental issues. When Mrs. McCullers' fifth novel, *Clock Without Hands,* was published recently, the old, familiar charges—of strangeness, of sensationalism, of morbidity, of artificiality, of obsession with the aberrations of human behavior—were all revived ("An odd book," *The Reporter* said about it, and J. N. Hartt, in *The Yale Review,* lamented the fact that Mrs. McCullers had found it necessary to add, in the character of Jester Clane, yet another homosexual to her gallery of grotesques); and, just for good measure, a few new ones were introduced. Thus, Irving Howe complained in *The New York Times* of a "lethargic flatness" in the style and an "absence of inner conviction and imaginative energy"; the novel, he said, is poorly constructed and does not present an integrated vision of life but is instead "an unadorned and scrappy scenario for an as-yet-unwritten novel."

Side by side with these largely negative judgments there has existed, from the very first, a solid corpus of favorable, even enthusiastic criticism: Richard Wright, in 1940, lauded the "astonishing humanity that enables a white writer, for the first time in Southern fiction, to handle Negro characters with as much ease and justice as those of her own race"; six years later Diana Trilling, in *The Nation,* noted that Mrs. McCullers displayed "powers of observation and recollection quite beyond the ordinary, and an equally extraordinary facility in translating remembered experience into language"; Paul Engle, in 1950, wrote admiringly of her "genuine insight and proved emotion"; and within the last two years we have had the opinions of Gore Vidal (in *The Reporter*) that "of all the Southern writers she is the most likely to endure" and that of Tennessee Williams (in *The Saturday Review*) that Mrs. McCullers is "the greatest living writer of our country, if not of the world." Meanwhile from across the Atlantic have come kudos from V. S. Pritchett ("the most remarkable novelist, I think, to come out of America for a generation"); from David Garnett ("the best living American writer"); and from Dame Edith Sitwell ("a great poet's eye and mind and senses, together with a great prose writer's sense of construction and character"). On the same Sunday that Mr. Howe smashed *Clock Without Hands* in *The New York Times,* Rumer Godden, in the *Herald Tribune,* gave it the most prominent place in the house ("Not a word could be added to or taken away from this marvel of a novel").

What is one to make of all this? The praise, one notes, has come mostly from other novelists, or from poets and playwrights; it is therefore tempting to label Mrs. McCullers a "writer's writer" and let it go at that. But the explanation is not so simple, for, on the one hand, she has enjoyed a fairly large popular audience from time to time, and, on the other, Edmund Wilson is not a critic whose judgment is easy to ignore.

II

There are, I think, three reasons why Mrs. McCullers' work is not more widely appreciated. The first is psychological, and has to do with her "message"— what she has to say. In her best work, Mrs. McCullers has always been concerned with exploring what Hawthorne called the "labyrinths of the human heart," and what she has found therein has not always proved cause for rejoicing. What she conceives to be the truth about human nature is a melancholy truth: each man is surrounded by a "zone of loneliness," serving a life sentence of solitary confinement. The only way in which he can communicate with his fellow prisoners is through love—this affords him a certain measure of relief, but the relief is incomplete and temporary since love is seldom a completely mutual experience and is also subject to time, diminishing with the death of the loved one. This view of life and love received its most pessimistic statement in what is probably the most formally perfect of all Mrs. McCullers' works, *The Ballad of the Sad Café;* here she attempted to demonstrate not only that no love is actually reciprocal but that in most cases the beloved actually "fears and hates" the lover: "and with the best of reasons, for the lover is forever trying to strip bare his beloved . . . the lover craves any possible relation with the beloved, even if this experience can cause him only pain." A flaw thus exists in the very nature of love, and frustration is the lot of man.

These are not popular ideas. They do not flatter the reader. They are uncomfortable to live with. We are reluctant to acknowledge that they may correspond to reality—and our very reluctance may be evidence of a sneaking suspicion that they do. This, I believe, is the reason for much of the embarrassment that many readers feel toward Mrs. McCullers' work, and in this respect her situation is somewhat similar to that of another controversial writer who, though the critics have not always been kind, has certainly not lacked a popular success: Tennessee Williams.

The second reason Mrs. McCullers has suffered unfavorable criticism is her choice of characters and situations. It must be admitted that her characters are not always the kind one is likely to encounter in ordinary experience, and that the situations in which she places them are frequently uncommon, even implausible. But there is a reason for this, and a good one. Mrs. McCullers' theme, as I have said, is spiritual isolation, and it should be obvious that any kind of deviation, physical or psychological, increases this sense of isolation. It is not because Mrs. McCullers is indulging a taste for the freakish that she causes Singer, in *The Heart Is a Lonely Hunter,* to be a deaf-mute; it is because, being such, he constitutes an ideal symbol of man's inability to communicate with his neighbor. Similarly with Captain Penderton in *Reflections in a Golden Eye* and the dwarf in *The Ballad of the Sad Café:* their mutilations are not irrelevant but symbolize the factors that make for the loneliness of Everyman. To call Mrs. McCullers' work Gothic is to misuse the term, for Gothic horror is horror for its own sake, and while Faulkner has occasionally been guilty of this, notably in *Sanctuary,* Mrs. McCullers has not.

As for her situations, if they sometimes have an artificial, stylized quality it is because they have been contrived deliberately to illustrate a thesis, not to imitate situations in real life. Thus, Mrs. McCullers' notion that "the most outlandish people can be the stimulus for love . . . the value and quality of any love is determined by the lover himself" is illustrated by Singer's love for the half-witted Antonapoulos in *The Heart Is a Lonely Hunter* and by Amelia's love for the dwarf in *The Ballad of the Sad Café.* Since frustration is a constant theme, and since of all frustrations frustrated love is the most painful, Mrs. McCullers prefers situations that lead inevitably to disappointment in love: love, the attempt at ideal communication, is usually unreturned, unrecognized, mistaken for its opposite, or made difficult if not impossible by social and sometimes even biological considerations.

I have indicated two reasons for the controversy over Mrs. McCullers that are perhaps more discrediting to her critics than to herself. But the third and most important reason, which has to do with her favorite form (allegory), is one that does not altogether absolve her of blame. In allegory the realistic level, while coherent, must always be secondary to the symbolic. In Kafka, for example, the realistic level is negligible: the reader understands from the first that it is not to be taken as seriously as the symbolic, and if his characters are less convincing as human beings than Mrs. McCullers' they are for that reason more effective as symbols. The trouble with Mrs. McCullers is that she writes almost as well on the realistic as on the allegorical level. No other living American writer of allegorical fiction is so thoroughly in command of the devices of realism (as witness her dialogue, which is marvelously authentic), and though this is an achievement many another writer might envy her, it has worked to her disadvantage, for there is an ever-present temptation to read her largely on the realistic level and thus to overlook the allegorical scheme. In much of her work one is conscious of a struggle between the two levels, and this makes for a certain unevenness. Even the most conscientious reader can be distracted from the proper subject of a book by too dazzling a display of surface brilliance.

The Ballad of the Sad Café does not suffer from this defect, but *The Heart Is a Lonely Hunter,* for all its astonishing richness and beauty, does: so also, I think, does *Clock Without Hands,* an otherwise powerful novel in which Mrs. McCullers relates her familiar theme of isolation to the "existential crisis"—the achievement of identity through engagement and moral choice. The search for identity is the real subject of this book, and its three main characters go about it in their separate ways. Malone, a pharmacist dying of leukemia, who has passively allowed others to manage his life for him, gets his opportunity when, at a drawing of lots to determine who shall bomb the house of a Negro recently moved into a white neighborhood, the job falls to him and he refuses. Jester, a nineteen-year-old tempted by the need to identify himself with something bigger than himself and outside himself, decides (on learning his lawyer-father committed suicide after losing a case in which he defended a Negro client in a trial that proved a mockery of justice) that he too will become a lawyer and take up the struggle where his father left off: his life thus achieves moral direction. Sherman Pew, the Negro, achieves his identity in martyrdom.

Relevant only in a mechanical way to the central allegory is old Judge Clane, Jester's grandfather, and yet he is handled with such marvelous realism, with his turnip greens and his classical allusions, that he dominates the book. He is Mrs. McCullers' most successful character to date, and though one is grateful for having met him, this is a pity, for the design of the novel requires that he play a relatively minor part. Of the three searchers, the protagonist ought to be Malone, who, living under the shadow of impending death (as we all do), possesses Everyman's weaknesses as well as his capacity for dignity and the moral life. But more space is devoted—and more interest attaches—to the doings of the old Judge, whom Mrs. McCullers has allowed to usurp his function. *Clock Without Hands* is an impressive novel, but it would have been even more successful if Mrs. McCullers had not permitted her gift for realistic characterization to compromise her didactic purpose.

I doubt if any American writer since Hawthorne and Melville has handled the difficult form of allegory quite as well as Mrs. McCullers, and it is ironical that her greatest defect has been an excess of talent in another direction. Many of the charges that have been brought against her spring, as I have shown, from an ignorance of her intentions; the unevenness, however, and the lack of proper emphasis and proportion of which many readers have justifiably complained, have this obtrusive talent for their source, and it should probably either be suppressed in an effort to return to the purity of her "middle period" or allowed full expression in a novel that does not aspire to maintain a consistent allegorical level.

[A Feminist Reading:
McCullers's *Heart Is a Lonely Hunter*]

GAYATRI CHAKRAVORTY SPIVAK*

INTRODUCTION

We are in trouble over sex, race, and class. Any intellectual, any reader, any teacher must try to understand the world, even if she must remind herself constantly of the perils of taking understanding as a privilege or a goal. If she is a feminist, she must try to change the world, even if she is cautious enough at every step to reiterate at least two things: the sense of a "world" is the ever-shifting and many-planed converging point of interminable determinations; and even a "change" conceived of as a restructuring must be called again and again into question.[1] Even within this careful framing she cannot ignore that the categories of the class struggle are the best developed tools for understanding and change. Her first reaction, hesitant though not adverse, is that these categories are *macro*-structural. When the sexual struggle is translated into the class struggle, or when it is understood as analogous to the class struggle, the *micro*-structural daily intercourse between and among the sexes in public and private is programmatically excluded.

The way in which power is exercised in personal relationships and the way in which the ruling sex explains it away is what constitutes the micro-structure. The articulation of normative macro-structures that produce the most majestic edifices of the patriarchy will not allow this inconvenient dimension to clutter up the sphere of public analysis. Merely to co-opt feminism into the macro-structures of class analysis is to give in to this impatience that will not recognize that the micro-structures of sexuality cut across the private and the public. Rather than accept this dismissal by labelling a concern for the politics of sex as an obsession with the personal, feminism should

*Excerpt reprinted from "Three Feminist Readings: McCullers, Drabble, Habermas," *Union Seminary Quarterly Review* 35.1&2 (Fall/Winter 1979–80): 15–34, by permission of the journal and the author.

redefine the personal as the micro-structurally political suppressed by the macro-structure. It should develop and act upon an analysis that is enriched by the class-component at every step, but is neither identical nor in contradiction to it.[2]

Any internationalist feminist must also consider the importance of the race struggle. In America, the race situation, except when the member of the racial minority or the ethnic group has been "tokenized" into the majority, can be identified with political oppression. The notion of the "class" (rather than the race) struggle as a collective effort as well as the cautions of "deconstructive activism" (regarding the limits of understanding and change mentioned in my opening paragraph) are alien to the white liberal feminist. A benevolent interest in the uplift of the races, however, has always been the genuine concern of Liberalism, even with a capital L, as in the nineteenth century movement in England. Its effects have been felt in the colonial theatre larger than the United States. Here the forces of Socialist Feminism can join with white liberal feminism without too much ado. Perhaps because of this alliance, or perhaps because of this incipient "vanguardism" of much Socialism in America, the internationalist approach to race-sexuality remains askew. It becomes "impractical" to recognize that the international informants of the American feminists are themselves marked by a privilege that allows them channels of communication with the ruling races.[3] It is also overlooked that in Asia and Africa the situation of racialism is not domestically identical with the situation of political oppression; or that the internecine caste-class oppression in underdeveloped economies cannot be identified merely with the massive exploitation of the Third World countries by the First/Second Worlds, where the superpowers are white.[4] It is further overlooked that, as a result of racialism, in those Third World countries the model of an unexamined white feminism is becoming, like riding, tennis, or clubwomanship, at worst a fashion of the privileged elite and at best not far different from the ideologically ambiguous missionary and colonial impulse toward "native women's education." Apart from, yet deeply and asymmetrically involved in all these complications, the micro-structural and often brutal politics of sex continues its work across the social spectrum, there as here.

If orthodox Socialist Feminism must privilege the macro-structure of class analysis in the interest of a cleaner and more feasible practice, orthodox Internationalist Feminism must privilege its "vanguardism" by a predictable refusal to recognize its own "ideological fix." Indeed, any critique of that ideology must begin its work through the great macro-structures of the history of colonialism. And yet, if the micro-structural questions and cautions are given up, practicing such a critique becomes useless for a feminist, who forgets at her peril that sex straddles the private and the public. Feminism, it seems, must work with the personal and the political as they disguise themselves to foreclose the micro- and the macro-structures. To misunderstand this as a mere class-based personalization of the political might be to resist understanding, to resist change.

These issues are broader than the scope of Carson McCullers's *The Heart is a Lonely Hunter* and Margaret Drabble's *The Waterfall*. Yet, as these issues inform my days, it is in terms of them that I have read these books.

I

One of the chief concerns of Carson McCullers's first book, *The Heart Is a Lonely Hunter* (1940), is that people cannot discover a common bond.

> One night soon after Christmas all four of the [main characters] chanced to visit [the central character—a deaf-mute named Singer] at the same time. But something was wrong. . . . Always each of them had so much to say. Yet now that they were together they were silent. When they came in he had expected an outburst of some kind. In a vague way he had expected this to be the end of something. But in the room there was only a feeling of strain. His hands worked nervously as though they were pulling things unseen from the air and binding them together.[5]

This failure of collectivity remains McCullers's lasting concern. But, by the time she comes to write *The Ballad of the Sad Café* (1943) or *The Member of the Wedding* (1946) the concern becomes the theme of individual loneliness, growing pains, social or physical marginality. In the first book, however, the irreducible separation is based on race-, class-, and sex-struggle.

Let us first consider the story of the struggle of the growing girl, Mick Kelly. Her story is the most accessible to a depoliticized American reader. It allows this tough and strange novel to be described, as in the Bantam paperback blurb, as "a searching and sensitive novel of innocence lost." The book is an account of a few months of Mick's thirteenth year. She is ferociously independent and her creative impulses are concentrated in a passion for music. She situates this passion in her "inside room." Through it she hopes to transcend the subject-object dichotomy and time itself by way of a vicarious autoeroticism: "This music was her. . . . The whole world was this music and she could not listen hard enough. . . . It did not have anything to do with time going by at all. . . . The whole world was this symphony, and there was not enough of her to listen. . . . Now that [the symphony] was over there was only her heart like a rabbit and this terrible hurt" (100–101). Yet music, she hopes, will also get her to the great outside world: to foreign countries of splendid opulence. It will give her class mobility and thus launch her into the "outside" world: in hiding near a "cultured home," she listens to the symphonies. It will permit her to place her unique name within the hierarchy of power. Among her first gestures in the novel is inscribing the following list on the walls of a new and empty house: EDISON, DICK TRACY, MUSSOLINI. "Then in each corner with the largest letters of all, made with green and outlined in red, she wrote her initials—M. K." The female genitals as male obscenity, the prohibited object of pornographic consumption is included on the list. "She crossed over to the opposite wall and wrote a very bad word—PUSSY, and beneath that she put her initials, too." Finally, "quickly she wrote the fellow's name at the very top of the list—MOTSART" (31).

An orthodox literary critic might comment that a list such as this is overdetermined—that it carries different investments of meanings in the different contexts endorsed by even a fairly simple reading of our novel. It can just as easily "mean" a *differentiation* of music *from,* rather than its *inclusion in* the world of technology, individual enterprise, politics, sexuality-as-commodity, selfhood. Since the reader is asked to provide the connectives among the items on the list, the critic might point out that two incompatible, mutually self-destructive points of view can be produced from the list. It seems more important to us to notice that on Mick's list politics, sex, art, power, music, and the proper name are *assembled,* though the syntactic connections are left open. The "inside room" is the way to the real outside—the man's world, where the only viable female commodity is sex. It is not surprising that Mick uses music to identify with her elder brother, and to distinguish herself from her sisters, who are typically "feminine."

Halfway through the book, Mick loses her virginity. Harry Minowitz, a Jew, the only politically aware boy in Mick's crowd, takes responsibility for his act, worries about Mother seeing his sin in his eyes, and leaves town. The subtle process of Mick's growing up has begun. McCullers shows her caught in the body-mind bind again and again. Her first orgasm is "like her head was broke off from her body and thrown away. And her eyes looked up straight into the blinding sun while she counted something in her mind. And then this was the way. This was how it was" (235). Her desire couples her body to her brother's, and she worries about familial strictures upon love as she is exasperated by the constrictions of a legalistic (male) rationality based on evidence and demonstration.[6] "The room was quiet and dark and George was asleep. She pinched him and twisted his ear. He groaned but did not awake. She fitted in close to him and pressed her face against his hot little naked shoulders. . . . 'Suppose I wasn't your sister. Would you love me then?' . . . 'I reckon I would like you all right. But I still say you can't prove—' 'Prove! You got that word on the brain. *Prove and trick*'" (268–269). And then she thinks of the deaf-mute—Mr. Singer—and feels a love that bypasses family or body. "Mister Singer, Mister Singer. She said his name over and over. She loved him better than anyone in the family, better even than George or her Dad. It was a different love. It was not like anything she had ever felt in her life before" (268).

It is not her sex-predicament but her class-predicament that finally defeats her. The book laments not so much her loss of innocence as her entry into the work force. Her dreams are the dreams of a classbound free spirit, a girl who can think cannily about herself and her family: "They were mighty near as poor as factory folks. Only nobody could look down on them" (203). At the end of the book she is out of school and working in the Costume Jewelry section of Woolworth's. She is "shut out from the inside room," although she is still not "the kind of common girl that would wear cotton stockings" (301, 300). She has accepted the system in undirected anger and resentment and has no recourse left but to talk of herself in vain reassurance:

> It was like she was mad all the time. . . . Only there was nothing to be mad at. Unless the store. But the store hadn't asked her to take the job. So there was nothing to be mad at. It was like she was cheated. Only nobody had cheated her. So there was nobody to take it out on. However, just the same she had that feeling. Cheated. . . . What the hell good had it all been—the way she felt about music and the plans she had made in the inside room? It had to be some good if anything made sense. And it was too and it was too and it was too and it was too. It was some good. All right! O.K.! Some good. (304)

Those last two words carry a deep colloquial ambiguity. Perhaps in terms of the sex-struggle McCullers's Mick is merely conventional; perhaps the most we can say, knowing what we know, is that a girl of Mick's spirit has much less of a chance than a boy. But McCullers's class instinct is, in this one novel, intact. She does not make the liberal mistake of saying that one can *choose* to work in a factory rather than make music and the difference between the two is that the first obliges you to read Marx whereas the second involves making an American revolution while having fun.[7]

The real intrusion of the sex-struggle into *The Heart Is a Lonely Hunter* is much more mysterious. It is a micro-structural experiment in the text that I can relate to the macro-structural impulse that leaves its signature in generic and traditional negative utopias, such as *Gulliver's Travels*.[8] In this experiment we read of a human relationship of love and sexuality at furthest remove from so-called "normal" relationships. All details of a plausible heterosexual fiction have been filtered out. It is an unconsummated and, indeed, sexually unacknowledged relationship between two deaf-mute male homosexuals of completely incompatible personalities. Why and in what respect does this relationship still seem to carry the distinguishing mark of what the Western world has for so long celebrated in the "straight" scenario of love?

As in *La Vita nuova* or *To the Lighthouse*, it is a story of communication willingly given up.[9] "When he was twenty-two he had come South to this town from Chicago and he met Antonapoulos immediately. Since that time he had never spoken with his mouth again, because with his friend there was no need for this" (8). As in *La Vita nuova* or Yeats's "Ego Dominus Tuus," the absence of the beloved object not only does not hamper the narrative but advances it: if the book begins with an entry into that world of coupling that seems hardly real—"In the town there were two mutes, and they were always together" (1)—just six pages later Antonapoulos is taken away to the mental asylum, without his friend knowing "just what he really understood."

Singer writes many letters to Antonapoulos, but never sends them. This can remind us not only specifically of *La Vita nuova* and Love's mediation there, but also of the many odes, epistles, minnesongs, sonnet sequences, and epistolary novels—not to mention invocations to the Muse—with the narrative of letters *publicly* addressed to, and sometimes exchanged with, the beloved, that crowd the literature of the West.[10] It can make us begin to suspect that perhaps the "other" in those canonical and publicized exchanges has always been "really" like Antonapoulos in this story: mute, muted, distanced, displaced, imprisoned, mysterious, uncommunicative, and so unlike her "self" that she might as well be mad. The feminist must redefine those frozen signals of micro-structural intercourse; perhaps a reading such as this, of a text such as McCullers's, can contribute, even if minimally, to that collective project.

Singer's unsent letters are elaborate and serious, and indeed the one we are given in full (eleven long paragraphs) provides an analysis of that failure of collectivity which pervades the book:

> Yah Freedom and pirates. Yah Capital and Democrats, says the ugly one with the mustache. Then he contradicts himself and says, Freedom is the greatest of all ideals. I just got to get a chance to write this music in me and be a musician. I got to have a chance, says the girl. We are not allowed to serve, says the black Doctor. That is the Godlike need of my people. Aha, says the owner of the New York Cafe. . . . You know how I have always said that to be rude and not attend to the feelings of others is wrong. . . . I write it to you because I think you will understand. . . . I am not meant to be alone and without you who understand. (183, 184, 185)

It is of course possible to remark that such a letter, a piece of transparent self-deception on "the register of exactitude," brings an indispensable effect of anacoluthon in the text even as it insists that the intended uncomprehending non-recipient of the letter must be written to because he understands.[11] More important to this paper is the next significant exchange between the two men: in a dream an undisclosed phallus ("something held above the head") remains the object of worship as well as the mysterious unifier of the book's world. The final exchange between them shows us a childlike and idolized Antonapoulos who, indefinitely displaced through mutism, homosexuality, and idiocy, reveals the brutal image foreclosed by all the "normally" objectified love-goddesses of the world.

This is part of the dream:

> Antonapoulos kneeled at the top of these steps. He was naked and he fumbled with something that he held above his head and gazed at it as though in prayer. He himself knelt halfway down the steps. He was naked and cold and could not take his eyes from Antonapoulos and the thing he held above him. Behind him on the ground he felt the one with the moustache and the girl and the black man and the last one. They knelt naked and he felt their eyes on him. And behind him there were uncounted crowds of people in the darkness. (185)

Antonapoulos is, in part, described as the child-idiot-idol to whom Singer brings the offering of Mickey Mouse and Popeye films:

> Antonapoulos! . . . He wore a scarlet dressing-gown and green silk pajamas and a turquoise ring. . . . When Singer stood before him he smiled serenely, without surprise, and held out his jeweled hand. . . . His head was immense against the white pillow. The placid composure of his face was so profound that he seemed hardly to be aware that Singer was with him. . . . His fat little feet had untucked the cover at the bottom of the bed. His smile faded and he kicked contemptuously at the blanket. . . . When [the nurse] had straightened the bed to his liking the big Greek inclined his head so deliberately that the gesture seemed one of benediction rather than a simple nod of thanks. . . . Antonapoulos watched [Singer] with his dark, drowsy eyes. Sitting motionless in his bright, rich garments he seemed like some wise king from a legend. (187, 188, 190)

The unsent letters are the fiction of a paradoxically impure pure signifier that will never be sublated—that is, contradicted and preserved in a higher form—through its own contradiction and become a meaning-filled signified because the addressee receives it. In this encounter in the hospital we are shown a paradoxically impure *completed* exchange that is purely inter-objective—Narcissus forever unfulfilled—and paradigmatic of the relationship: "The eyes of his friend were moist and dark, and in them he saw the little rectangled pictures of himself that he had watched a thousand times" (187). In this moment the verdict on "romantic love" is complete and sexual difference is seen as difference-as-such, which love must narcissistically deny. It is not at all surprising that at the death of the image-object-beloved the lover must methodically put a bullet through his chest.

As a heterosexual feminist, I have read this love-legend *in extremis* as a commentary on the ideology of "normal love" that is the sustaining glory of literature. I have suggested that the commentary consists of structural irreducibles that remain even after a fictional operation of distancing from "normality" has been performed. These irreducibles help us re-read and re-write not merely the literary but also the psycho-political canon. The love-legend can, of course, be a reminder of yet another sexual differential: the differential between the heterosexual and the homosexual worlds. Although women and male homosexuals are both marginal as "non-serious" versions of the male norm, the woman has a recognized use in the male economy of reproduction, genealogy, and the passage of property. The male homosexual, on the other hand, has only the unrecognized use of sustaining as criminal or monstrous the tremendous force of the repressed homoeroticism of the patriarchy. The latter part of this argument is developed in Jacques Derrida's *Glas* (Paris, 1974). Carson McCullers is certainly no Jean Genet, the homosexual play-wright on the occasion of whom Derrida writes. Her homosexuality, like Woolf's, could find no socially collective voice and could not be macro-structurally endorsed like race or class. Yet in this alternate reading of Singer's story, it is not a transcendental androgynous model that stands as the book's god, but rather the male homosexual as the institutionalized insane. The depiction of Mick remains largely caught within the literary tradition of innocence-experience novels. That moving sentimentality seems to be utterly separate from the bizarre grandeur of this story of Singer and Antonapoulos.

Whether Singer's story is read as the irreducible and undisclosed description of the "straight" love stories with which the ruling sex animates the literary tradition, or as a more obviously historically determined represen-tation of the absolute otherness (alterity) of homosexual love, we have here once again a situation of two unresolvable readings. I cannot really say that the text engenders both readings. How unorthodox a reading the text can *convincingly* be made to engender depends sometimes on the vested authority and power of the critic within the system of academic patronage. I can merely say that the cautions of deconstructive activism would prime the feminist reader toward a both/as-well reading, as well as an either/or reading. The next step would be to question the tight opposition between figural (formal-ist) and empirical (moralist) readings and suggest that these two versions of the Singer-Antonapoulos story might well constitute part of a practice that will see the predicaments of heterosexual feminists and homosexuals as *forms* of the sex-struggle, micro-structurally differentiated though macro-struc-turally pulling together in collectivities.

The race-class scenes are woven together and have little or nothing to do with the sex scene in the book. Benedict Copeland is a fanatically devoted black doctor who wants to raise his race into self-conscious self-governance. Jake Blount is a lower middle-class autodidact whose introduction into social justice was through an elderly schoolmistress. Copeland, wishing to make his children exemplary, named them Karl Marx, Alexander Hamilton, and Por-tia, but had no understanding of the pedagogic and affective nature of the family. His children remained *his* project alone and his wife stole them from him and foiled his plan. Blount's non-relationship to women can be crypti-cally indicated by the following multiply overdetermined example: Jake is addressing his working-class neighbors, whom he cannot touch, and of whom he thinks as "the don't knows." " 'Come on, everybody,' he roars, 'Come one, come all. I'll settle you three at a time.' 'That's right, Honey,' a whore called" (245). This nameless prostitute, like Copeland's daughter Portia, remains typecast: the good working-class whore who situates Jake's thwarted revolutionary impulse as childish machismo, and the solid black earth-mother who situates Copeland's thwarted socialist impulse as childish intransigence.

Copeland's and Blount's problem is putting theory into practice. They are both men of words—Jake much more so. McCullers gives to Copeland the profession of a doctor who has selflessly helped his prolific people while trying to teach them birth control. Jake's efforts at "organizing" have resulted in comic-opera pranks and confusion (132). Copeland is shown as suffering tremendous indignities at the hands of the police; his son's feet are cut off because of gangrene contracted through brutal punishment in prison. By contrast, Blount in a panic will still yell "Order! Help! Police!" and at the end of the book will still say "it felt good to be sitting safe in a booth and to have just eaten a good meal" (289, 297). For him "there was hope . . . and soon perhaps the outline of his journey would take form" (299). Copeland's story ends as he is being taken back to the farm on a mule-wagon driven by his father-in-law: "He felt the fire in him and he could not be still. He wanted to sit up and speak in a loud voice—yet when he tried to raise himself he could not find the strength. The words in his heart grew big and they would not be silent. But the old man had ceased to listen and there was no one to hear him" (287).

There is a dialogue between Blount and Copeland toward the end of the book. It is a discussion of theory and practice. Copeland is very sick, Blount very drunk. After a lifetime of patience, Copeland has realized that "the most fatal thing a man can do is try to stand alone" (259). His dream now is of a black march upon Washington. Blount's idea is to take Copeland's maimed son around in a cart as an object lesson and "give a talk on the dialectics of capitalism—and show up all of its lies" (260). For him the problem of the black is too special an interest. "The only way to solve the Negro problem under capitalism is to geld every one of the fifteen million black men in these states. . . . Who cares whether you and your thousand Negroes struggle up to that stinking cesspool of a place called Washington? What difference does it make? What do a few people matter—a few thousand people, black, white, good or bad? When the whole of our society is built on a foundation of black lies" (261). His solutions are fully macro-structural. Copeland pants out a broken plea for the individual but, of course, the question of micro-structural politics is not within his ken either: "The soul of the meanest and most evil of us on this earth is worth more in the sight of justice than—"(261).

If the letter from Singer to Antonapoulos is structurally so open as to be a dead end, this conversation, structurally a dead end, carries many open-ended moments of suspension in its texture. It begins at an indefinite time.

Copeland asks Blount to leave because he is "a white man and a stranger." Jake does not go. There is a sub-section break in the typography. It is "long past midnight." A "long, exhausting dialogue" is mentioned, but not quoted. "And now a pause had come" (253).

It is in this many-times-suspended interstitial pause that Jake makes a portentious-seeming beginning: " 'So the time is ready for—' " But this moment too is lost. Copeland interrupts him. Some meaningless courtesies are exchanged, each urging the other to go on. In that further suspension Jake gives us this *alternate* opening: " 'Well—. . . I won't say what I started to say. Instead. . . ' " (254). There is, in other words, some other topic, which we shall never know, for which the time was ready. This one is merely a substitute.

Slowly the internationalist turns "a cheap globe of the world that served as a paperweight . . . in his hands. . . . 'If you was to ask me to point out the most uncivilized area on the face of this globe I would point here—' 'Watch sharp,' said Doctor Copeland. 'You're out in the ocean' " (254). Again a double-take and Jake chooses the thirteen states. The conversation proceeds through long speeches by Jake frantically interrupted by Copeland: " 'Mr. Singer is a Jew.' 'No, you're wrong there.' 'But I am positive that he is. The name, Singer. I recognized his race the first time I saw him. From his eyes. Besides, he told me so. I'm certain. Absolutely.' 'Very well,' said Doctor Copeland. 'We will not quarrel' " (257). A long tense pause ensues. Copeland breaks this suspense. Once again they interrupt each other. Once again, after mutual concessions, Jake takes the lead. " 'The only solution is for people to *know*' " (258). He proposes chain letters. Mr. Copeland tries many times to speak out. Finally the by now far from unique words emerge. " 'Do not attempt to stand alone.' " This time Jake's interruption does not work. " '*But*, nothing,' said Doctor Copeland didactically. 'The most fatal thing a man can do is try to stand alone' " (259). He now makes a plea for a practice that would reconcile the macro- and the micro-structural, but, once again, the micro-structural dimension is understood not as an arena of politics and the exchange of power, but as the individual soul: " 'Do not attempt to stand alone. . . . But once you enter this it must be all. . . . You must give of your whole self without stint, without hope of personal return, without rest or hope of rest' " (260). It is after this that Blount's brutal "internationalist" perspective on the question of the black is expressed.

What does this rhetoric of suspension, hesitation, substitution, iteration signify, represent, dramatize? One can not know. Let us say—a discontinuous dialogue, of course, but also a disarticulation between views of social justice based on class struggle as seen from a primitive internationalist "vanguardist" perspective, and on the race struggle as seen from the domestic perspective of the colonized. I am suggesting that a fully politicized feminism, far from being a special interest, can bring a consideration of the power-structure of the interstices of such a discussion within reach of practical analyses. I should like to think that McCullers's text gives a shadowy hint of support to such a view, when it makes of a character like Singer—totally divorced from his all-consuming sexuality—the mysterious bond among the characters. He understands nothing, yet they feel he understands. It is also a comment on the American Ideology, where both collective (macro-structural) efforts and demystified personal (micro-structural) relations are seen as threatening. A figure like Singer can be seen as fulfilling an empty dream of mysterious rather than historical "solutions":

> An old Negro women told hundreds of people that he knew the ways of spirits come back from the dead. A certain piece-worker claimed that he had worked with the mute at another mill somewhere else in that state—and the tales he told were unique. The rich thought that he was rich and the poor considered him a poor man like themselves. And as there was no way to disprove these rumors they grew *marvelous and very real*. Each man described the mute as he wished him to be. (190; italics mine)

There is one person who does not need to create quite so much of a spell out of Singer and even wonders "why . . . everyone persist[ed] in thinking the mute was exactly as they wanted him to be—when most likely it was all a very queer mistake?" (191). His name is Biff Brannon. He is taken by everyone to be the picture of reasonableness. Yet he is impotent, has a crush on Mick as long as she is the half-grown boy-girl, and the most vivid story about him is that he had farted in a dark room full of people thinking he was alone and that his subsequent embarrassment had been as great as his response to his mother's death (202). He is conservative in politics and his icon is the cash register, behind which he is most often to be seen. He is the ever-vigilant bureau of investigations which, until it reaches federal proportions, can seem merely curious and idiosyncratic: he keeps his restaurant open day and night, although it is far from profitable to do so, and he has filing cabinets full of newspapers "chronologically from October 27, 1918, on up to the present date" (113). Of course I am doing an injustice to his personal goodwill when I describe him so harshly. Perhaps the best verdict is Jake's: " 'You been very reasonable. And since I think about it you're a right decent guy—from the personal perspective, that is' " (295). But the personal defined as if it can be undetermined and ideology-free is indeed not political enough. The very end of the book shows us Biff unable to accept a schizophrenia that I would read as a predicament that might be the only solution to a system—"the counter glass"—that separates the personal and the political:

> In a swift radiance of illumination he saw a glimpse of human struggle and of valor. Of the endless fluid passage of humanity through endless time. And of those who labor and of those who—one word—love. His soul expanded. But for a moment only. For in him he felt a warning, a shaft of terror. . . . He saw that he was looking at his own face in the counter glass before him. . . . One eye was opened wider than the other. The left eye delved narrowly into the

past while the right gazed wide and affrighted into a future of blackness, error, and ruin. . . . But, motherogod, was he a sensible man or was he not? And how could this terror throttle him like this when he didn't even know what caused it? And would he just stand there like a jittery ninny or would he pull himself together and be reasonable? For after all *was* he a sensible man or was he not? . . . Somehow he remembered that the awning [of the cafe] had not yet been raised. As he went to the door his walk gained steadiness. And when at last he was inside again he composed himself soberly to await the morning sun. (306-307)

This is the careful glance into history and the broad glance into the future; on another register, it is the relationship between theory (knowing) and practice (doing). In yet another register, not quite the same but a similar one, it must be recognized that both knowing and doing are undermined, yet made possible, by the micro-structural network of an ever-fractured sense of being. A politicized socialist and inter-racialist feminism will work at redefining the personal as the micro-structural network of being that undermines as it makes possible the production of both theory and practice. McCullers's book is unable to provide a coherent redefinition. But the kaleidoscope of the micro-structure "changes minute by minute," and its motives come from many places at once; indeed, a recognition of the micro-structure might disclose that a *coherent* redefinition is impossible. *The Heart* at least dramatizes the incoherence: the simple story of an adolescent girl victimized by her class; the mysterious and secret story of the nature of sex as such and/or marginal sex; the political story of the lack of contact between race- and class-politics; the hopeless story of idolatry; the safe story of the recovery of reason. The questions at the end of the passage just quoted—which is indeed the end of the book—mark an edge between literature and ideology that can be discovered at any moment. The ideological charge of the reading depends on how we answer Biff's rallying questions to himself. As a feminist reader, I take it seriously that the questions are addressed to "motherogod." I should be able to answer: "there are no more blessed virgins to give you your security, my son." It is the jittery hysterical ninnies who would insist that to want merely to know causes, only to be sensible, demystified, and reasonable at all costs, is to insist upon the safety and convenience of *macro*-structural analyses that will not suffice—simply because even the most dedicated activist ticks to the minute micro-structure of the moment divided among the neural twitch, the heart beat, and the blink of two eyes.

. . .

Within the manifold problematics of sex, race, and class, we should read books like *The Heart Is a Lonely Hunter* and *The Waterfall* together. McCullers maps for us an entire network of problems—but the place of "our sister" is left virtually empty. Drabble fills that void with meticulous and helpful articulation, though she seems thwarted in any serious presentation of the problems of race and class, and of the marginality of sex. Both of them, however, seem to engage in that micro-structural dystopia, the sexual situation in extremis, that begins to seem more and more a part of women's work. If we are involved in a taxonomic rather than exclusivist practice, we will not ask writers or ourselves to do more than they or we can, but rather will put things together, move within a collectivity where our role is not that of the leader. Our motto, then, will not be Drabble's Jane's "I prefer to suffer, I think"— the privatist cry of heroic liberal women; it might be McCullers's Copeland's "Do not attempt to stand alone," however already undone that directive might always be.

I realize in writing this I might be accused of Pierre Macherey's "normative fallacy."[12] I am projecting an ideal whole that subsumes novels and social problematics *and* our lives as fragmented texts. It is only half in jest (and half in mortification) that I say that a choice of words can halt that accusation. It is "intertextuality" that I am engaged in, weaving in texts of "book," "world," and "life." Refusing to acknowledge the inside and the outside of these three compartments, I am honoring, necessarily somewhat in the breach, the dictim: "There is no outside-of-the-text."

What is one man's "intertextuality" can, alas, be diagnosed as another woman's "moralism."

. . .

Notes

1.   The broad methodological presuppositions of this essay are much influenced by my understanding of a deconstructive theory of practice. Although Derrida has written since then, the pieces that illuminate this theory best for me remain "Signature Event Context," *Glyph* I, 1977, and "Limited inc abc," *Glyph* II, 1977.

2.   Sheila Rowbotham's "The Women's Movement and Organizing for Socialism," *Radical America* XIII, 5, September-October, 1979, was brought to my attention after I had completed this essay.

3.   In the case of anthropology, the problem of the status of the informant and the conditioning of the informant's response by the structure of the investigator's question is lucidly discussed and critiqued by Pierre Bourdieu in *Outline of a Theory of Practice,* trans. Richard Nice, Cambridge, 1977.

4.   In the case I know best, that of India, the contrast between the structures of domestic and international oppression can be appreciated if one compares Mahasveta Devi's *Agnigarbha,* Calcutta, 1978, with T. Nagi Reddy's *India Mortgaged: A Marxist-Leninist Appraisal,* Anantapuram, 1978.

5.   Carson McCullers, *The Heart Is a Lonely Hunter* (New York: Bantam, 1953), pp. 178–179. Subsequent references included in text.

6.   A reading of McCullers with reference to psychoanalytic thematics would consider the prevalence of little boy-elder sister relationships in her text. The most obvious example is John Henry West and Frankie in *The Member of the Wedding.*

7.   Marcia Deihl and Pat Ouelette in Pam Annas, "The Politics of Music—Carrying It On: An Interview with the New Harmony Sisterhood Band," *Radical Teacher* XIII, March, 1979, pp. 19–20.

8.   Mary Shelley's *Frankenstein* is a text where a micro- and a macro-structural dystopia converge. The macro-structural experiment is the science-fiction possibility of the experiment itself and the investigation into the nature of social ostracism. The micro-structural issues are the male intellectual's womb-envy, which makes him want to make a human being without a mother, and his egotism, which makes him think the monster's revenge will fall upon himself.

9.   The present essay will form part of a larger work on feminist criticism. The references to *La Vita nuova*, "Ego Dominus Tuus," *To the Lighthouse, Glas,* the origin of the family, and numerous other arguments relate to other parts of that study. When, two sentences later in my text, I speak of the "narrative" of "Ego Dominus Tuus," it should be remembered that the narrative energy of a Yeatsian poetic dialogue works rather differently from a Dantean sonnet sequence or a modern American novel.

10.   The relationship of Bram Stoker's *Dracula* or Saul Bellow's *Herzog* to the thematics of sexual objectification would not be uninteresting to contemplate.

11.   Paul de Man, *Allegories of Reading,* New Haven, 1979, p. 300.

12.   Pierre Macherey, *A Theory of Literary Production,* trans. Geoffrey Wall, London, 1978, p. 19 and passim.

Carson McCullers, Lonely Huntress:
[*Reflections in a Golden Eye*]

HUGO MCPHERSON*

· · ·

There can be little doubt that Carson McCullers's vision is profoundly affected
by the monstrous spectre of racial inequality in the South. Her portraits of
Berenice in *The Member of the Wedding* and the Copeland family in *The Heart Is a
Lonely Hunter* leave us in no doubt of her sympathy for the Negro, the "square"
who is excluded from the circle of Society City. But the colour-bar is only a symbol of the larger human problem. The question is whether *any* man should be
denied the opportunity to live fully, whatever his "colour". *Reflections in a Golden
Eye* (1941)—Mrs. McCullers's greatest achievement—is a macabre dramatization of this problem as it affects the white society of the South.

The setting of this extraordinary work is a Southern military camp in
peacetime, a class society in which the conventions exercise an absolute rule.
Anacleto, a Filipino houseboy who shares with the Negro a menial role in this
society, find an image to describe its life: he sees "A peacock of a sort of ghastly
green. With one immense golden eye. And in it these reflections of something
tiny and . . . grotesque." But the regimented creatures of the camp, bound by
their "code," are unaware of the ironic gaze of the bird of evil omen. They do
not *know* their own natures, and when the shattering missiles of their inner
warfare burst through the calm surface of their lives, they are lost.

The persons of the story (there is not a superfluous character or incident)
form two opposed triads. In the first we have Leonora Penderton, the eternal
female—voluptuous, passionate, "a little feebleminded." Her husband, an
army Captain, is a man of considerable intelligence, but the pressures of army
conformity and of irrational pride (the chief legacy of Southern aristocrats to
their impoverished heirs) combine to make him a pettifogging coward who at
once envies and *loves* the virility of his wife's lovers. His alter-ego is Private
Elgee Williams, a faun-like soldier who grooms Leonora's stallion, Firebird.
Private Williams, uninitiated in the rites of sex, spends long nights crouching
in Leonora's bedroom, watching the sleeping beauty with a piercing but
unfulfilled delight.

*Excerpt reprinted from "Carson McCullers: Lonely Huntress," *Tamarack Review* 11 (1959): 28–40.

143

The second trio—and this is the way of parables—lives next door. Major Morris Langdon is the complete male—athletic, hearty, sentimental, selfish; for some time he has been Leonora Penderton's lover. His wife, Alison, is the female counterpart of Captain Penderton, an intelligent woman whose sensibility is constantly outraged by her husband's obtuseness and gross physical energy. The Filipino houseboy, Anacleto, is Alison's alter-ego; he imitates her in all things, improves upon her fantasies, and understands her every thought.

The catastrophe which engulfs these six people is so bizarre that we are tempted to dismiss it as a particularly unpleasant episode in the eternal war of the sexes; but the sureness of Mrs. McCullers's writing, and the tenacity with which her story grips the memory convince us that this is more than mere sensationalism. Like "The Ballad of the Sad Café" and *The Heart Is a Lonely Hunter,* this narrative is a parable. Given this perception, we recognize that the Langdon and Penderton households present two variations on a single theme. Captain Penderton is the perceptive male (a military tactician) attempting to achieve recognition in a narrowly conformist society. Alison Langdon is the perceptive female, similarly struggling to find her place in the scheme of "army" life. By contrast, Major Langdon and Leonora Penderton are average, healthy animals, the most viable types that their world produces; the life of the senses is enough for them. But since both Leonora and the Major are incapable of understanding their mates, they turn to each other. And this adulterous alliance drives both Alison and Captain Penderton (the extremes of male and female sensibility) to turn to the thing that they lack most acutely. What the Captain both desires and fears is the joy of a "natural," instinctive sexuality, a force which is symbolized for him in the unselfconscious virility of Private Elgee Williams and the untamed power of Firebird. Gross men like Major Langdon take the "privates" for granted, and ride daily. But Captain Penderton, who has never really had confidence in his authority, is afraid of Firebird; and the Private who grooms this creatures is an innocent who keeps a vigil of desire beside Leonora's bed. Alison, on the other hand, abandons her hope that the Major will ever share her love of imaginative things, and turns obsessively to her "foreign", mercurial houseboy, Anacleto, the figure who represents the imagination. Needless to say, the Major, by nature, hates this fairy.

Mrs. McCullers does not comment upon the alienation of sprit and flesh, imagination and the senses, which make both of these marriages unhappy; instead she dramatizes the problem in two nightmarish incidents. First, Captain Penderton finally decides that he will ride his wife's stallion. To his terror, the horse runs away with him, but soon he begins to enjoy the experience: "The Captain knew no terror now; he had soared to that rare level of consciousness where the mystic feels that the earth is he and that he is the earth." For a moment he is master of the fiery steed; but when it comes to an exhausted standstill, he ties it to a tree and whips it mercilessly. Private

Williams, who has been sunbathing naked on a rock nearby, appears and silently leads the horse away. Captain Penderton has rejected the instinctive power of sex; he has punished the creature which has given him his greatest moment of happiness. But his obsession does not die; from this point on, he nourishes a compulsive love-hate for the animal's primitive keeper, Private Williams.

Second, Alison Langdon believed that her marriage with the materialistic and sensory world that the Major represents would be productive; but the Major showed no feeling for the child of their union; and when the infant died he regarded Alison's grief as morbid, and turned to the purely sensual embraces of Leonora. When Alison could bear this rejection no longer, she went home one night and "cut off the tender nipples of her breasts with the garden shears." She rejected altogether, that is, the possibility of a union with her husband's world, and retired to the sickroom of her imagination where Anacleto (an . . . embodiment of the Tiresias-image) nursed her and talked to her of music, painting, and poetry.

Given this double history of incapability and frustration, we can almost predict the dénouement of the tale. During her sleepless nights, Alison has become aware of the shadow of Elgee Williams hovering about the Penderton's house. One night, shortly after the Captain's experience with Firebird, she boldly enters her neighbour's house and surprises Private Williams at his vigil in Leonora's room. Since her own experience of love has been crass and brutal, she fails to understand the natural, clean passion which the innocent Private symbolizes. She scornfully tells the Captain to "go up to your wife's room," and then informs the Major that Leonora deceives both her husband and her lover—"and with an enlisted man." The Major's codified instincts, however, reassure him that Leonora would no more be capable of understanding and loving her innocent groom that he would be capable of communion with the imaginative houseboy Anacleto. He decides, therefore, that Alison is mad, and confines her to a mental hospital. Soon after, Captain Penderton discovers Private Williams in his wife's room and shoots him dead. The force that he has both loved and feared—the "natural" man—has at last been annihilated, just as the imaginative force, Anacleto, has been put to flight by Major Langdon.

The novel leaves us, then, in a tragic impasse. Captain Penderton, the cleverest man in the Southern army camp, has irrevocably denied his manhood. He will not be a creative force in his community. And the imaginative Alison, with her houseboy, has been banished. Ironically enough, the Major longs to have Anacleto back; the conquering Captain looks like a broken puppet; and the feeble-minded Leonora, who has slept comfortably throughout the whole tragi-comedy, will presumably live on in her fecund sterility.

These futile and grotesque "reflections" of life afford something less than a reassuring picture of Southern, or Western, society. Captain Penderton and Alison Langdon, the perceptive people who might have learned the full meaning of love, have failed to discover and assert their own natures; perhaps in a society where people like Leonora and the Major dominate there can be no fulfilment for individuals like Alison—or like Biff Brannon, and Mick Kelly. Anacleto and Elgee Williams, the symbols of intuition and "natural" sexuality respectively, perish. Only the vacuous animals for whom life is a waking dream escape unscathed.

The "reflections" are not complete, however, without a word about a seventh character of the story—a person who, Mrs. McCullers assures us, "was of no consequence to anyone on the post." He is Lieutenant Weincheck, an impoverished subaltern who is paying for the education of a younger brother. This man plays the violin and loves nature and art, but he is unworldly in a way that arouses the scorn of all officers on the post. Alison Langdon and Anacleto love him dearly, but they are powerless to advance his position. As the story ends, we learn that the authorities have requested his retirement. Lieutenant Weincheck might conceivably be a suitable partner for Alison, but even this possibility, in an army society, is closed, for he is not a self-assertive character. The ranks of Major, Captain, Lieutenant, and Private indicate unmistakably the value which society attaches to various kinds of talent. Carson McCullers does not say more; the reader must interpret the "reflections" for himself.

. . .

Fighting for Life

SANDRA M. GILBERT AND SUSAN GUBAR*

. . . even while women in the 1920s and 1930s continued to infiltrate the public sphere—gaining the vote, achieving university degrees, entering the work force—the feminist-modernist vision of a female moment of triumph, a vision perhaps most optimistically as well as comically elaborated in "Indissoluble Matrimony," began to darken. And, curiously, such darkening was manifested in women's texts by what would seem at first glance to be a healthy impulse to depict women actively fighting their male opponents rather than just passively resisting them.

From C. L. Moore's "Shambleau" (1933) to Ann Petry's *The Street* (1946) and Carson McCullers's "The Ballad of the Sad Café" (1951), women's fictions of sexual struggle in the 1930s and 1940s portray female characters who are physically powerful enough to inaugurate and sustain combat against men.[1] Ultimately, however, this aggressive power is shown to be not a badge of courage but a horrifying necessity, born of escalating male bellicosity and inexorably leading to female defeat. In addition, it is consistently characterized as tragic, freakish, or monstrous. For, as male writers like Faulkner, Miller, and Wylie mounted intensified attacks on female autonomy, their female contemporaries defended themselves with aggressive fantasies of physical power, a power that the plots of their stories define as necessary for survival. At the same time, these postmodernist women of letters do not seem to have been able to imagine such physical force as effective, for their women combatants are regularly haunted by guilt and frequently punished by defeat. Indeed, the plots constructed by these writers are often so critical of or punitive towards their female protagonists that their authors would seem to have internalized just the horror at independent womanhood which marks the writings of literary men from Faulkner to Wylie.

. . .

Where in the science fiction and black traditions species warfare and racial combat are conflated with sexual battle, the southern Gothic mode allows Carson McCullers to depict sexual conflict with equal extravagance through the

*Excerpt reprinted, by permission, from *The War of the Words,* vol. 1 of *No Man's Land: The Place of the Woman Writer in the Twentieth Century* (Yale University Press, 1988), 100–12. Copyright © 1988 by Yale University.

creation of characters who are in their own way at least as freakish as Petry's Mrs. Hedges and C. L. Moore's Shambleau, and through the recounting of the sort of grotesque events that are usually the subjects of tall tales or folk ballads. Even more dramatically than Moore and Petry, however, McCullers shows in her dreamlike mythic narrative of "The Ballad of the Sad Café" the culturally determined psychic logic that condemns the autonomous woman as a freak who must necessarily be sentenced to the defeat that is femininity. In fact, like her friend and contemporary Tennessee Williams, Carson McCullers seems to stand outside the constructs of gender in order to demonstrate, as Williams did in *Streetcar,* the pain of what Adrienne Rich has called "compulsory heterosexuality."[2] But even more than Williams does in *Streetcar,* McCullers focuses in "Ballad" on the terrifying revenge that the law of the phallus inflicts on those (women) who defy its imperatives. Specifically, she dramatizes the punishment meted out to a woman who has arrogantly supposed that she could live in a no man's land—first without a real man, and then with a dwarfish no-man.

At the beginning of "Ballad," Miss Amelia Evans has the kind of physical power, intellectual authority, and personal autonomy that characterize Rebecca West's Evadne Silverton, but, unlike Evadne, she does not need men at all, even as instruments of her own pleasure. Six feet two inches tall, frequently "dressed in overalls and gumboots," the thirty-year-old Amelia Evans is "a woman with bones and muscles like a man," who has parlayed an inheritance from her father into a fortune that makes her "the richest woman for miles around," for she is the proprietor of a store and a still (where she makes "the best liquor in the county") and the possessor of "mortgages on crops and property, a sawmill [and] money in the bank (45)."[3] In addition, she is an extraordinarily skillful healer, a kind of self-taught general practitioner about whom McCullers observes that "no disease was so terrible but what she would undertake to cure it" (17).

That Miss Amelia's success is associated with a culturally problematic eccentricity is shown not only by her masculine and peculiar physical appearance (besides being unusually tall and strong for a woman, she is cross-eyed, "dark and somewhat queer of face" [14]) but also by her anti-social nature (it is "only with people that Miss Amelia [is] not at ease" [5]), by her litigiousness (only her proclivity for lawsuits keeps her from being "as rich as a congressman" [5]), and, most important, by her one failing as a "doctor":

> If a patient came with a female complaint she could do nothing. Indeed, at the mere mention of the words her face would slowly darken with shame, and she would stand there craning her neck against the collar of her shirt, or rubbing her swamp boots together, for all the world like a great, shamed, dumb-tongued child. (17)

Taken together, all these traits illustrate this woman's rebellious desire to rule rather than to be ruled. Alienated from the community which she in some sense governs, the indomitable Miss Amelia manipulates social law in order to transcend it, and she refuses to acknowledge the biological law that governs her own body.

Inevitably, then, when Miss Amelia marries one Marvin Macy—for reasons that remain mysterious to the townsfolk as well as to the reader but which seem to have the inexplicable force that motivates actions in fairy tales—the wedding leads to immediate disaster. During the ceremony itself, Miss Amelia rubs "the palm of her right hand down the side of her satin wedding gown" as if "reaching for the pocket of her overalls," and afterwards she hurries out of the church, "walking at least two paces ahead" of her bridegroom (30). But the couple's wedding night is even more catastrophic. Though the townsfolk had "counted on the marriage to tone down Miss Amelia's temper, to put a bit of bride-fat on her, and to change her at last into a calculable woman" (30–31), this incalculable bride refuses to sleep with her husband, instead "stomp[ing] down the stairs in breeches and a khaki jacket" and spending the night, "feet up on the kitchen stove," smoking her father's pipe (31). Worse still, when the humiliated Marvin Macy—who has for love of her transformed himself from the handsome town ne'er-do-well to an exemplary suitor—seeks to placate his resistant wife with presents from "Society City," she offers them for sale in her store; when he signs "over to her the whole of his worldly goods . . . ten acres of timberland," she studies the paper "sternly" and files it away "soberly"; and when, driven to drunkenness by her recalcitrance, he approaches her humbly, she swings "once with her fist and hit[s] his face so hard that he [is] thrown back against the wall and one of his front teeth [is] broken" (32). After ten days of marriage, she turns him off her property and, following much public suffering, he leaves town, writing her a "wild love letter" in which "were also included threats" and vows of revenge (33).

At this point, Miss Amelia seems invincible, not only in her battle with her groom but also in her social and sexual eccentricity. Yet, oddly enough, she can only speak of Marvin Macy "with a terrible and spiteful bitterness" (33) that would not appear to be the natural response of the victor to the vanquished. Given Miss Amelia's fierce independence, along with her excessive hostility to Marvin Macy, it is almost predictable that, having rejected a he-man, she now embraces a no-man like Lymon Willis, the mysterious hunchbacked dwarf who claims to be her cousin. Coming out of nowhere from no one but asserting common ancestry with hers, this physically deformed and spiritually dissolute but emotionally compelling creature is destined, in his consumptive way, to consume most of Miss Amelia's worldly goods, and, significantly, he resembles not only the dwarfish "sewer rat" Loerke in Lawrence's *Women in Love* but also the spiteful cripple Doyle in Nathanael West's *Miss Lonelyhearts,* both paradigmatic no-men who represent for their authors all that is socially bankrupt in contemporary culture.

But while Lawrence and West characterize the dwarf as from first to last a decadent whose perversity signals the end of the species of man, McCullers implies that, at least in the beginning of their relationship, Miss Amelia's Cousin Lymon is an empowering figure for her. Knitting her into the community, he facilitates her creation of the cafe in which her rare liquor can teach its drinkers how to read the truths of their own souls. Offering her (or, more accurately, allowing her to offer) love and friendship, he functions as the family, and hence the identity, she lost when her "Big Papa" died; and that she gives him not only her father's snuff box but her father's (master) bedroom suggests again the dwarf's connection with her patrilineage. Tiny as a child yet charismatic as any gigolo, he seems to be her son and her lover, a link to the ancestral past who might provide her with the future she repudiated when she rejected Marvin Macy. Yet, as McCullers's text gradually and grimly reveals, Miss Amelia's Cousin Lymon is, in the deepest sense, a lie-man, a no-man whose manhood is really a lie. In fact, nebulously related to her mother (ostensibly the son of her mother's half-sister), he is not in any way associated with her patrilineage. Rather, pale and vampiric, he is in Freudian terms the (false) baby as false phallus, whose deformity and fake masculinity represent the deformity and fakery that (as Miss Amelia must learn) are associated with her own self-deluding male impersonation. If she wants a member instead of a wedding, she has to discover that this treacherous imposter is what she will get.

That Lymon as phallus is a lie becomes clear with the liberation of Marvin Macy from the penitentiary where, after Miss Amelia's rejection, he had been incarcerated for a number of years. Unlike George Silverton in Rebecca West's "Indissoluble Matrimony," who had been pruriently obsessed with his wife's supposed adultery and whose no-manhood had led him to the edge of madness, Lymon becomes instantly enthralled to his patroness's unknown husband, with whom he exchanges a look "like the look of two criminals who recognize each other" (47). But once the no-man Lymon, who as the fake thing recognizes the real thing, weds himself to the he-man Marvin, Miss Amelia begins to go into a bizarre decline, a decline that presages a defeat even more radical than Evadne's victory. Relinquishing her overalls for the red dress that she had previously reserved only for Sundays, Miss Amelia has lost her falsely instrumental Lymon Willis and is now, therefore, will-less. Moreover, caught between two phallic beings—the one exploitative, the other vengeful—she tries to please one and poison the other, but in both cases she fails: mendacious cousin Lymon becomes a mad man who is increasingly flirtatious toward Marvin Macy, while Marvin Macy becomes a bad man whose gradual usurpation of the very house and grounds she had granted to the dwarf signifies that, even if the rebellious woman desires the false phallus that she can control, the true phallus will eventually repossess her and all her worldly goods in an ultimate act of masculinist retribution. Indeed, as McCullers shows, though Miss Amelia tries to resist her "mortal enemy," "everything she trie[s] to do against Marvin Macy rebound[s] on herself" (60).

Since the terms of the psychodrama unfolding in McCullers's sad cafe are so inexorable, Miss Amelia is doomed from the start to lose the physical battle with Macy which constitutes the novella's climax. Because she has given up her bed to Lymon (who has given up his to Marvin Macy), her only bed has been an uncomfortable sofa, and perhaps, we are told, "lack of sleep . . . clouded her wits." But in itself, as McCullers makes clear, neither sleeplessness nor the stress of having her house invaded would necessarily have been enough to guarantee Miss Amelia's defeat. "A fine fighter," this powerful woman "know[s] all manner of mean holds and squeezes," so that "the town [is] betting on" her victory, remembering "the great fight between Miss Amelia and a Fork Falls lawyer who had tried to cheat her . . . a huge strapping fellow [who] was left three quarters dead when she had finished with him. And it was not only her talent as a boxer that had impressed everyone—she could demoralize her enemy by making terrifying faces and fierce noises" (61). In spite of Miss Amelia's unnatural strength, though, the sexual subtext represented by the grotesque triangle in which she is involved dooms her to defeat.

For, as McCullers describes it, the spectacular fight in which Marvin Macy and Miss Amelia engage before a mass of spectators in the cleared cafe at seven P.M. on Ground Hog Day is not just a jealous struggle for power over Lymon, it is the primal scene of sexual consummation which did not take place on their wedding night. Stripped for action—Miss Amelia barefoot in overalls rolled up to the knees, Marvin Macy "naked to the waist and heavily greased"—the combatants present themselves as the central figures in a bizarre but ancient ritual, "walk[ing] toward each other with no haste, their fists already gripped, and their eyes like the eyes of dreamers" (66). But as they come together in the match, the specifically sexual nature of this ritual becomes clear, for McCullers's language, whether intentionally or not, is heavy with double entendres. At the beginning of the fight, when the strange and estranged husband and wife are said to produce "the sound of knocks, panting, and thumpings on the floor" as they are "experimenting with various positions" (66), McCullers evokes the idiom of foreplay. Then, when Miss Amelia gets "a grasp around [Marvin Macy's] waist" and "the real fight" begins, the wrestling couple's thrashings not only recall the wrestling match between the unnaturally virile Bertha Mason Rochester and her captor husband but also plainly suggest that, besides being sexual, the battle *is* sex: "For a while the fighters grappled muscle to muscle, their hipbones braced against each other. Backward and forward, from side to side, they swayed in this way" (67).

Unlike Rochester, however, who is so confident in his mastery that he will not "strike," he will "only wrestle," Marvin Macy appears to be on the verge of losing the fight and his manhood, for though he is "tricky to grasp," Miss Amelia is "stronger" (67). In fact, as their bout reaches its climax, she bends "him over backward, and inch by inch she force[s] him to the floor" until she has "him down, and straddled; her strong big hands . . . on his throat" (67). At just this moment of imminent female victory, however, the phallic retribution that must punish Miss Amelia's transgressive behavior is exacted. The hunchback, who has been watching the fight from an elevated position on the counter of the cafe, suddenly utters "a cry . . . that caused a shrill bright shiver to run down the spine" (67) and sails "through the air as though he had grown hawk wings" (68) to land like an incubus on Miss Amelia's back and to allow Marvin Macy to leave her "sprawled on the floor, her arms flung outward and motionless."

Why is the hunchback the agent of Miss Amelia's symbolic defloration as well as her literal defeat and thus the instrument of Marvin Macy's sexual triumph? And why is his leap into the fray accompanied by a mysterious cry? McCullers's text is so complex that we have to read it as overdetermined. From one perspective, if we take the hunchback to represent the false phallus associated with Miss Amelia's presumptuous usurpation of masculine privilege—with, that is, what Freud would call her "penis envy" and her "masculinity complex"—then his intervention in the fight signals the moment when she must be forced to confront the delusional quality of her pseudo-virility.[4] Deformed himself, Lymon lands on her back to dramatize the way in which his physical deformity echoes her sexual deformity. In this reading, then, as Miss Amelia is made to surrender her pretensions to power, true masculinity reasserts itself with a victorious war whoop that sends a shiver down the spines of the onlookers, who realize that they are present at a solemn cultural event.

From another perspective, if we see the hunchback as representing the "little man" that is the female clitoris or, in a more generalized sense, the authentic if truncated female libido that Miss Amelia has refused to acknowledge, then the intervention of the hunchback in the fight signals the moment when she has been forced to confront her desire for Marvin Macy. Certainly from the day Macy returned to town, her behavior has notably changed: abandoning overalls for a dress, feeding Macy at her table, and finally bedding him down in her private quarters, she might almost "[seem] to have lost her will" (53) because she is in a kind of erotic trance, and the hunchback's open flirtation with Marvin Macy might well express her own secret enthrallment. In this reading, therefore, the mysterious cry is a cry of female orgasmic surrender which sends a shiver down the spine of onlookers because they realize that they are voyeurs witnessing a ceremonial sexual event.

Finally, from yet a third perspective, if we define the hunchback not simply as an anatomical or allegorical aspect of Miss Amelia but rather as an autonomous male character, then his intervention in the fight signals the moment when, by eliminating Amelia as a rival, he achieves a homosexual union with the man whom he has been trying to seduce since the moment when they exchanged their first gaze of secret complicity. In this reading, then—a reading that supposes McCullers's text to be haunted by female anxiety about male social and sexual bonding—Miss Amelia is simply the medium whose house and flesh provide the opportunity for Lymon and Marvin Macy to come together, and the mysterious cry at the end of the fight expresses their homoerotic orgasm while sending a shiver down the spines of onlookers because they realize they are witnessing a perverse and subversive event. Moreover, that the two men leave town together after destroying most of Miss Amelia's property reiterates the point that she not only is no longer necessary to them but that their union requires her obliteration.

Whether one subscribes to all or none of these readings, it is clear that at the conclusion of "Ballad" Miss Amelia has been metamorphosed from a woman warrior to a helpless madwoman. Her very body has shriveled, for she is "thin as old maids are thin when they go crazy"; her eyes emphasize her isolation because they are "more crossed . . . as though they sought each other out to exchange a little glance of grief and lonely recognition"; and her voice is "broken, soft, and sad" (70). Bereft of her once legendary physical strength, she has also lost her social, intellectual, and economic authority; her cafe is closed; her house is boarded up; and all her "wise doctoring" is over, for she tells "one-half of her patients that they [are] going to die outright, and to the remaining half she recommend[s] cures so far-fetched and agonizing that no one in his right mind would consider them for a moment" (69–70). Incarcerated in a wasteland of a town where "the soul rots with boredom," she resembles not only such paradigmatic mad spinsters as Miss Havisham in Dickens's *Great Expectations* and Miss Emily in Faulkner's "A Rose for Emily" but also a female version of T. S. Eliot's wounded Fisher King.

Even the male prisoners in the novella's mysterious epilogue—a brief coda entitled "THE TWELVE MORTAL MEN"—are happier on their chain gang than is this prisoner of sex in her sad cafe, for as she sits in silence beside the one window of her house "which is not boarded" and turns toward the empty street "a face like the terrible dim faces known in dreams," their voices swell together "until at last it seems that the sound does not come from the twelve men on the gang, but from the earth itself, or the wide sky" (3, 71). Even in the penitentiary, McCullers implies, men are sustained by their own community while a woman like Miss Amelia—who, even at her most powerful, never had a community of women—has been inexorably condemned to the solitary confinement such a singular anomaly deserves.

Notes

1. Moore, "Shambleau," in *The Best of C. L. Moore,* ed. Lester Del Rey (New York: Ballantine, 1975), 1–32; Petry, *The Street* (New York: Pyramid, 1961); McCullers, *The Ballad of the Sad Café and Other Stories* (New York: Bantam, 1981; further references will be to this edition, and page numbers will appear in the text).

2. Rich's essay, "Compulsory Heterosexuality and Lesbian Existence," originally appeared in *Signs* (1980) and is reprinted in *Women: Sex and Sexuality,* ed. Catharine R. Stimpson and Ethel Spector Person (Chicago: University of Chicago Press, 1980), 62–91.

3. Claire Kahane offers a brief discussion of this point in "The Gothic Mirror," in *The (M)other Tongue: Essays in Feminist Psychoanalytic Interpretation,* ed. Shirley Nelson Garner, Claire Kahane, and Madelon Sprengnether (Ithaca: Cornell University Press, 1985), 347–48.

4. See Freud, "Female Sexuality" (1931), in *Sexuality and the Psychology of Love,* ed. Philip Rieff (New York: Collier, 1963), 98–99.

Tomboys and Revolting Femininity

LOUISE WESTLING*

Memory plays very little part in the lives of Carson McCullers's heroines, and they live in a world practically devoid of traditional Southern femininity. . . . Surrounded by the tawdry everyday life of modern Southern towns, they seem to exist in a void, alienated from the few models of femininity available to them. The only warmth provided by women comes from Negro cooks. Mick Kelly's mother rarely appears in *The Heart Is a Lonely Hunter,* and then only to issue impatient or dispirited orders about Mick's baby-sitting chores or the management of the family's boardinghouse. She is a scarcely believable stick figure by comparison with the vivid presence of Portia. The cook's vigorous and compassionate views of the world provide the only adult guidance for Mick and her little brothers, yet Portia is more like a practical older sister or aunt for Mick than a mother. The real maternal figure in the novel is the androgynous cafe keeper Biff Brannon, but Mick shies away from his solicitations. In *The Ballad of the Sad Café* Miss Amelia Evans has been raised motherless and has lost even her father long before the action of the novella begins. Frankie Addams of *The Member of the Wedding* knows her mother only as a timid and sad-looking picture shut up under the handkerchiefs in her father's bureau drawer. Berenice the cook is the wise black mammy figure who has raised the motherless child, but her race prohibits Frankie from following her example as a woman. Without mothers, these feminine protagonists define themselves most comfortably in masculine terms. The crisis for each of them comes as social pressures force them to abandon masculine independence and accept a feminine identity increasingly fraught with anxiety as McCullers progresses in her exploration of the problem from novel to novel.

Anne Goodwyn Jones has described the relation between the absence of mother figures and ambivalence about feminine identity in Southern women's writing from 1859 to 1936. Surely this problem is an expression of profound discomfort with the traditions of Southern womanhood. One of the best tactics for ignoring conventions is to omit their exemplars, in this case the mothers who represent what the daughters are trying to escape. In

*Excerpt reprinted, by permission, from *Southern Humanities Review* 14 (1980): 339–50, as revised and reprinted in *Sacred Groves and Ravaged Gardens: The Fiction of Eudora Welty, Carson McCullers, and Flannery O'Connor,* by Louise Westling (University of Georgia Press, 1985), 110–32. © 1985 by the University of Georgia Press.

Reinventing Womanhood, Carolyn Heilbrun explains that the rejection of the mother and identification with the father is a typical pattern for assertive, successful women; the distinctive heritage of white Southern women . . . makes this an especially tangled process for them. McCullers's own situation is an extreme example of both the strength of matriarchal tendencies in Southern life and the difficult problem of self-definition for the Southern girl who wants to become a writer. . . . [H]er mother dominated her childhood and hovered solicitously nearby through most of her life. Yet, as her brother suggested, perhaps the force of their mother's personality was too powerful for the daughter to contemplate; Carson McCullers remained a Southern woman whose imagination was frozen in collision with society's expectations. In Mick and Frankie she presents ambitious, artistic girls who are disoriented and terrified when they are forced to identify themselves as female at puberty. Because she performed the radical experiment of creating the grotesque amazon Amelia Evans, between *The Heart Is a Lonely Hunter* and *The Member of the Wedding,* the images which define this crisis for Frankie Addams are the images of sexual freaks in an ambience of androgynous longings, homosexuality, and transvestitism.[1]

Such imagery is directly related to the tradition of the tomboy so dear to the hearts of English and American fathers from late Victorian times. In childhood, a lively girl could romp with boys, wear their clothes, and cut her hair short. She had complete physical freedom and often served as a lively companion for her father, a temporary stand-in for a son. As Bertram Wyatt-Brown explains, this tradition seems to have been especially prevalent in the American South. In frontier days, girls were raised without much sexual differentiation from males until puberty. Later in the antebellum period a similar childhood liberty was common, contrasting sharply with the absolute restrictions the patriarchy placed on adult women in marriage. We remember Mary Chesnut's bitter description of herself and her fellow Southern women as slaves, but before marriage many young ladies "could ride as well as their brothers, and not a few of them could handle firearms with great accuracy and skill," according to a nineteenth-century commentator.[2]

All that changed when the time came for courtship. Kate Chopin immortalized the Southern tomboy type and her problem of sexual adjustment in her short story "Charlie." One of seven daughters of a handsome widower, Charlotte is her father's favorite. With her boy's nickname, short hair, and wild temperament, she is a charming oddity galloping about the plantation in "trouserlets" on a black horse. Her physical courage and her ability to ride and shoot and fish coincide with another talent: she is a natural poet. Thus Chopin has made a conjunction between the tomboy's physical assertiveness and literary talent, a connection Carson McCullers would make in the character of Frankie Addams and one very close to the relation of musical ambition and tomboyishness in Mick Kelly.

. . .

Ambitions are the psychological equivalents for the physical assertiveness of the tomboy, and again the requirements of submissiveness and restraint for the Southern lady have traditionally discouraged the pursuit of professional, artistic, or political goals. In modern life these pressures exert themselves subtly, woven as they are throughout the texture of adolescent experience. But they produce a fear that to be female and to dare to achieve is to venture into dangerous territory, to violate one's gender, to become a kind of freak. The girl who insists on following her ambitions almost inevitably pays the price of shame and guilt as an adult; she must live with a troubled sense of herself as a woman because she has abandoned the familiar boundaries of her gender. Women writers since the early nineteenth century have documented the problem, and Virginia Woolf spent an important part of her creative life describing the waste and distortion of character resulting from the narrowly restricted lives forced upon gifted women because of their sex. Woolf gained her own independence more easily than her predecessors, but for her as for ambitious women of later generations, there are still "many ghosts to fight, many prejudices to overcome."[3] This has been particularly true in the South, and McCullers began to discover the horrifying dimensions of the problem as she progressively explored feminine independence in the portraits of Mick Kelly, Amelia Evans, and Frankie Addams.

Virginia Woolf's ghosts are the phantoms of guilt which cripple the imagination, focusing the most sensitive women writers' attention on negative self-images and preventing professional women from confident assertion of their gender. Barbara Clarke Mossberg has shown how the writing of both Emily Dickinson and Gertrude Stein is obsessed by the need to come to terms with the hatred for almost everything conventionally female which they have absorbed from dominant social attitudes. As people who rejected the devalued and restricted intellectual life of their sex, each was nevertheless bound by the inescapable fact of living in a female body and being judged as a woman by those around her. Similar ambivalence troubles contemporary women poets, as Sandra Gilbert points out. Poets like Diane Wakoski, Adrienne Rich, and Sylvia Plath see themselves in a strange confusion of contradictory images: an arrow, a blackbird, an androgyne, a watercolor that washes off, a bone scepter, "a naked man fleeing across the roofs," a guerrilla fighter, a tree, a pig. Sylvia Plath may write, "I / Have a self to recover, a queen," but she never really succeeds, and neither do the others. This failure of imagination to supply positive self-images applies not only to the confessional poetic self but also to the public image of the successful woman. Carolyn Heilbrun argues that "women writers (and women politicians, academics, psychoanalysts) have been unable to imagine for other women, fictional or real, the self they have in fact achieved." As psychoanalysts they have not developed theories which embody their own female strengths; as writers they have not created female characters as independent as themselves; as academics they have not encouraged women students to aspire to what they as women have achieved. They have had to adopt the perspective of their masculine colleagues and function professionally as males.[4]

Understanding these problems of self-definition, we should have no trouble interpreting the psychic paralysis of Sylvia Plath's gifted young writer in *The Bell Jar,* whose talent is rewarded not by serious literary regard but by a summer of luncheons and fashion shows on the staff of *Mademoiselle.* Esther Greenwood's real interests are drowned in a sea of cosmetics, flowers, perfumes, fashionable hats, and piles of flouncy dresses. This conflict between serious ambition and the pressure of conventional femininity is exactly the problem that confronts Mick Kelly and Frankie Addams in Carson McCullers's fiction. McCullers's portrayal of their dilemma is especially valuable because she concentrates on puberty, the time when demands for "femininity" first press in upon a girl, and she allows her protagonists to be more sharply aware of their choices than Plath allows Esther Greenwood to be. Esther is paralyzed because she cannot even look at the contrary impulses within herself. She tries to escape them by blotting herself out, in a sense accepting the verdict implied by *Mademoiselle*'s refusal to acknowledge her identity as a serious writer. Mick and Frankie have the immense advantage of tomboy self-reliance and a habit of scrappy assertiveness. Their passage into womanhood may be acutely painful, but at least childhood experience helps them to confront their confusion head-on. Through Mick and Frankie, McCullers provides an unusually perceptive treatment of the problem which warps so many gifted women's lives, but between them she makes the grotesque experiment of picturing a tomboy who refuses to acknowledge it.

Another woman writer had very likely helped to show her the way by suggesting means for objectifying the self-reliance and assertiveness of a tomboy with artistic ambitions. Several of the images Willa Cather used in *The Song of the Lark* to reveal Thea Kronberg's restless energies reappear in *The Heart Is a Lonely Hunter.* The picture of Thea pulling her baby brother Thor all over her Colorado town in an express wagon is an effective way of objectifying the frustrating domestic responsibilities imposed on this adventuresome girl. Rather than stay home passively baby-sitting, Thea roams and explores, dragging her burden behind her, just as Mick Kelly will do with her brother Ralph in McCullers's novel. Thea has a secret life of books and artistic dreams in her attic room, apart from the mundane activities of her family. This is another effective motif which McCullers seems to echo in describing Mick's "inside room" of imagination where she tries to write music and dreams of becoming a great composer. Finally, both girls physically express their vague new energies by roaming the streets at night. Cather describes Thea in terms which reveal the correspondence between physical restlessness and psychological confusion: "Many a night she left Dr. Archie's office with a desire to run and run about those quiet streets until she wore out her shoes, or wore out the streets themselves; when her chest ached and it seemed as if her heart were spreading all over the desert."[5] Mick similarly wanders along dark sidewalks, defying the fears which she knows keep most girls indoors. But, unlike Thea, she loses this freedom when she accepts her sexual status as a woman. She becomes afraid of the dark.

. . .

Not long after the dramatic success of this first novel, Carson McCullers began another one with a similar girl as her main character. The story which would eventually become *The Member of the Wedding* began with twelve-year-old tomboy Frankie Addams suddenly beset by terrifying but nameless anxieties which make her life seem freakish. This book took McCullers more than five years to write and caused her considerable pain, at least in part because the problems of sexual ambivalence which are central to Frankie's confusion were shared by McCullers in her tangled relation with her husband Reeves.[6] After struggling for two years with what she then called "The Bride and Her Brother," McCullers paused to write a new tale which explored Frankie Addams's anxiety in a bold new way. For it she created her two greatest freaks—a huge, mannish Amazon and her twisted, dwarfish lover—in a nightmare vision of the tomboy grown up, without any concessions to social demands for sexual conformity.

. . .

The real force of *The Ballad of the Sad Café* lies in its depiction of a masculine Amazon whose transgression of conventional sexual boundaries brings catastrophic male retribution. Unlike Dinesen, who portrayed an uneasy compromise between proud female autonomy and reluctant masculine homage, McCullers sought to deny the feminine entirely and allow a woman to function successfully as a man. She could not sustain her vision, because she knew it was impossible.

The consequences of her experiment in this novella play a part in determining the final form of *The Member of the Wedding,* which inexorably moves Frankie toward an acceptance of conventional femininity. After writing *The Ballad of the Sad Café* in only a few months, when McCullers returned to her long struggle with the materials of *The Member of the Wedding,* she knew that Frankie would have to submit as Miss Amelia had not. The conclusions she reached in her nightmarish folktale must have contributed profoundly to the undercurrent of fear McCullers creates in *The Member of the Wedding* through the image of the freak show which haunts Frankie's mind and indeed the whole novel.

With the character of Frankie Addams we return to the type of the ambitious tomboy on the brink of puberty, baffled by incomprehensible changes in her life. This time the heroine's ambitions are literary rather than musical; Frankie Addams writes plays and dreams of becoming a great poet. Her ambitions are not blighted as Mick's are, but it could be argued that Frankie's attitude toward writing has changed significantly by the end of the novel. However, the focus of McCullers's attention in this book is not on the protagonist's dreams of fame but rather on the psychological trauma she suffers when required to accept her femininity. By the end of the novel she has passed from childhood into adolescence with an acceptance of the facts of adult sex. In the process of attaining her new status, she follows the same general pattern as Mick Kelly. We meet her as a twelve-year-old tomboy with a boy's name and haircut, who wears shorts and a B.V.D. undershirt. She is an expert knife-thrower and has the toughest bare feet in town. Toward the middle of the story, she transforms herself by changing her name to F. Jasmine and putting on a pink organdy dress, lipstick, and Sweet Serenade perfume. She has made herself into a romantic caricature of a female, much as Mick Kelly did for her prom party. As she parades around town in her finery, F. Jasmine meets a soldier who takes her for much older than she is, and with him she has her first adult sexual encounter. This dismaying experience forces her to admit to what men and women do together. Her last illusions are shattered when her brother and his bride refuse to let her go along on their honeymoon. At the end of the book we find her completely changed into a giddy teenager, having accepted her femininity and her real name, Frances.

Before this transformation can occur, however, Frankie suffers agonies of loneliness, feelings of entrapment, and fears of freakishness which hover around her in the shapes of the prodigies she has seen at the fair. There are several kinds of freaks which Frankie and her little cousin John Henry West visit at the Chattahoochee Exposition. She is afraid of all of them, but Ellen Moers is right to single out the hermaphrodite as the most important, for it is the quintessential symbol of Frankie's danger. Images of sexual ambivalence are carefully cultivated throughout the novel in the Negro transvestite Lily Mae Jenkins, the Utopias invented by Frankie and John Henry where one could change sex at will or be half male and half female, and John Henry's interest in dolls and dressing in women's clothes. Always such hermaphroditic or androgynous references are placed in a negative frame, for the novel's entire movement is towards Frankie's ultimate submission to the inexorable demand that she accept her sex as female. Just after telling Frankie about Lily Mae Jenkins, wise old Berenice urges her to start looking for beaus and acting feminine. "Now you belong to change from being so rough and greedy and big. You ought to fix yourself up nice in your dresses. And speak sweetly and act sly."[7] Berenice also refuses to countenance sexual transformation in the Utopian dreams she and Frankie and John Henry spin on summer afternoons. Children may play at exchanging sex roles, but adults may not, unless they are to be regarded as grotesques fit only for sideshow displays.

This truth begins to force itself upon Frankie Addams in the "green and crazy summer" of her twelfth year. "Frankie had become an unjoined person who hung around in doorways, and she was afraid." McCullers emphasizes the element of fear so rhythmically that the novel's opening pages swim in a fevered, hallucinatory atmosphere. The central setting is the sad and ugly kitchen, like the room of a crazy house, its walls covered with John Henry's freakish drawings. Here a vague terror squeezes

Frankie's heart. And here she, Berenice, and John Henry constitute a strange family or private world cut off from any other. The real doorway where Frankie lingers in baffled fright is the passage between childhood and the clearly defined sexual world of grown-ups which she must enter, for almost all of the specific sources of her anxiety turn out to be sexual. The older girls who have shut her out of their club are preoccupied with boys and gossip about adult sex which Frankie angrily dismisses as "nasty lies" (pp. 1–11).

Yet even she has participated in a secret and unknown sin with a neighborhood boy in his garage, and she is sickened with guilt. Her father has decided she is too old to sleep with him, but she is afraid in her bed by herself. Her most vividly realized fear derives from the changes in her body which she epitomizes in her height. At her present rate of growth she calculates that she will end up over nine feet tall—a freak.

Frankie's fear of freaks surely indicates some subconscious understanding of the qualities within herself which make her peculiar in the eyes of the normal world. McCullers uses the motif of unfinished music to underline and intensify Frankie's dilemma, suggesting the proper resolution to her confused view of herself. In Part 1, Frankie hears a grieving blues tune on "the sad horn of some colored boy" at night. The disembodied sound expresses her own feelings, for she herself is a piece of unfinished music. Just as the tune approaches its conclusion, the horn suddenly stops playing. The music's incompleteness drives Frankie wild, trapping inside her the unbearable emotions it has drawn to a focus (pp. 41–42). Like Mick Kelly, Frankie tries to find release through masochism, beating her head with her fist, as she will do again several times in the story. When she changes her name to the romantic F. Jasmine in Part 2 and waltzes around town in a dress, telling everyone she meets that her brother and his bride will take her away with them on their wedding trip, the unfinished music is resolved in her mind. Her stories about the wedding sound inside her "as the last chord of a guitar murmurs a long time after the strings are struck." Unfortunately, her fantasies of the wedding are doomed to disappointment. We know this long before the event because McCullers returns to the motif of unfinished music, this time in the sound made by a piano tuner at work, which embodies F. Jasmine's romantic dream. "Then in a *dreaming way* a chain of chords climbed slowly upward *like a flight of castle stairs:* but just at the end, when the eighth chord should have sounded and the scale made complete, there was a stop" (p. 81, my emphasis).

The only event that resolves the unfinished music as well as the frantic, disjointed activities of F. Jasmine, John Henry, and Berenice is the transcendent moment when a group of older girls file slowly through the backyard in clean, fresh dresses and are turned golden by the slanting rays of the evening sun. These girls are a sublime vision of Frankie—F. Jasmine's destiny, a vision of ideal feminine grace before which the group in the kitchen stands transfixed in hushed awe. The piano tuner is silent. F. Jasmine's growing body and the outside world demand that she complete herself in the terms of this vision, but she will not submit until her fantasies of escape are smashed.

The meaning of the unfinished music is closely linked to Frankie's spiritual kinship with the blacks of her little Southern town. Both are made clear in the person of Honey Brown, Berenice's young, light-skinned foster brother. Too intelligent and restless to live comfortably in the circumscribed world of Sugarville, the black section of town, he periodically explodes: "Honey played the horn, and he had been first in his studies at the colored high school. He ordered a French book from Atlanta and learned himself some French. At the same time he would suddenly run hog-wild all over Sugarville and tear around for several days, until his friends would bring him home more dead than living" (p. 122). The old black fortune-teller Big Mama explains that God withdrew His hand before Honey was completed, leaving him eternally unsatisfied. It must have been Honey's sad blues horn that Frankie heard in the night, the horn that stopped playing just short of the music's resolution. Big Mama's explanation of Honey's plight describes his frustration clearly enough, but the real cause of Honey's problems is the fact that he, like Frankie, does not fit the categories imposed on him by his Southern town.

Frankie shares a sense of entrapment with Honey and Berenice, but hers is not finally as severe, even though it is more vividly realized in the novel. At first she longs to escape from her hot, stultified town to the cold, snowy peace of Alaska. At the end of Part 1, however, she fixes on the wedding in Winter Hill as the means of escape. The old question of who she is and what she will become ceases to torment her when she decides to be a member of the wedding and go out into the world with her brother and his bride. This absurd fantasy is a denial of the adult sexuality which Frankie cannot bear to acknowledge, but her attraction to it is obvious in her infatuation with the engaged couple. McCullers associates the returning motif of unfinished music with the imagery of prison to show that F. Jasmine's romantic dream will not bring escape. The evening before the wedding, when the piano tuner repeats again and again his unfinished chords, "the bars of sunlight crossed the back yard like the bars of a bright strange jail" (p. 75). In the crazily disoriented recent months, Frankie had feared the eyes of the prisoners in the town jail because she sensed that they, like the freaks at the fair, recognized her as one of them. Even as F. Jasmine, she is closer to them than she knows. Berenice explains that all human beings are imprisoned in their separate bodies and separate minds, blacks even more extremely than others.

> We all of us somehow caught. We born this way or that way and we don't know why. But we caught anyhow. I born Berenice. You born Frankie, John Henry born John Henry. And maybe we wants to widen and bust free. But no matter what we do we still caught. . . . But they done drawn completely extra bounds around all colored people. They done squeezed us off in one

corner by ourself. . . . Sometimes a boy like Honey feel like he just can't breathe no more. He feel like he got to break something or break himself. (pp. 113–14)

F. Jasmine feels like breaking things too, but her frustration usually expresses itself rather harmlessly in perverse moods. She is ultimately able to accept the limitations of her sex, which of course are far less cramped than the restrictions of segregation in the 1940s. But McCullers is making a traditional association between the oppression of women and that of blacks, an association most obvious in Harriet Beecher Stowe's *Uncle Tom's Cabin* in the nineteenth century, but also very clear in the relationship of the recent feminist movement to the Civil Rights Movement of the 1960s.[8]

Frankie is caught in a blossoming female body which she must recognize and accept. She must also face the fact that grown men and women make love, and that her body makes her desirable to men. As a younger child she had unwittingly walked in on the lovemaking of a man and his wife who were boarders in her house. Uncomprehending, she thought the man was having a fit. Even at twelve she does not understand the nature of his convulsions, just as she refuses to listen to the "nasty lies" of the older girls and tries not to think of her own wicked experience in the neighbor boy's garage. This innocence makes her dangerously vulnerable when as F. Jasmine she wanders through the town looking older and wiser than her years. The toughness that had served her well as a tomboy betrays her now, so that the soldier she meets in the Blue Moon Cafe assumes she is willing to be seduced. F. Jasmine is paralyzed with horror as the soldier embraces her in his cheap hotel room. She feels she is in the Crazy House at the fair or in the insane asylum at Milledgeville. At the last minute she knocks him out with a pitcher and makes her getaway down the fire escape. Not until late the next night, after the disaster of the wedding, does her mind accept the meaning of this encounter and its relation to her veiled sexual memories and anxieties. By then her brother and his bride have rejected her and she has suffered the humiliation of being pulled screaming from the steering wheel of their car. Back home, she has made a futile attempt to run away and has been recovered by her father in the Blue Moon Cafe, where she had felt she was drowning.

The Member of the Wedding ends in a new world, with Frances reborn as a giddy adolescent. The environment of her childhood has been dismantled completely—John Henry has died horribly of meningitis, Berenice has resigned herself to marriage and quit her job, and Frances is preparing to move to a new house with her father. The final scene takes place in the kitchen, now remodeled so that it is unrecognizable as the freakish prison of the terrible summer. Frances is making dainty sandwiches to serve her new soulmate, an artistic girl two years her senior. No longer a frightened alien, she is united with her friend through a mutual infatuation with poetry and art.

Significantly, the time of the greatest changes in her life coincided with the fair's annual visit to town. As her childhood world collapsed and John Henry lay screaming and dying in a dark room, Frances blithely visited the fair with her friend Mary Littlejohn, this time avoiding the Freak Pavilion which had so fascinated her and John Henry the year before. She no longer feels any association with the freaks, for she is secure in her new feminine identity. Paradoxically, however, there is another kind of freak whose existence she never really confronts. Instead of the exotic monsters at the fair, the new and much grimmer freak is the dying John Henry, his little body hideously twisted and his eyeballs "walled up in a corner stuck and blind" (p. 152). McCullers makes the connection between John Henry and the freaks at the fair by describing them together in one important paragraph very near the end of the novel. But Frances is too happily absorbed in her new friendship and her passion for Tennyson and Michelangelo to give much thought to the sufferings of the little cousin who had been her patient companion during the crazy summer. Nor does she have time to consider the plight of Honey Brown, whose last explosion of frustration landed him in prison about the time of the fair. McCullers has rather ruthlessly removed the "deviants" from Frances's life so that safe conformity can triumph.

The price for this relief from the tensions of strangeness has been high, perhaps too high. Frances is less attractive at the end of the novel than she was as frightened tomboy Frankie. She has become a silly girl who no longer produces her own juvenile works of art—the shows and plays she used to write—but instead gushes sentimental nonsense about the Great Masters. The hard edge of her mind is gone, and all that is left is froth. The struggle against conformity which had identified her with Honey Brown had been a struggle to assert artistic sensibility and intelligence in a world which refused to accept those qualities in a woman or a black man. Honey had expressed his needs by learning French and playing the trumpet, but his music remained unfinished, and he ended up in prison for trying to "bust free" of the narrow limits around his life. Frances avoids such drastic disappointment by giving up and hiding beneath the protective coloration of giddy young womanhood. But if Frances's intelligence is not destroyed, we might speculate that, like Sylvia Plath or Adrienne Rich, she will someday feel the old conflict again and awaken to a fearful "sense of drift, of being pulled along on a current which called itself my destiny, but in which I seemed to be losing touch with who-ever I had been, with the girl who had experienced her own will and energy almost ecstatically at times."[9] Without McCullers's two portraits of the artistic twelve-year-old girl and her telling images of sexual freakishness, we could never understand so clearly why "a thinking woman sleeps with monsters" or how those monsters function in the minds of talented girls emerging from childhood.

Notes

1.　Anne Goodwyn Jones, *Tomorrow Is Another Day: The Woman Writer in the South, 1859–1936* (Baton Rouge: Louisiana State University Press, 1981), 355; Carolyn G. Heilbrun, *Reinventing Womanhood* (New York: Norton, 1979), 106–08; Karen Horney, *Feminine Psychology,* ed. Harold Kelman (New York: Norton, 1967), 54–70. For previous discussions of sexual ambivalence in these works, see Leslie Fiedler, *Love and Death in the American Novel* (New York: Dell, 1969), 333, 484–85; Ellen Moers, *Literary Women* (New York: Doubleday, 1976), 108–09; and Patricia S. Box, "Androgyny and the Musical Vision: A Study of Two Novels by Carson McCullers," *Southern Quarterly* 16 (January 1978): 117–23.

2.　Quoted in Bertram Wyatt-Brown, *Southern Honor: Ethics and Behavior in the Old South* (New York: Oxford University Press, 1982), 231–33.

3.　Virginia Woolf, "Professions for Women," in *The Death of the Moth and Other Essays* (London: Hogarth Press, 1942), 153. Woolf's most famous description of the crippling difficulties women face is of course *A Room of One's Own,* but she illustrated the assertions of that work in the whole body of her essays and in her treatment of women characters like Mrs. Ramsay and Lily Briscoe in her novels. For scholarly examination of the presentation of these problems in women's writing since the early nineteenth century, see Moers; Elaine Showalter, *A Literature of Their Own: British Women Novelists from Brontë to Lessing* (Princeton: Princeton University Press, 1977); and Sandra M. Gilbert and Susan Gubar, *The Madwoman in the Attic: The Woman Writer and the Nineteenth-Century Literary Imagination* (New Haven: Yale University Press, 1979).

4.　Barbara Clarke Mossberg, "Slant Truths and Bandaged Secrets: The Art of Deceit in Emily Dickinson and Gertrude Stein," Paper presented at the MLA convention, New York, December 1978; Barbara Clarke Mossberg, *Emily Dickinson: When a Writer Is a Daughter* (Bloomington: Indiana University Press, 1982); Sandra M. Gilbert, " 'My Name Is Darkness': The Poetry of Self-Definition," *Contemporary Literature* 18 (Autumn 1977): 443–57, and especially 446–47; Heilbrun, 72. See also Heilbrun, 105–24. Karen Horney is a notable exception, as Heilbrun points out (99), but her daring resulted in ostracism by her professional colleagues.

5.　Willa Cather, *The Song of the Lark* (Boston: Houghton Mifflin, 1915), 140.

6.　Virginia Spencer Carr, *The Lonely Hunter: A Biography of Carson McCullers* (Garden City, N.Y.: Doubleday, 1975), 570–73.

7.　Moers, 109; *The Member of the Wedding,* in *The Ballad of the Sad Café: The Novels and Stories of Carson McCullers* (Boston: Houghton Mifflin, 1951), 77–78. Subsequent references will be indicated parenthetically by page number in my text.

8.　See Moers, 19–41.

9.　Adrienne Rich, "When We Dead Awaken" and "Snapshots of a Daughter-in-Law," *Adrienne Rich's Poetry* (New York: Norton, 1975), 95, 12.

[A Materialist Reading of *Clock Without Hands*]

CICELY PALSER HAVELY*

Margaret Drabble has been particularly highly praised by British critics. Because the range of her early work was so narrowly domestic, she was frequently compared with Jane Austen—but those who praised her in those terms were too often only invoking gentle Jane. In effect, Margaret Drabble was being praised for sticking to what women are supposed to know best, *Kinder, Küche* and private *Angst*. Then something happened. In *The Realms of Gold* (1975) she made her heroine a successful and famous archaeologist, thus enlarging both the temporal and spatial range of her themes, though it was still clear that she was more at ease loading the dishwasher in Putney, or unearthing family history in the provinces. Then in *The Ice Age* (1977) with an exhilaration which effectively challenges the despair in the novel, she took on the corruption at the heart of the British collusion between capitalism and socialism—a decisive move into the heart of male-dominated territory. But in her latest novel, *The Middle Years* (1980) she has gone back to the old, safe "female" provinces. I had hoped that a novelist in whom I find so much to admire would go forward to some more progressive mixture of male and female concerns. Virginia Woolf expressed similar hopes for the novels that would be written by then newly emancipated women:

> . . . her attention is being directed away from the personal centre which engaged it exclusively in the past to the impersonal, and her novels [will] naturally become more critical of society, less analytical of individual lives . . . The novel will cease to be the dumping ground for the personal emotions.[1]

But her novels were more, not less directed to "the personal centre" than those of George Eliot, or Mrs. Gaskell, or the author of *Shirley;* and they roused Mrs. Leavis to a famous attack:

> One's own kitchen and nursery, and not the drawing-room and dinner table where tired professional men relax among the ladies (thus Mrs. Woolf) is the realm where living takes place, and I see no profit in letting our servants live for us.[2]

*Excerpt reprinted from "Two Women Novelists: Carson McCullers and Flannery O'Connor," *The Uses of Fiction: Essays on the Modern Novel in Honour of Arnold Kettle,* ed. Douglas Jefferson and Graham Martin (Open University Press, 1982), 115-24, by permission of the author.

She adds "I myself . . . have generally had to produce contributions for this review with one hand, while actually stirring the pot, or something of that kind, with the other." She might have been writing a manifesto for the Drabbleasian school. Yet how few of its members have really set out a balanced response to the wisdom of Mrs. Leavis's point of view. The hand that stirs the pot has got its due, but not the hand that writes the review, or operates a machine or does any of the things that a woman must set her other hand to. While women of all classes (not just the women who have always worked outside the home) have gradually achieved a fuller share in the public life of the community, the reflection of their lives in the novel has tended to narrow, and to concentrate on the domestic and interior aspects to a degree that was actually much less often found in the nineteenth-century novel, when the servants of middle-class women did so much of their living for them. Then so many women novelists, not just the famous, used the novel to participate in all the major public controversies of their time, barred as they were from pulpit and parliament.

This concentration on the inner and private life is sometimes most marked where it appears least likely to be so. Doris Lessing's work is partly valued for the record it contains of the political climate of post-war Britain. But this record is only to be read through thick veils of highly individualized consciousness. In *The Four Gated City* (1972) Martha Quest works for and has an affair with a vaguely political figure who, like Mr. Rochester, has a mad wife. But in this novel madness is a welcomed experience rather than the fearful excess that it is in *Jane Eyre*. Unlike Jane, Martha Quest falls in love with the mad wife and it is with her that the richer relationship develops, opening the way to Martha's own incipient insanity. Jane Eyre's subjective point of view looks like the most detached objectivity compared with the view of the world through Martha Quest's tortured and abnormal consciousness. *The Four Gated City* is extremely impressive but it is a mistake to think of it as a political novel simply because its characters attend political rallies. In choosing to elaborate on the familiar subjective formula of *Jane Eyre* Doris Lessing actually draws attention to how deep within the eccentric private self is the source of her point of view.

Some of the most ingrained traditions of the novel have helped to make such narrow concentration on the private self, and especially the sexual aspects of the private self, difficult to escape from. *Pamela* and *Clarissa* have remained powerful models, and the tensions and patterns of sexual behaviour have become inextricably involved with the structures of the novel. A reader without our cultural antecedents might think that the destruction of Le Voreux was climax enough for *Germinal;* it is possible to imagine Pip suffering just as badly from expectations that did not include Estella; and Insarov's biographer would probably relegate Elena to a footnote. The importance of sex in the novel, the sheer amount of novel time it takes up, is blatantly unrealistic—even in the Victorian "realists." All kinds of themes are developed through the expression of the protagonists' sexuality. Daniel Deronda looked for "the blending of a complete personal love in one current with a larger duty" and found Zionism not only through Mirah, but inseparable from her. Hardy was one of the still very few novelists to give any attention to the working lives of his characters, but crises in their working lives are invariably indicative of crises in their inner and sexual lives as well. D. H. Lawrence effectively tied the knot with his insistence that the sexual aspects of the lives of men and women are not only of central importance, but that everything else that might seem to be separate in their lives relates to their sexuality. And because he embodied such ideas in his novels, still heavily influenced by the traditions of nineteenth-century realism, he effectively cemented a bond between the expression of sexuality and the novel form itself which has proved to be almost unbreakable. Nadine Gordimer (like Doris Lessing) is an explicitly "political" novelist. Yet she too expresses the tensions and conflicts of South African society in terms of very private individual relationships and locates the critical points of these tensions within the ultimate intimacy of sexual love. This is less an undistorted reflection of the ways in which a society works, than a formula proceeding from the traditional novel itself, subsuming in sexual relationships all the various crises of moral behaviour that men and women endure.

The novel as our culture has derived it from Richardson's prototypes is a forum of the emotional, rather than the rational life. The emotions have been supposed to be the province of women, rationality that of men. In so far as there is any value in this distinction, the novel has become a "feminine" form, predisposed to the inner life; and though by no means only women novelists explore such material for their fiction, there is a more urgent need for them to break from it. Men writing about the inner life must (in a sense) enter a foreign country; but women have no other well-established territory to move into. Like so many of the snares that beset women, the entanglement is complex. One of the things that feminists want to tell the male-dominated world is that being barred from the public world has trapped women within their inner lives. But the available form accommodates the treatment of the inner life so readily that the necessary political perspective is too often lost. There can be nothing wrong with any writer's desire to give the fullest possible account of an exclusively female experience or point of view. But the danger in the situation is that so much women's writing about women tends to consolidate the unhappy status quo, and not to advance the claims of women to a fuller life in every respect.

The better the thing is done, the easier it is to believe that this is the thing that women do best, and from there it is too easy a step to believing that it is the only thing they can do. This is why I want to look at the work of two women writers of the generation before this who have been very much neglected in Britain: Flannery O'Connor and Carson McCullers. Both achieved in their writing a degree of balance between the inner life and the public world which suggests that there is a way forward which has been missed.

. . .

Carson McCullers achieved fame through subtle delineations of eccentric inner landscapes, as in *The Heart Is a Lonely Hunter* (1940) and *The Member of the Wedding* (1946). In *Clock Without Hands* (1961) she went beyond her earlier achievement by relating four such inner landscapes to each other and to the complex social and political situation which involves them all. The unwilling desegregation of the South is not mere "context." It impinges directly and violently on her characters' lives even though the particular events they are involved in have little historical consequence. The novel achieves a rare and impressive balance between the demands of private feelings and the claims and pressures of the public world.

Clock Without Hands is about the relationships between blacks and whites in a small Georgia town. All the main characters are men. J. T. Malone, the pharmacist, is dying of leukaemia at the age of 40. His friend, Judge Clane, formerly a Congressman and "fixed star in the galaxy of Southern Statesmanship"[3] is in his eighties, weighs three hundred pounds and is losing his reason; but he is still shockingly vigorous. His present passion is that the Government should redeem the Confederate currency, of which he has ten million dollars' worth, and pay restitution for freed slaves. With dazzling insensitivity he employs as a secretary for this project Sherman Pew, the half-white son of a black man sentenced to death. Sherman refuses to write the letters, and enraged into action, moves into a white neighbourhood. The judge, who misses the "white sheeted meetings at Pine Mountain" that are now illegal, calls the foremost citizens to the pharmacy where they decide that Sherman Pew's house must be bombed. The lot falls to the mortally sick Malone who is a weak-spirited creature, with prejudices of his own against Germans and Jews as well as blacks. But with more courage than he has ever shown in his life before, he refuses:

> "Gentlemen, I am too near death to sin, to murder." He was excruciatingly embarrassed. (p. 195)

The preacher at the church Malone attends (for purely conventional reasons) likes to preach about "drawing a bead on death," yet he is as embarrassed about Malone's individual death as Malone. In a direly comic interview the immortality that confronts him is defined by the preacher as "an extension of earthly life, but more intensified." (p. 137) Malone is appalled: he "thought of the drabness of his life and wondered if it could be more intensified." With no particular excitement or horror he comes to realize that though no-one has noticed, he has already lost his life; which save for one remarkably trouble-free act of adultery, has been undistinguished by either vice or virtue. His refusal to bomb Sherman Pew's house is the most positive act of his drab life.

But it is ineffective. The task is joyfully taken on by Sammy Lank, a poor white with a large family, who, as the Judge says, has "only . . . the Nigra to look down on." (p. 191) The Judge's grandson, Jester Clane, takes the assassin up in a plane in order to shoot him. But Lank reveals that his life's ambition is still unfulfilled. He wanted to father quins, and has produced no better than triplets. Grotesquely pathetic though this revelation is, Jester can no longer kill a man who has become, by making it, more than the impersonal agent of a hateful cause. So he lands Sammy Lank safely "to brag to his family that he is such a well-known man that even Jester Clane has taken him on an airplane ride." (p. 202) Thus ironically a small choice against violence comes to be seen as a gesture approving it. The progress of justice is almost invisibly slow. The novel was begun in 1954, the year in which it is set, and at that time a less restrained optimism would not have been realistic.

Nor is Malone consciously fulfilled or redeemed by his action. Instead, he worries that the good-will value of the pharmacy may have been jeopardized. He dies the day the Supreme Court decides that schools must be integrated. The Judge decides to start his resistance with a radio broadcast which will have all the impact of Lincoln's Gettysburg address but "the other way round." But he can think of nothing to say: "vile words, cuss words unsuitable for the radio . . . raged in his mind" (p. 207) and when he gets to the microphone Lincoln's words are the only ones he can get out. The last act of Malone's mind is to understand that what has happened is "nothing that was not a long time in the making." Even a dyed-in-the-wool reactionary like the Judge must now march to the music of Lincoln's tune, the last thing in the world he wants to do.

So the progress which Carson McCullers discerns does not reveal itself in dramatic acts of heroism performed by individuals whose heroism will inspire others. It consists of small, half-understood or even involuntary actions which added together suggest an evolution towards justice of geological slowness but of geological sureness too. Near the beginning of his year of dying Malone contemplates the old pestle ("grey and smooth with use") which he bought from his predecessor with the other effects of the pharmacy. Possibly a relic of Indian times, it will outlast him. The prejudice which corrodes the South cannot be ground down in a single life time.

Both Flannery O'Connor and Carson McCullers got beyond what Patricia Stubbs recently called "the tyranny of the intensely personal."[4] In *Clock Without Hands* as in O'Connor's short story the vividly realized inner lives of the protagonists are firmly set in a well observed and well analysed social context which is being subjected to great pressures from without. She is able to take a long view of her subject without loss of detail in the foreground. There may still be people who believe that women are constitutionally unable to take a long view and I feel unhappily obliged to concede that women novelists have not recently done much to disabuse them. So many of the generation of writers who have succeeded McCullers and O'Connor seem to have lost or deliberately abandoned their broad perspectives and turned inwards to the private world. Talented women like Mary McCarthy, Doris Lessing, Edna O'Brien, Fay Weldon, Erica Jong, Marilyn French and Lisa Alther write almost exclusively about the private lives of their own sex. Why did Margaret Drabble take a couple of steps into a broader (I do not say better) world and then scuttle back into safe, familiar territory in *The Middle Years*? Their attitude is not so much chauvinistic as nationalistic. They proclaim the pleasures and pains of their own territories, their own cultures, and exclude all the rest. In this respect feminists are not the only isolationists. There is a similar tendency towards the highly particularized private life among Jewish American writers today, and perhaps it is a characteristic of the writing of other minority groups in search of their identity as well.[5]

In an essay of this length one is bound to appear more divisive than one wishes to be. I do not want to attack good novels of any kind, and I have derived much pleasure, instruction and sisterly reassurance from the novelists I have listed. But I think their vein is nearly exhausted. It is not a critic's business to tell novelists what to do next. But these women, whether they call themselves feminists or not, have chosen to write novels which expound a cause, and I think I am as entitled to exhort them about their cause as any woman—and not a few men. The majority of women's novels about women are only a fragment of the truth. They concentrate on the home, and on intimate relationships. They are for the most part about middle-class, highly educated women, professional people, if they work at all. Of course this area of experience is as entitled to its literature as any other, but vast areas of women's experience are still unexplored—and areas where women's experience meets that of men. There is no reason why women today should not be able to combine the impressive humane understanding they undoubtedly possess with the broader political perspectives of—say—Paul Scott or V. S. Naipaul. It cannot be because they still have only limited access to the public world. The only limits to a woman's vision are conventional, not real, but they are much harder to break through if they are self-imposed as well.

Notes

1. Virginia Woolf, *Women & Fiction,* Collected Essays Vol. 2 (The Hogarth Press, London 1966), 147–8.

2. Q. D. Leavis, "Caterpillars of the Commonwealth Unite!" *Scrutiny,* Vol. 7, No. 3 (September 1938): 210.

3. This, and subsequent quotations from *Clock Without Hands,* are taken from the Penguin edition, 1977. It was first published in New York, 1961.

4. Patricia Stubbs, *Women and Fiction,* 1979, p. 233.

5. And yet Toni Morrison's *Song of Solomon* (1978) seems to have achieved the kind of balance between the private and public worlds exemplified in the writings of O'Connor and McCullers.

Freaking Out:
The Short Stories of Carson McCullers

Robert Phillips*

For Irving Malin

The work of Carson McCullers is whole cloth. Few writers have maintained such a consistent vision. Moreover, few writers have such a clear conception of their preoccupations and themes. In "The Flowering Dream: Notes on Writing" (included in *The Mortgaged Heart,* edited by Margarita G. Smith) McCullers wrote:

> Spiritual isolation is the basis of most of my themes. My first book was concerned with this, almost entirely, and all of my books since, in one way or another. Love, and especially love of a person who is incapable of receiving it, is at the heart of my selection of grotesque figures to write about—people whose physical incapacity is a symbol of their spiritual incapacity to love or receive love—their spiritual isolation.

There, in one paragraph, McCullers answered satisfactorily all the queries raised concerning *why* in her novels she wrote almost exclusively of grotesques. Elsewhere, in "A Personal Preface" to her second play, *The Square Root of Wonderful,* she again stated, "I suppose my central theme is the theme of spiritual isolation. Certainly I have always felt alone."

Now if we take the lady at her word, and I believe we should, this theme of spiritual isolation is the cornerstone to her house of fiction. One of the smallest rooms of that house is the region of her short stories. While there already is a considerable body of criticism concerning her four novels and the fifth novella, very little has been said about her shorter fiction—particularly the fourteen stories published in the posthumous collection, *The Mortgaged Heart.* Which is a pity, because of the total of nineteen stories to be found there and in the earlier omnibus collection, *The Ballad of the Sad Café,* several are quite superb fiction. Certainly all are typical McCullers, with this exception: they are all less likely to be labeled "Gothic" or "grotesque" when compared to her novels. For whatever reason, there is less physical abnormality in

*Reprinted from *Southwest Review* 63 (Winter 1978): 65–73, by permission of the author.

the stories. Instead of mutes and dwarfs, what we generally encounter here are people isolated by circumstance rather than physical appearance or malady. Instead of freaks we find an inner freaking-out.

What does Carson McCullers mean by "spiritual isolation"? I have taken the phrase to mean, simply, personal dissociation—the feeling of being severed from society, disunited from others, lonely, separate, different, apart. Certainly that state characterizes Frankie Addams of *The Member of the Wedding,* one of McCullers's more "normal" characters, just as it does Cousin Lymon of the *Ballad,* a more "abnormal" one. Obviously the term "spiritual isolation" applies to the freaked-out as well as to the freaks.

One of the amazing things in considering McCullers is not only how many variations she played upon this theme in book after book, story after story, and two plays, but also how early that vision was formulated. It is to be found in her very first story, "Sucker," written when she was a seventeen-year-old school girl. There the title character, Sucker, is an orphan, and therefore unrelated to the family with whom he lives. The young author described him beautifully: "his face had the look of a kid who is watching a game and waiting to be asked to play." Sucker desperately wants to be loved, to become a member of the family. In this respect he is a young Frankie Addams, who wanted so very much a "we of me."

At first "Sucker" seems to be the story of the narrator, Pete, and the pull between *agape* (Pete and Sucker) and *eros* (Pete and Maybelle). But by the time of the story's climax, the awful scene in which Pete tells Sucker he doesn't care for him one bit, we realize the story bears the correct title after all. It *is* Sucker's story, the story of an outsider who tries to fit in. In one epiphany he is made to realize he never will, and thus he freaks out and becomes a hardened rebel.

Though it was her first story, "Sucker" contains the seeds of the later McCullers's philosophy of love, which she expounded upon in a famous passage in *The Ballad of the Sad Café.* In "Sucker" she tells us, "There is one thing I have learned, but it makes me feel guilty and is hard to figure out. If a person admires you a lot you despise him and don't care—and it is the person who doesn't notice you that you are apt to admire. This is not easy to realize."

Years later, in the *Ballad,* she wrote in part,

love is a joint experience between two persons—but the fact that it is a joint experience does not mean that it is a similar experience to the two people involved. There are the lover and the beloved, but these two come from different countries . . . most of us would rather love than be loved. Almost everyone wants to be the lover. And the curt truth is that, in a deep way, the state of being beloved is intolerable to many. The beloved fears and hates the lover, and with the best of reasons. For the lover is forever trying to strip bare his beloved. The lover craves any possible relation with the beloved, even if this experience can cause him only pain.

Given this world view, is it any wonder her characters freak out?

Being an orphan, then, was McCullers's first projection of a spiritually isolated being. She used the same projection in "The Orphanage." Yet another early story, "Breath from the Sky," depicts a young woman orphaned from her family not by parental death, but by her own invalidism. Both her shorn hair and the cut flowers are symbolic of the sapping of her strength, the nipping of the bloom of her youth. The story centers on her realization of the helplessness of her situation. She is overcome by the lustiness of her brother and sister, and even the bounding, healthy dog. While a move three hundred miles north to Mountain Heights is supposed to help her, the simple move from the inside of the house to the yard has in itself made her feel enervated and stricken. The trip surely will estrange her both in body and in spirit.

Some of Carson McCullers's most successful characterizations of the isolated individual are, of course, her adolescents—characters like Mick Kelly and Frankie Addams, who belong neither to the adult world nor to the world of childhood. One such in-betweener is the thirteen-year-old younger sister in the early story "Like That." Perceiving the pain of growing into womanhood experienced by her older sister, she resists rather than embraces maturation. Like Sucker, she rebels, only her rebellion is against such overwhelming forces as menstruation, sexuality, premature death.

Another adolescent is the heroine of "Correspondence," a slight epistolary story of a one-way correspondence undertaken by a Frankie Addams type, here named Henrietta Evans. Henrietta, estranged from her fellow freshmen, seeks release through a South American pen pal. He never answers, and the psychic changes inflicted upon the girl are reflected in changes in her signature—she transforms herself from "Henky Evans" to "Henrietta Evans" to "Miss Henrietta Hill Evans"—a ploy also practiced by F. Jasmine Addams, formerly known as Frankie. This little story clearly illustrates McCullers's theme of man's revolt against his own inner isolation and his urge to express himself as fully as possible. That there is no response from the other country is indicative of McCullers's negative world view.

Not all of McCullers's suffering adolescents are female. In the long "Untitled Piece" a boy called Andrew Leander seems a male Frankie, and his father is also a jeweler. The action takes place during one crazy summer, and Berenice Sadie Brown has somehow been transmogrified into a younger black named Vitalis. In his attempt to become joined to something, Andrew commits an act of unpremeditated miscegenation with Vitalis, then flees the town in guilt. His one act of union and love has forced his separation and fear. A later story, "The Haunted Boy," depicts a teenager named Hugh who is also isolated, in his case in the knowledge that his mother is mad and that he may once again discover her in a suicide attempt. The story is marred by a pat ending, but Hugh's fear is made extraordinarily real. One does not soon forget his terror at the simple act of opening the upstairs bathroom door.

Another category of McCullers's characterizations of young people is that of the adolescent as musician. As if being adolescent were not sufficiently special and disjoining, McCullers knew that for an adolescent who studied music the situation would certainly be exacerbated. "Wunderkind" is one of the most famous of all her stories, even though there are several that are better. It concerns the realization of a fifteen-year-old music student that she simply does not possess the emotional capacity to match her facile pianistic technique. Outside she is all glitter; inside, she knows she is empty. There is no sensationalism here, yet the epiphany is as traumatic as Alison's severing her own nipples with garden shears (in *Reflections in a Golden Eye*). In the novels McCullers strove for grand moments; in the stories, for quiet occasions which nevertheless are vital occasions. When the washed-up *wunderkind* flees her piano teacher's studio and hurries "down the street that had become confused with noise and bicycles and the games of other children," the reader comprehends the loss of the girl's childhood, sacrificed to the music she cannot really play well. She is an emotional freak who is outwardly normal.

Another youthful musician appears in "Poldi," an early tale of hopeless love. The young protagonist admires and perhaps even loves an older cellist, who in turn, naturally, thinks of him merely as "a little brother." The cellist, in turn, loves a pianist named Kurt, whom she has seen only three times in her life. It is the McCullers love formula at work again. As in "Sucker," "The Haunted Boy," and the "Untitled Piece," McCullers successfully transforms herself into a young male. That her ability to do this may have roots deeper than mere considerations of technique and point of view is suggested by the revelations of Virginia Spencer Carr's exhaustive biography of the author, *The Lonely Hunter.*

Bridging the generation gap between the author's younger and older short story protagonists is the eighteen-year-old university student in the early tale "Court in the West Eighties." This is a character who neither acts nor is acted upon, but merely records the scenes about her in an apartment house which serves as a microcosm of the macrocosm. She seems to make a God figure of one inhabitant, a serene, red-headed man: "The sun made a haze of light around his bright hair that was almost like a sort of halo." He is perhaps an early precursor of John Singer of *The Heart Is a Lonely Hunter.* He is also a demiurge, looking on unfeelingly while a young jobless couple living across the court slowly starve. McCullers injects a potent symbol into the story in the form of a balloon man—that is, a man made of balloons, bearing a silly grin and hanging perpetually from one apartment window. He is an effigy mocking mankind and man's helplessness. In the world of McCullers's imagination we are all dangling, hanged men.

In McCullers's stories portraying adults confronting adult problems—or rather not confronting them, since most either freak out or flee the situation rather than face it—the characters are occasionally absolutely normal in appearance. Later, however, they are rendered symbolically grotesque, as in "Instant of the Hour After," a mood piece in which a young married couple's love for one another is inexplicably destroying them. In the story's chief symbol they are seen as two figures in a bottle—small, perfect, yet white and exhausted, like "fleshly specimens in a laboratory." This image is quite akin to that of the pickled fetus in "The Orphanage." The story also predates the conflict of the later and vastly superior "A Domestic Dilemma."

In "A Domestic Dilemma," the isolated character is a housewife, physically transplanted from Alabama to New York. Unable to adjust to the changes involved in the move or to make friends, she seeks escape through drinking. Without the artifice of alcohol her interior life is insufficient. Just as the son in "The Haunted Boy" lives in fear that his crazy mother may again harm herself, so too this suburban housewife's husband is haunted by her earlier drunken accident with one of the children and by the possibility that it could happen again. A threat of undefined disaster underlies his days. Far worse is his fear that her daily drunken behavior is causing invisible psychic damage to the two children—damage which can only increase as the immunity of incomprehension passes. In this, my personal favorite of her shorter fiction, McCullers explores love/hate relationships in marriage and what she calls "the immense complexity of love."

This inability to adjust to physical change signals a state of spiritual isolation in several of the best stories by McCullers, including "The Sojourner" and "A Tree. A Rock. A Cloud," as well as the more superficial "Art and Mr. Mahoney."

"The Sojourner" is a meditation on what McCullers terms "the improvisation of human existence." Some people adjust to life's variations, some do not. John Ferris, this story's protagonist, has not adjusted to the anxieties of transience and solitude brought about by his divorce. On the other hand, his former wife has adjusted, and he makes the discovery of his own emotional poverty during a visit to her and her new family. It is as traumatic for him as the *wunderkind*'s discovery of her own shortcomings. He perceives immediately that his ex-wife has created a rich new life for herself, with two children and a second husband. He, by contrast, has put down no roots. Recently even his father has died, reminding him of wasted years and death, cancelling out the past in a life which has no present or future. Physically he is an expatriate from America; emotionally he is an expatriate from the human heart. At the end he is vowing to reach out, to create a meaningful relationship with his mistress's son, an act he may or may not be able to accomplish.

The disintegration of a marriage also creates another dis-integrated soul in "A Tree. A Rock. A Cloud." The story relates the encounter in a café of a twelve-year-old boy and an old cuckold. It is not so much a plotted story as the plodded meditations of the old man on the nature of love—surely one of Mrs. McCullers's favorite topics. Love here is expounded as a condition which must be achieved through small steps. Rather than presuming to begin one's love life with a woman—what the old man (and McCullers) calls "the most dangerous and sacred experience in God's earth"—we should instead begin in very small ways, loving tiny inanimate objects first: a tree, a rock, a cloud. Only when we can relate to the minimal can we hope to possess the maximal.

That the old man's experience of losing his wife has stunted him emotionally is undeniable. His science of love can be taken as mere justification of his remaining womanless. Like Coleridge's ancient mariner, he is forever having to unburden himself upon strangers. But there is something more to be said for his love-science. That McCullers sides with him is made clear by the actions she attributes to Leo, the café owner. Leo not only treats his regular customers stingily, but also does not love himself enough to nourish his body adequately. He grudges himself a bun. But then, in McCullers's love affairs, everyone seems to be grudging their buns.

The twelve-year-old paperboy listener, drinking his coffee in a café of adults drinking their beer, is another McCullers alien. He is as out of his element in the café as Ferris is in Paris. The paperboy is further endowed with a physical difference. One shoulder is lower than the other, from the weight of the paper sack. This qualifies him as a freak in a café which prefigures Miss Amelia's place, in the *Ballad,* as a place of fellowship and understanding.

Mr. Mahoney's inability to adjust, in "Art and Mr. Mahoney," is less dramatic. He is a man of great cultural pretensions and little education to back them up. Inadvertently he reveals his ignorance by clapping at the wrong time in a piano concert. "I should think that anybody with a grain of sense knows enough not to clap until everybody else is clapping," his wife hisses, forgetting, of course, that if this were so, there would never be any applause. Ultimately Mr. Mahoney must face the realization that he belongs more to the town's coarser elements than to the refined. The sound of his applause in the silent auditorium symbolizes his interior isolation. His little embarrassment, however, can in no way be compared to the illuminations experienced by the *wunderkind* and Ferris and the haunted boy, and "Art and Mr. Mahoney" remains a trivial story.

A more traumatic dissociation takes the form of writer's block in "Who Has Seen the Wind?" and pathological lying in "Madame Zilensky and the King of Finland." "Who Has Seen the Wind?" is the rather melodramatic tale of Ken, a writer who is blocked after two books. His inability to communicate is driving him mad. His is a much more severe case of the blues experienced by Henrietta Evans in "Correspondence." In the story's best moment Ken experiences, in the act of trying to talk out the plot of his third unwritten novel to a friend at a party, an extreme case of *déjà vu:* seven or eight years before, he had told the same friend the same plot at the same kind of party. Just as no one has "seen" the wind, creative inspiration goes and comes, is ungraspable. Ken's unreturned correspondence with the muse is another example of McCullers's use of the writer's art as the means by which an individual rebels against isolation and silence.

The tale of "Madame Zilensky" is a superb one of a woman so dedicated to music that she is alien to the rest of the world, consequently compensating through lies—living vicariously the experiences she never had time to experience. The action of the story revolves about her forced confrontation with the truth, an encounter in which she manages to gain the upper hand and preserve her precious illusions. Madame Zilensky's need for illusions in order to exist is greater than her unmasker's need for truth. Indeed, he feels he will have killed her if he continues to confront her.

In a curious final paragraph, McCullers makes a comment on the nature of what passes for "reality." When the Madame's accuser thinks he sees a dog running backward in the street, we perceive that reality is events refracted through the human brain, and each person's reality is relative to his own mental state at the time.

In "The Aliens," which is a sketch rather than a story, we are given speculations on the nature of grief from the mouth of a wandering Jew. There once was a time, I hear, when many provincial people thought a Jew was a freak, with horns and a tail. McCullers's Jew has neither horns nor tail, and can in no way qualify as a freak. She uses his Jewishness to emphasize his displacement. He is an alien on the bus of life, as it were—rootless and totally other.

This brings us through eighteen of McCullers's nineteen short stories, and if one discounts a paperboy with a lowered shoulder, we have yet to encounter a freak, in the physical sense. That would disappoint many of McCullers's critics, who seem to think she wrote of nothing else. But with the nineteenth story (nineteenth only in my survey, not in the order of their writing), we do find a freakish fellow. He is the title character in "The Jockey." With his diminutive physical stature and his life of mandatory dietary deprivation, he is a man-child in the world of men. A freak.

But more than size and diet separates this jockey from his peers. He is morally outraged by the behavior of the trainer, the bookie, and the rich man who populate the story. Their insensitivity is typified by the grossness of their appetites. When the jockey takes a mouthful of their french fries and spits it out, he symbolically rejects their values.

In contrast to the physical and material values of these men, McCullers posits a symbol of the soul—green-white August moths which flutter about the clear candle flames. The soulful jockey and the moths are one. The image is a good one, because in this gallery of wanderers and aliens, failures and outcasts in a world in which all traditional values are, if not reversed, unrecognizable, all are seeking but one thing—the freedom of the moth, the unification of the spirit with the environment, the soul with the body of this earth. In these nineteen short stories, with only one certified freak among them, Carson McCullers depicts this quest with less sensationalism than in the novels, and often with true distinction.

Two Planetary Systems

Robert Aldridge*

In an unfortunate metaphor in *The New Yorker,* August 3, 1968, Penelope Gilliatt described the film of *The Heart Is a Lonely Hunter* as a hippopotamus which had swallowed a tiny, shining minnow, Carson McCullers's prized 1940 novel. The minnow is obviously the hero of the metaphor; the hippo is the villain. But the conception is inaccurate about who is ingesting whom. The book contains a far wider and more complex range of theme, plot, and characterization, as well as McCullers's undeniable genius. The motion picture is more modest in range and is devoid of even claim to genius, except perhaps the acting of Alan Arkin. If either has been swallowed up, it is surely this nearly forgotten 1968 film. Yet, as shall be discussed, the movie of *The Heart Is a Lonely Hunter* deserves respect—as a quiet, principled complement to McCullers's vision rather than as the animalist antagonist of Gilliatt's tortured formulation.

Originally called *The Mute,* the novel *The Heart Is a Lonely Hunter* appeared in 1940 to almost universal applause. The critics agreed that here was a sizable talent and that McCullers's insights into human suffering were far beyond her twenty-three years. Klaus Mann (son of Thomas Mann) referred to the book as "the melancholy by that strange girl, Carson McCullers. . . . An abysmal sadness yet remarkably devoid of sentimentality. Rather grim and concise. What astounding insight into the ultimate inconsolability and incurability of the human soul." He described Carson McCullers herself as "uncannily versed in the secret of all freaks and pariahs. . . ."[1]

McCullers's book places a series of interrelated stories within the frame tale of deaf-mute John Singer's intense devotion to another deaf-mute, Spiros Antonapolous, who has the mind and temperament of a child. Spiros must be committed to an institution, where eventually he dies. Deprived of his reason for living, Singer commits suicide. Within this frame are the lives of four major characters touched by Singer: Mick Kelly, a lonely adolescent girl; Biff Brannon, a cafe owner who is widowed early in the novel; Jake Blount, a roving revolutionary outraged over the oppression of laborers by capitalist

*Reprinted from *The Modern American Novel and the Movies,* ed. Gerald Peary and Roger Shatzkin (Ungar, 1978), 119-30, by permission of the author.

bosses; and Dr. Copeland, a black physician who has struggled bitterly throughout his career to inspire other blacks to rise from their oppression.

The essential tension between the outer and inner stories is that Singer actually has found meaning in his life (Antonapolous) before losing it: the others seek endlessly for the resolution of sweeping social conflicts (Jake and Dr. Copeland) or for self-fulfillment and identity (Mick and Biff). But because they never learn of the Singer-Antanapolous relationship—it is a tale without words—the message of Singer's suicide remains a puzzle to them. Even though Biff Brannon realizes in a flash of revelation that "love" is the hope of man, none of the characters has grasped the secret lesson of the deaf-mute who passed through their lives.

The 1968 filmmakers faced an ominous task in making *The Heart Is a Lonely Hunter*. Screenwriter Thomas C. Ryan, producers Marc Nelson and Joel Freeman, and director Robert Ellis Miller had to consider the twenty-eight year difference in milieu, the large cast of characters (there are at least thirteen developed personages in the novel, in addition to a sizable supporting cast), and McCullers's multitude of orbital themes surrounding her central one (to be discussed later). The result was perhaps the best it could be—a more tightly focused story which omits most of the 1930s topicality (except for the race issue) but which retains much of the lyricism and, most important, the central theme of the book: that individual human communication based upon love and compassion is the most powerful of weapons.

Characterization: The young girl Mick is the dominant character in both novel and film. She grows and changes as a character in both, pushing toward maturation and adulthood, and there are unmistakable parallels between her and her creator Carson McCullers (for example, the love of music and the sensitive and yearning nature). But it is John Singer who provides a center of gravity for the orbiting characters in their various quests. He provides the key to the relationship between characters and plot, though in the novel he occupies less narrative space than Mick.

The Singer of the novel is both close to and removed from the other characters. He cares for Mick, Jake, Biff, and Dr. Copeland as people, and he can feel their deep unhappiness. But he cannot understand the full meaning of their lonely quests. In his letter to Antonapolous (who, of course, cannot read), he describes the others: about Jake he says, "The one with the mustache I think is crazy. . . . He thinks he and I have a secret together but I do not know what it is"; about Dr. Copeland he says, "This black man frightens me sometimes. His eyes are hot and bright. . . . He has many books"; about Mick he says, "She is not yet a young lady. . . . She likes music. I wish I knew what it is she hears"; and about Biff, "He watches. . . . Aha, says the owner of the New York Cafe. He is a thoughtful one." (This last statement is prophetic, for after Singer's death, it is Biff who senses the significance of the Singer-Antonapolous relationship without really knowing that it even existed.)

By contrast, the Singer of the film—played by Alan Arkin—has a more personal relationship to the major characters who revolve about him. He shares their loneliness. He is, as in the novel, a listener; but he is also more than that, he is a friend to each: Mick, Dr. Copeland, Jake. And Mick and Dr. Copeland, at least, know more about him than they do in the novel. They realize his isolation (Mick especially) and they offer mutual comfort.

The relationships that Singer has established provide, by their rapport, for the best scenes of the film, all without parallel moments in the novel. Perhaps the finest sequence in the picture occurs when Mick suddenly realizes that Singer is as lonely as she is. She attempts to share her love of music with him by standing before the phonograph and conducting. She talks to Mr. Singer with her hands, instead of her lips; and though he does not grasp the rhythms of music, he understands her physical expressions of compassion. Another excellent scene is the one in which Dr. Copeland shows Singer the x-ray which conveys to Dr. Copeland news of his own impending death; but it is not because of his x-ray or his words, but because of his poignant facial expressions and physical gestures that Singer understands that the doctor will die.

Other characters are missing from the film. The black characters orbiting Dr. Copeland have been homogenized into a nearly silent mass—all save Portia, his daughter, and Willie, Portia's simple-minded, accepting, gentle husband. The pharmacist Marshall Nicolls (soft-spoken, polite acquaintance of Copeland, neither revolutionary nor Uncle Tom) is gone; perhaps he would have done little for the film, which is, at 124 minutes, a rather long one. But more important, the tragically fated Lancy Davis has been removed. His militancy and bitterness lifted him above the other blacks of the novel, and his meaningless, untimely death added the hardest strokes of pathos. Of all absent characters, he is perhaps the most sorely missed in the film. Unless, that is, one considers Biff Brannon, reduced here to a background role, a "missing character."

Even before the death of his wife Alice in the novel (she is missing from the film), Biff is perhaps the most desolate character of all. His unrequited love for Mick and his sad realization that she has changed and moved away from him are among the most heartfelt elements in the novel. Biff's almost androgynous personality—in contrast to his rough appearance he enjoys pretty things and domestic duties—establishes a parallel with the tomboy Mick, but one that is never carried through in personal terms. But in the film a character named Biff Brannon appears merely as the owner of the New York Cafe (without Alice, his sister-in-law Lucille, and his niece Baby Wilson, all from the novel) and as a "freak fancier" who is kind to Singer. But in a sense Biff's identity is not missing from the movie: he is merged with his soulmate Mick. She alone carries the burden of the quest for fulfillment and meaning in the film version. And it is Mick who articulates the theme, although she may not know it, when she utters her epilogue over the grave of Singer.

There are three other important characters who are changed significantly in the film: Dr. Copeland, Portia, and Jake Blount. Benedict Mady Copeland and Jake Blount are restless, bitter, probably doomed characters in the novel. Dr. Copeland, hopelessly tubercular, drives himself relentlessly, despite illness, in his effort to pull the Negroes up out of despair and degradation. Jake cannot avoid violence in his frustrated struggle against capitalist exploitation—he is both outwardly and inwardly destructive. Both remain pitiably isolated in the novel. Because of their single-mindedness and strident zeal, neither can communicate with the other, and neither sees his dreams come to fruition: Dr. Copeland is moved to the country by his own family, probably to die. And Jake, as has apparently been his life pattern, vanishes from the scene, violence on his heels, heading perhaps toward more violence.

In the film, Dr. Copeland's fate is rather definite: he knows he will die soon, and he has time to prepare. He also has the friendship and sympathy of Singer; and through Singer's friendship, this proud black man—tempestuous and driven like Lear and culturally alienated like Shylock—is reunited with his daughter, whom he named Portia. This, it would seem, makes for a much more optimistic ending: some frustrated dreams, yes, and a too early death; but also reconciliation and peace.

Jake is much less realized as a film character. As in McCullers's novel, he is a secretive, bitter, violent man, although we learn less of his past and of the nature of his quest. He vanishes quite early in the film (not until the end of the novel), having provided a touch of humor, some insight into Singer, and a look at the brutal nature of racism, but never seeming to merge with the core idea of the film. He is almost, as he quotes the judge, "irrelevant and immaterial."

And then, Portia. It is tempting to say that the character was changed to suit the talents of Cicely Tyson: it is difficult to imagine Tyson as the religious, stoically accepting Portia of the novel, who says after Willie's mutilation, "Nothing us could do would make no difference. Best thing we can do is keep our mouth shut." And after Mick says she wishes she could kill the men who did it: "that ain't no Christian way to talk. . . . Us can just rest back and know they going to be chopped up with pitchforks and fried everlasting by Satan." Obviously, the Portia of the film is quite different: bitter, strong-minded, capable of intense love and loyalty and also of hatred. The harsh scenes in which she relates Willie's mutilation and in which she promises her father that she will learn to despise him are particularly illustrative of her changed, outspoken screen character. Willie merges the Willie (her brother) and the Highboy (her husband) of the book; but the effect is the same simple, uneducated innocence, working against the worldly, knowledgeable Portias of both versions.

Plot Structure: The important question becomes: what is the major difference in the overall plot structures? In McCullers's novel, the central, solar figure of Singer is orbited by two pairs of planets: each pair is bound in trajectory by parallel characterization; first, there are the two inner planets Mick and Biff, inner because they are representative of the lonely quest for beauty and meaning and therefore closest to the emotional nature of Singer (whose only drive in life is to love); and second, there are the outer planets, Jake and Dr. Copeland, outer because their quest is for social justice, in terms of masses of people and generalized ideologies. Neither pair is successful in altering their paths to achieve the goal, or one might say grail, of their quest. Yet each pair senses some central core of meaning radiating from Singer, something *beyond* the quest—akin to it perhaps, but overwhelmingly simple and more beautiful.

In the film we find another planetary system—Singer again as sun; but instead of paired planets in each orbit, we now have individual planets revolving about him: Mick, Dr. Copeland, Jake. It is not simply the overwhelming performance of Alan Arkin which lends this great importance to the character of Singer (an idea suggested by numerous critics); it is the plot structure itself which makes the character so pivotal.

In Mick he arouses sympathy and a deepened understanding of the suffering of others (again—the scene with the phonograph). In Jake he fosters a sense of confidence and sensitivity to those directly around him (at least a need to notice his own irrelevance). And he lightens the bitterness of Dr. Copeland and brings him together with Portia.

In both versions the episodes are tightly bound together: in the novel by the parallel characterizations and by characters who link more than one line of action (such as Portia, Biff, and Mick, whose lives touch on several quests), and in the film—in addition to the powerful gravital force of Singer—by meaningful joining of episodes through transitional devices, primarily strategic uses of the dissolve to link the various personages. Two examples: (1) the dissolve from the scene of Mick conducting the record for Singer to a deaf-mute black boy on the porch, with Singer acting as sign-language interpreter (hence, the connection made by linking two scenes of nonverbal communication), and (2) the dissolve from the stunning brightness of the blank x-ray screen in Copeland's office to the hot summer sky above the creek bank where Mick has her first sexual encounter (two scenes depicting the transition from illusion to reality).

Milieu: The novel bristles with the major issues of the late Depression in the United States and the growing possibility of war in Europe. Poverty, bigotry, Marxism, anti-Semitism, Fascism—these were the issues when the book appeared, and should they be less significant twenty-eight years later in 1968? Of these themes, racial bigotry *was* considered by the filmmakers to be of paramount importance, hence Dr. Copeland remains a key ideological figure in the film, just as he had been in the novel. The year 1968 was marked by the assassination of Dr. Martin Luther King, and some of this movie was filmed in the town he made famous, Selma, Alabama.

But the other topics were considered passé or irrelevant by Hollywood in 1968, at least when compared with the urgency with which Carson

McCullers had treated them. So Harry Minowitz becomes, in the screen version, a handsome Southern white, instead of the restless Southern Jew of the novel who is eager to be off to the new war and kill Hitler. His chief function in the film is to introduce Mick to the world of dating and then, with almost contradictory innocence, to that favorite topic of fiction and film: the first sexual experience.

Labor reform, too, had no real place in this 1968 film. It was *the* central injustice of Jake Blount's world view in the book; Jake's near-religious zeal for a revolution among the proletariat could not radiate as much power in a film made during the period of the greatest prosperity workers in America had (or have) ever enjoyed. His words from the novel would connote something very different in 1968: "The only solution is for the people to *know*," he tells Dr. Copeland. "Once they know the truth they can be oppressed no longer." He means one kind of truth, obviously, in 1940; but there would be a different kind of truth in the era of George Meany, James Hoffa, Lyndon Johnson, and the Great Society.

And what about the South? Jake Blount's "strangled . . . wasted . . . slavish South" of the late Depression, the South that Carson McCullers knew firsthand, has become in the film a scenic background, a shallow movie set. Southern accents are amusing, and the stereotypes predictable, timid, and unserious. Even the cynical, insensate sheriff of the novel has lost any pretense to other than verbal cruelty in the film. (Dr. Copeland is beaten and jailed in the novel when he insists upon seeing the judge. In the film he is only ridiculed and tricked.) Of race prejudice there remains the racially motivated mutilation of Willie, though reduced from the loss of both feet to the loss of one leg. Through the vehicle of Cicely Tyson's compelling portrayal of Portia, in which she exhibits a rare gift for combining a steely dignity with bitter indignation, all the dread and repulsion of this act of unspeakable brutality are preserved intact from the novel. This is "reported violence" of the finest kind, reminiscent of speeches of harrowing off-stage deaths in Greek tragedy. The bigotry, then, is the only truly Southern theme in the film; and so Dr. Copeland and Portia and Willie and the sheriff are the only truly Southern characters. Except for those funny accents and passing stereotypes, the other characters are universals: a change in speech patterns could place them in Iowa, Colorado, California, or New England.

And what of the anti-Semitism and Fascism? Neither had vanished from the land or the world in 1968, but the treatment of both in the novel had been so closely tied to Hitler, Mussolini, and the war that reintegration in the film would have been clumsy and inappropriate. The same is true of repeating the deeply felt anti-Fascist sentiment of the 1940 novel.

Poverty was one key issue in the milieu of the novel which was transferred almost *per se* to the film, but the transition is a shaky one. Mick does not seem to be the daughter in a desperately poor family. For one thing, in McCullers's book there are other boarders in the house and their presence is mandatory for the survival of the Kelly family. And there is the Baby Wilson episode—when Mick's brother Bubber has shot Baby in the head with his pellet gun and the family must deplete whatever small financial security they have to pay the medical costs. There is also the general novelistic framework of the Depression, which lends instant credibility to financial deprivation. But the Kelly family in the film enjoys sway over their rather spacious domain (a house which most Americans of 1968 might welcome for personal living space). In addition, Mick's position in the society of the little town is misleading—she mingles with the elite as though there were no other difference than a little money. In short, it seems unconvincing that Mick must drop out of school to help the family to continue on.

The book's Marxist motif (which originates with Dr. Copeland and his attempts to educate the poor blacks about Marx's ideas) predictably is missing from the film. There is no mention of the fact that Dr. Copeland has a child named Karl Marx, and the image of him as teacher is absent. So too is the marvelous Christmas scene from the novel and Dr. Copeland's Christmas lecture: "It is natural for us to share with each other. We have long realized that it is more blessed to give than to receive. The words of Karl Marx have always been known in our hearts: 'From each according to his ability, to each according to his needs.'" This speech in the film might have established one interesting and pungent parallel between two decades, a parallel to Dr. King's social concerns perhaps; but Dr. King's message was democratic reform, not Marxist class warfare. And to change Dr. Copeland to suit the parallel would have required bold liberties.

But what is the effect of all this rearrangement of topicality? The proposition here is that the filmmakers were, in the main, right in their decision to emphasize the race issue above all and to concentrate most heavily upon Mick's quest for beauty and meaning in a puzzling, lonely universe and Singer's silent answer to that quest—love.

Revelation of Theme: There is a sense of rushing at the end of both the novel and the film, with theme coalescing rapidly. In the novel all flies asunder at the suicide of Singer; the center of gravity is released with awesome suddenness and simplicity by McCullers (reminiscent of E. A. Robinson's "Richard Cory"): "Then when he had washed the ash tray and the glass he brought out a pistol from his pocket and put a bullet in his chest." In the film the rising tempo begins earlier, with the departure of Jake Blount, and continues through Dr. Copeland's revelation to Portia of his approaching death, the financial collapse of Mick's family, her loss of innocence, the death of Antonapolous, and the suicide of Singer, which is portrayed with much the same suddenness and deliberateness as in the novel.

Both use epilogues to drive home their points: in the book McCullers carries us through the full course of a single day a month after Singer's funeral (in August, 1939—significantly, the month before Hitler's invasion of Poland and the beginning of World War II). In a section called "Morning," we see the departure of Dr. Copeland for the country and for eventual death. In "After-noon," we witness the flight of Jake Blount from the violence which has cost the life of Lancy Davis. And in "Evening," we behold the terrible epiphany of Biff Brannon, alone in his New York Cafe, listening to the radio from which he hears only mystifying and ominous foreign voices:

> Then suddenly he felt a quickening in him. . . . For in a swift radiance of illu-mination he saw a glimpse of human struggle and of valor. Of the endless fluid passage of humanity through endless time. And of those who labor and of those who—one word—love. His soul expanded. But for a moment only. . . . For in him he felt a warning, a shaft of terror. And he was suspended between radiance and darkness. Between bitter irony and faith. Sharply he turned away.

The epilogue of the film takes place in the cemetery beside Singer's grave. Dr. Copeland (who is still practicing in the town) and Mick meet and ponder the mystery of Singer's death. Then Mick is left alone at the grave. She, too, is suspended between two worlds: she does not understand the enig-matic sadness of life as it has been revealed to her during the course of this one summer. But she seems to realize the secret power of Singer, the one word which Biff saw in his flash of revelation in the novel. And it is she now who articulates the central theme of both book and film when she says. "I loved you, Mr. Singer. I loved you."

The theme of love—individual love—is preserved, then, realized by Biff Brannon in the novel, Mick Kelly in the film. It is this singular love between people which can transcend the misery of living, which can supply meaning and purpose in the midst of the chaos of war, oppression, and violence. But even this love is transitory, and the misery is still there. For McCullers *and* her adaptors, the heart remains a lonely hunter.

Note

1.   Virginia Spencer Carr, *The Lonely Hunter: A Biography of Carson McCullers* (Garden City, N.Y., 1975), 100.

Carson McCullers's *The Ballad of the Sad Café:* A Song Half Sung, Misogyny, and "Ganging Up"

SUZANNE MORROW PAULSON*

1

Most commentators see the chain gang at the start and end of Carson McCullers's *The Ballad of the Sad Café* as representing harmony in human relationships.[1] A perverse frame for a love ballad, the chain gang is initially presented as a sort of entertainment and a means of countering small-town alienation. And for a short time, the prisoners' voices *do* come together, harmoniously uniting in song, even overcoming racial differences. The "twelve mortal men who are together" do not notice that "seven of them [are] black and five of them white boys" (72).[2] But most importantly, McCullers is saying, "the whole gang" (71) does *not* (the community does *not*) overcome gender differences.[3]

The prisoners' song is "half sung, and like an unanswered question" because half of the human community is ignored and, most obviously in the case of Amelia, denigrated. The "silence" (72) remaining after the chain gang stops singing is poignant. Indeed, the *Ballad* community silences women, in particular McCullers's protagonist Amelia. Woman's song is a solo heard only once in the tale: "Somewhere in the darkness a woman sang in a high wild voice and the tune had no start and no finish and was made up of only three notes which went on and on and on" (41). Of a masculine type, there is also the "one lonely voice" (71) that momentarily remains after the chain gang tires of singing. And after his return from prison, Marvin Macy (McCullers's antagonist) sings—his "voice . . . slimy," his "tunes [gliding] slowly from his throat like eels" (62). But Marvin sings no song of loneliness and alienation—

---

*This essay was written for this volume and is published here for the first time by permission of the author.

a touch that might have made his purported love for Amelia more believable. The majority of men in this tale are not lonely (the feminine man, Morris Finestein, an exception). It is rather women who are alienated—the protagonist Amelia who suffers loneliness. Marvin and Lymon, the pair who "went off *together*, the two of them" (69) and the men in the chain gang who are "together" (72—the last word of the novella) are a terrible contrast to the abandoned Amelia.

Ultimately, the androgynous Amelia does not express her femininity constructively because the community associates women with weakness, men with power and physical aggression. Amelia's suffering amounts to "The Rejection of the Feminine," as Panthea Reid Broughton rightly has it, but even more truly the *murder* of the feminine in a male-dominated community.[4]

McCullers's sad ballad depicts a heroic woman's struggle to contribute actively to a misogynist community, to control her own destiny, and to earn respect from the men who "gang up" to destroy her. We should consider the masculine and aggressive tenor of the word *gang,* which is repeated seven times in the coda, "The Twelve Mortal Men." McCullers might have termed the prisoners a "chorus" at least once in the saga, especially given her musical background, but instead she consistently relates "men" and "boys" to various "gangs."

This word, *gang,* is a "rayword," as Bakhtin puts it in another context— a rayword "shot through by shared thoughts."[5] McCullers's gangs effectively commit a gang bang; the author does not encourage her readers to admire the chain gang—the "boys" who are "chained at the ankles" (71).[6] Nor should the reader admire those who defeat Amelia and destroy the community *togetherness* inspired by Amelia's love for Lymon. Reader admiration for the chain gang in fact may be one of the reasons McCullers saw her novel as a failure. Virginia Spencer Carr's disparaging biography contributes to the confusion regarding lines of sympathy here—to the lack of sympathy for Amelia. Carr felt that her "biography substantiated much of what 'people' guessed through reading Carson's fiction," as the biographer put it during one of her many lectures on McCullers.[7]

Perhaps the fear of biography as gossip and literary criticism as sensationalized biography forced "Carson" to sing her feminist *ballad* pianissimo (not to mention the problem of taking a feminist stand in the conservative society of the author's upbringing). At any rate, this novel attacks what Eve Kosofsky Sedgwick calls "homosocial desire" in a society that admires and rewards aggressive, even violent, men.[8] Further, community admiration of male criminal loners, aggressive male collectives, and "homosocial" male pairs clarifies the decentered status of all women in the *Ballad* community, not just that of Amelia.

Even though they are criminals, those in the chain gang still breathe the outside air freely and are far less imprisoned than the defeated Amelia, who is banished to her "deserted" house, "boarded up completely" (3). She is "gender-locked" in the female body.[9] The chain gang represents a destructive force in an American society grounded in misogyny and the acceptance, indeed the celebration, of homosocial groups, masculine aggression, and criminality.[10]

2

The most crucial enquiry, then, is the question McCullers explicitly posits as the last sentence of her novel: "What kind of gang *is* this" (72, my italics) that walks the main street of Amelia's community and McCullers's fictional world?[11] Analyzing the powerful male collectives in this novel is essential to understanding Amelia's plight. In addition to "The Twelve Mortal Men," we should consider various other male citizens who act aggressively together and another mixed-gender group appearing at the start. When Lymon wanders into town, the manly Amelia, now an insider, functions as a member of the community welcoming committee of five porch-sitting people. Besides Amelia, this welcoming committee includes the "timid," "gentle," "nervous," and feminine Henry Macy, brother of the criminal Marvin Macy, and three manly men, Stumpy MacPhail and the Rainey twins. The latter strictly masculine contingent of three gangs up on Lymon, the "prissy" (9), when he "suddenly [begins] to cry" after "claiming kin with Miss Amelia" (7)—kinship determined by his maternal line—his mother being a half-sister of Amelia's mother.

At this point, the gentle Henry leaves because he expects the aggressive Amelia (rather than the three bullies) to devastate the hunchbacked intruder. Then the bullies viciously attack the newcomer for being "afflicted," like Morris Finestein, who "cried if you called him Christkiller" (9). The stereotype of the feminine and suffering Jew here prefigures Amelia's suffering. The feminine man is a positive figure in *The Ballad of the Sad Café,* the chain gang a negative figure. McCullers's *Ballad* indeed is a "satire" (237), "indicting not the Jew but the society" (238), as Carr's biography paraphrases McCullers's unpublished letter defending herself against an anonymous reader's charge of anti-Semitism. McCullers clearly indicts the male society that dominates both purportedly weak, feminine men and women; she associates "poor Morris Finestein" (44) with Henry: the feminine "good soul" (8) of the Jekyll/Hyde brother pair. And the author associates men like Marvin with evil spirits and racist communities, not only in the South but in Europe as well (Hitler's persecution of the Jews profoundly affected McCullers while she was writing this novel).

Amelia's tenuous membership in the first battery of porch-sitting men is clear when she invites Lymon into her home and heart as if to spite those who reject the crippled and helpless beseecher. Thus, she rebels against the misogynist community that ridicules weak and weepy men. The men in the community resent Amelia's actions and achievements because she is a female non-conformist who does not accept her place as an inferior. She tries but cannot be a member of the porch-sitting gang for long. It is the gang (in the first instance the three-member group) that is the primary target of McCullers's satire, not Amelia—even though the author pokes fun at her protagonist's masculine/aggressive tendencies.

More cohesive than the porchsitters, the next gang appears as a lynch mob, "the delegation" (16), "a sorry bunch of gabbies" (17). They are nameless at first mention and in uniform like the chain gang. The "eight men [who] looked very much alike—all wearing blue overalls" (18)—are convinced that Amelia murdered Lymon. They pursue the worst possible criminal, Amelia, who is dangerous not merely because she may be a murderer but also because she dresses like a man and eats like a farm hand.

Whereas the gangs attack Amelia, there is an admirable feminine man in this story who supports her. The narrator first reveals a feminine aspect to his character when he explains the gossip about Amelia's presumed crime and sides with certain anonymous citizens not misogynistically inclined. He points to the "few sensible men [gender specified] who reasoned that Miss Amelia . . . would not go out of her way to murder a vagabond [male gender implied]" (14). These men of course are cynical and misogynist; they are right for the wrong reasons. The narrator then most certainly identifies with the "three good people [gender unclear] . . . [who] felt toward her something near to pity" (14). McCullers's diction constantly calls attention to gender.[12]

The narrator rightly deems the rumor that Amelia killed Lymon a "sickly tale," praising for the second time "the three good people," a small minority indeed, who did not want to condemn Amelia as Lymon's murderer. These three counterparts to the first three bullies and the lynch mob "judged Amelia in a different way from others" (14) and clarify the narrator's gentle nature, however inconsistently it may be expressed. Some of the time, of course, he conforms to patriarchal judgments.

McCullers identifies the real danger here as not the criminal, Amelia, but rather as male collectives and the misogyny that causes "men [to] gather and wait in this way" (16). Expressing the authorial view, the outsider/narrator dreads the time when "all together [the decidedly male mob] will act in unison, not from thought or from the will of any one man, but as though their instincts had merged together so that the decision belongs to no single one of them, but to the group as a whole" (16). When "[a]ll at once, as though moved by one will, they walked into [Amelia's] store," they are an undifferentiated, mindless mass, whose individual names are belatedly mentioned only after the gossip that Amelia killed Lymon has been disproven (20).[13]

Before Amelia's decisive battle with Marvin, other male collectives appear briefly: "Three young boys . . . from Society City" who attend "cock fights" (64) prefigure the "crowd" of mill workers and "riffraff" (65) cheering for Marvin during the battle when Amelia is defeated. All of these male groups prefigure the happy couple, Marvin and Lymon, who finally stride off at sunrise *together,* abandoning the hapless woman.

The "fork" in the Fork Falls Road, then, bifurcates life's travelers according to gender. The men and women in Amelia's community are far from a cohesive group. The plotline develops Amelia's fall from masculine authority to feminine alienation, or as Sandra M. Gilbert and Susan Gubar put it, "from a woman warrior to a helpless madwoman" (111). Of course, the narrative center of this novel is the essential change of the protagonist, Amelia. Before her defeat, she seems comfortable functioning in masculine, authoritarian roles: community father, town doctor, lawyer dickering over money, heartless banker/bill collector, and even wizardly brewmeister. We may condemn certain masculine behaviors Amelia acquires in order to assert herself and not be relegated to an unempowered place in a community of men—that is, her aggressive spells (at the worst in brute battle), her materialistic sense of competition, and at times her heartless suppression of feelings (when collecting debts or refusing to treat women patients, to cite the two primary instances). Nonetheless, McCullers portrays Amelia, her energy, and her capacity for love in a positive light. The tragedy is that her energies are not allowed full expression in a misogynist community. Her industriousness and inventiveness exemplify the spirit of America at its best until her defeat, when "her voice had lost its old vigor" (70) because she no longer taps the masculine energy epitomized by the chain gang. This stereotype of male power is another factor misleading readers to designate the chain gang a positive symbol.[14]

That the community seems for a short time to tolerate Amelia's assumption of masculine roles may be explained by the desire to keep the deviant in the public eye. Sedgwick studies this phenomenon in the context of terrorist attacks on homosexuals in the nineteenth century.[15] There were no pogroms then but rather a guarded and vicious tolerance. Amelia is tolerated only as long as town gossip militates against her deviance. And again as Sedgwick points out, men in the public eye attain respect, whereas women in the public eye suffer defeat (consider Brett Ashley encircled by male dancers in Ernest Hemingway's *The Sun Also Rises* and the grandmother, Baby Suggs, in Toni Morrison's *Beloved*).

3

Although the perplexed and perplexing narrator reveals a feminine aspect when he defends Amelia from the charge of murder, much of the time he conforms to the dominant perspective of the working-class masculine majority. Then he behaves as an insider reiterating manly truisms. He sees no value in the weak and feminine hunchback's belongings when Lymon collapses before

Amelia's porch: "junk," he declares, "odd rubbish that looked like parts out of a sewing machine, or something just as worthless" (8). He thereby denigrates woman's work, mentioned elsewhere only once when "women forgot to bring in the washing" (14).

Yet is it appropriate that cotton mill workers should deem sewing machine parts worthless? Amelia values her own "two Singer sewing machines in the parlor" (35) and chooses "a sewing machine in payment for a debt" (15). The narrator's attitude regarding woman's work reflects the community's masculine bias. He in fact outrageously vacillates between masculine and feminine perspectives, between the unreliable "gang" viewpoint and the reliable viewpoint revealing the author's insights regarding aggressive men and "ganging up."[16] Not that McCullers is a manhater. She sees everyone as subject to suffering, even the lynch mob; she notes that "all [of them have] wept and suffered" (20), a motif that echoes throughout the canon. Most particularly, McCullers focuses on suffering from mindless acceptance of gender codes that destroy the individual's more tender instincts and divide the community.

How *can* the reader distinguish between moments in the narration meant to ridicule the mindless romanticizing of aggressive behavior and moments when the narrator speaks for McCullers, the woman writer affirming the virtues of her androgynous heroine? This is a difficult problem that may not be easily and completely solved. We can say, nevertheless, that usually the narrator's flatly stated judgments represent the authorial view: Marvin Macy's brother Henry is consistently a "good soul" (8), who even seems maternal when he helps Amelia attend to the child suffering from a boil (39–40). Merlie Ryan, the idiot gossipmonger, is always represented as "not much account" (13). An uncomplicated monotone dominates the narrative voice when Marvin is declared "a terrible character who . . . caused ruin" (4) vaguely defined (Amelia's ruin, of course, the point). These passages refrain from hyperbole, irony, understatement, melodrama, sentimentality, and juxtaposition of contrary elements.

On the other hand, when a certain inflated diction, a heavy-handed ironic tone, and rhetorical flourish ("Nor did he want her because of her money . . .," 28) intrude, then the narrator simplistically parrots community truisms meant to sound silly: Amelia's marriage to Marvin Macy was "strange and dangerous" (4); her "sins . . . amounted to such a point that they can hardly be remembered all at once" (14); Marvin "reformed himself *completely*" (29, my italics) because wounded by Cupid's dart; all Marvin "had ever done was to make [Amelia] richer and to bring her love" (33). Moreover, an incongruous sequence of elements subtly pointing to the racist tendencies of the *Ballad* community undermines the credibility of this latter declaration of Marvin's complete innocence. More particularly, Marvin's purported innocence is overshadowed by the mention of his "Klansman's robe" (33). The community admonishes Amelia for cutting up poor Marvin's "Klansman's robe to cover her tobacco plants" (33), but Marvin is forgiven for belonging to the Klan.[17]

We should recognize the sardonic edge when the narrator relates the community view of Marvin Macy and tallies the reasons Amelia agrees to marry the brute (not least "to get herself some wedding presents," 30). We should not believe the narrator when he reports that "Marvin Macy chose Miss Amelia . . . solely out of love" (28). Shortly after this judgment is so emphatically presented, the narrator claims that "this is not a town to let white orphans perish in the road before your eyes" (28). Notice the sequencing and the understated racism. The sequence of ideas in this tale is critical because so many passages "weatherize," as Bakhtin puts it, one another. Marvin's declarations of love are radically undermined by his racism just as community truisms are undermined by community racism.

The narrator, then, stands in the community shadow but only during brief ironic, hyperbolic, melodramatic, and sometimes ludicrously poetic flareups—perhaps related to the ballad form as Dawson P. Gaillard suggests, but that form is manipulated so as to achieve ironic and satiric effects.[18] The narrator carefully distances himself from "the men of the group" (20) and the community gossip of "[s]ome" (30). For the most part, he reports that "the town was gratified" that Amelia married Marvin; the talespinner himself is never gratified when Amelia suffers.

In sum, the fact that the narrator is an ambiguous figure—conforming to patriarchal views at times and at other times demonstrating feminine compassion—implies how difficult it is for anyone to overcome conditioning determined by gender. This sort of destiny/fate best explains why "the characters often seem helplessly impelled toward a certain course of events," as Albert J. Griffith points out.[19]

When the narrator declares that the community was "wrong" (31) to think that the masculine woman would change, the reader should sense that this is a ludicrous statement considering how much Marvin and the community need to change. Should we really pity the groom because, as the narrator points out, "for three days \[Marvin] suffered" (32)? The brief duration of Marvin's "suffering" deserves a smirk. Amelia waits three years for Lymon to return after he abandons her. Marvin waits until the fourth day after Amelia's refusal and then decides that his strategies to buy her love have failed, despite the fact that "he signed over to her the whole of his worldly goods" in order to achieve sexual dominance. Then he downs "a quart bottle of whisky," approaches Amelia, and receives nothing except one blow "with her fist" (32). All of his approaches—including threatening her with his rifle and forcing his way into her house—appear to have taken less than a week before the "completely" (29) reformed Marvin, incensed and determined to seek revenge, leaves town. Lymon initially says he is "hunting Amelia" (7). Marvin's true character is also that of a predator. This is evident when "horrifying rumors"

(33) declare him "a criminal"—Marvin having committed robberies and murders and finally been imprisoned in the penitentiary.[20]

Subtly, McCullers warns against the greatest danger of all: the danger of losing one's individuality to the aggressive male collective that sees criminality as heroic and racism as acceptable. Marvin represents the brute masculine force of a misogynist and racist community, a brute force that is perpetuated by permissive and sentimental attitudes toward wayward white men. According to Carr, McCullers insisted that "no one hated prejudice and cruelty any more than she did" (*Lonely Hunter,* 237).[21]

Like blacks in the Southern community, Amelia is victimized by white males. She is *womanized* and *feminized;* more than once she nearly adopts a negative female role (subservient wife and fallen woman) but then rejects it. Later when threatened with the loss of her beloved, she again nearly conforms to stereotypes of weak femininity. She miscalculates the best strategy for overcoming Lymon's infatuation with Marvin when she relinquishes her overalls (the town uniform) and instead starts to wear "always the red dress" (53), a symbol of feminine weakness and sexual waywardness. This strategy of course is doomed to failure. Feminine weakness is exactly what the hunchback wishes to escape by associating himself with Marvin.

Feminine weakness, moreover, is what Amelia and everyone else in the tale subconsciously dreads. The hunchback transcends weakness when he progresses from being a Morris Finestein to becoming a "great mischief maker" (39; a good bad boy), a town gossip who "knew the intimate business of everybody" (40), and then the master of the house "goose-stepping about the café" (43). Amelia loses Lymon because he notices her female vulnerabilities and begins to identify with Marvin's masculine power. Similarly, Amelia had usurped power when she adopted her father's behaviors. Developing masculine characteristics allows both men and women to tap community powerlines more or less—men more, women less and tenuously.

Everyone wants to be the father and to belong to the gang (even, in this community, the Klan). Amelia wants to assume the identity of a tomboy without ridicule.[22] And everyone—whether man or woman—at some time suffers irrational repressed fears of the seemingly (to the infant) all-powerful mother.[23] In addition, the woman fears becoming the weaker sex victimized by the more powerful man.

In American society, the criminal is one of the most powerful and attractive figures: Butch Cassidy or the Sundance Kid might head a very long list. The heroics of aggressive men facing danger seem to be admired even if the hero himself is dangerous and evil. Marvin's *boyhood* crimes of murder ("For years, when he was a boy, he had carried about with him the dried and salted ear of a man he killed in a razor fight," 27) and his more mature crimes of abusing women are acknowledged only briefly in the short-term collective memory.

4

Narration of the storyline, then, differs considerably in tone from the mini-sermons and philosophical digressions strategically placed to undermine Marvin's character and to highlight Amelia's capacity for love, however misdirected. Since Amelia herself cannot be praised given the community's misogyny, the narrator instead muses over the virtues of Amelia's whisky. Then the treatise on the café (a place of communion more holy than a church) indirectly affirms Amelia's worth (23). Finally, the narrator's brief treatise on love helps the reader to understand the virtues of what Amelia feels for Lymon. Of course, this treatise follows the lines of Lysias's disparagement of love in Plato's *Phaedrus* but should be considered in the context of McCullers's *Ballad* and the ironies developed there.

The treatise on the café's success is the most important testimony to the virtues of love and the most important of the narrator's various philosophical asides. The narrator puzzles over who or what should be credited with the feat of revitalizing the community. First, the narrator mentions Marvin as playing "a part in the story of this café" (4), but then he credits Lymon with being "the person most responsible for the success and gaiety" of the café (4). Next he affirms that Amelia's whisky worked as a catalyst contributing to the café's success—her powerful brew revealing "that which is known only in the soul": "without [the whisky] there would never have been a café" (10). Finally, Amelia is directly credited several times with being "the cause" (23) of the wonderful "gathering[s]" (22) occasioned by what becomes not only a community hearth, but a kind of holy sanctuary.

The narrator assumes a preacherly voice when proclaiming that the café offers "fellowship" amounting to salvation because there folks discover "a certain gaiety and *grace* of behavior" (23, my italics). Those in the community do not need a hell-and-damnation sermon to achieve grace. The café feeds both body and soul, not to mention overcoming "the dull sameness in their lives, a sameness manifest in their collective lifestyle" (22).

The café in fact nearly overturns the dominant masculine collective lifestyle. "Fellowship" is at its peak when "[s]everal women" join the community even though they only half-heartedly imbibe "a swallow of [Amelia's] whisky" (22). During the time when the café thrives and community life is most harmonious, Amelia invites everyone into her store-turned-café with no thought of financial gain, a very unmasculine gesture. It is the feminine moralist/narrator who declares that the "proper café" reforms "[e]ven the richest, greediest old *rascal*" (22–23, my italics), a masculine designation. After digressions on Amelia's whiskey, the café, and love, after the history of Marvin's appearance and disappearance, during the most endearing moments of Amelia's and Lymon's romance, the hunchback is credited a second time with being the one "most responsible for the great popularity of the café"

(40). This is a circular treatment of how the café developed—starting and ending with Lymon—but the true source of community love is Amelia.

The tonal difference between the narrator's voice as he tells the story or mirrors the community will and his more gentle, preacherly voice praising Amelia's whisky and the café is important because it reveals McCullers's profound sympathy for her protagonist, a woman who suffers from love, a woman who unfortunately feels "shame" at her own womanhood (17), a woman sadly modeling herself in accordance with the aggressive and materialistic values of her masculine community, and a heroic figure undone by the "evil" (27) Marvin Macy, not to mention various insensitive collectives of misogynist men. Amelia is finally dethroned when Lymon and Marvin pair up against her not in the style of a "fly on the chariot wheel" (59) but as masters of nature leaving a wake of destruction. They seize the acorn symbolizing her father's procreative power. They seize the kidney stones symbolizing the excremental self Amelia associates with female weakness and the body;[24] she feels "fascination, *dubious respect,* and fear" (35, my italics) for these inert objects. Lymon and Marvin prevent Amelia from attaining both the power of the father and the procreative power of the mother.

Before the wrestling match between Amelia and Marvin Macy, we observe the three main players reacting to an unusual display of nature—snowfall. Amelia ignores the physical world here just as she ignored patients with female complaints. She cannot control the cycles of nature suffered by women. Her refusal to heal female ailments is her denial of her own gender, her own vulnerability to natural cycles. Marvin, on the other hand, masters nature (he "laid claim to the snowfall," 58), and Lymon basks "in the glory of Marvin Macy" (59). Nature indeed seems to fix the decisive match. Lymon comes aggressively to Marvin's defense, and the weaker sex is defeated.

Recourse to Sedgwick's analysis of homosocial bonds and love triangles is again useful here.[25] She cites René Girard's observation that "between the two active members of an erotic triangle . . . the bond that links the two rivals is as intense and potent as the bond that links either of the rivals to the beloved: that the bonds of 'rivalry' and 'love' . . . are equally powerful and in many senses equivalent" (20). Of course, Sedgwick analyzes Girard's concept of triangles "within the male-centered novelistic tradition of European high culture" and the usual case of "two males [who] are rivals for a female" (22). Nevertheless, her study is relevant because McCullers's *Ballad* depicts a society in which "it is the bond between the males that [is] most assiduously [uncovered]," as Sedgwick puts it (again in another context).

During the "Battle Royal" Amelia, then, stands in the place of the aggressive male and Lymon in the place of the feminine beloved, but the bond between the two men—the hawklike Lymon that strikes the blows defeating Amelia and the cruel Marvin—should be considered as the last example of male homosocial relationships assaulting the female would-be usurper of white masculine power.

5

So what was lost? We should notice the placement of the narrator's treatise on love as it follows the introduction to the Amelia/Lymon courtship and forms a transition to Marvin's pursuit of Amelia. The positive potential of love emerges in the first romance, the negative in the second disastrous courtship. That McCullers introduces Amelia and Lymon's relationship *before* focusing on Marvin's purported love for Amelia is a strange inversion of temporal sequence encouraging the reader to measure the short failed marriage of Marvin and Amelia against the Amelia/Lymon success, also short lived but encompassing years, not merely days.

At first, the Amelia/Lymon relationship truly does testify to the power of love, which staves off death and revitalizes the community. The Platonic aspect of this heterosexual love is crucial, but the physical aspects of love should not be ignored. Suspicious and strange as it seems to be, the narrator declares that "the good people" and "[a]ll sensible people" (25–26) approved of physical love in the case of Amelia and Lymon—affirmed the divine potential of this love as well. That the seemingly mismatched lovers "found some satisfaction of the flesh . . . was a matter concerning them and God alone" (26).[26] McCullers means to dramatize the value of Amelia's love for Lymon, which enlarges the whole community's capacity for love and acceptance of others regardless of financial status, race, or gender.[27]

And Amelia herself turns generous because of her love for Lymon. She is revitalized; she feels a creative surge of energy, even writing a story (45).[28] Love allows both the lover (Amelia) and the beloved (Lymon) to escape the "dangerous inward world" associated with the chain gang, the prisoners who work "at a certain dangerous place" (71). Amelia's good whisky (mostly men drink it) protects the townspeople from dreaming "themselves into a dangerous inward world" (71).

Both whisky and love are medicinal in this novel. Amelia's gift for healing is enhanced by her love for Lymon. Although his physical condition does not improve, it does not worsen, and his mental health radically improves. Amelia's patient responds as if for a time she cures him of his cold nature (37). She sets the example by sharing her intimate life with him; the lovers "sit for hours together by the fireplace in the parlor" (25).[29] At first, Lymon suffers "a deep fear of death," but Amelia's love helps to alleviate these fears. That is, she considers not only physical but also psychological ailments such as the emptiness felt when alone and "looking into the dark," acknowledging the mortal side of the self. Acting as town psychiatrist, Amelia does not want him "to suffer with this fright" (25).

Appreciating Amelia's devotion to Lymon, the narrator declares most convincingly that "the growth of the café came about mainly on this account: it was a thing that brought [Lymon] company" (25). It is Amelia's unselfish, contagious, loving attentions to Lymon that foster love on a grand scale.

Amelia's capacity for Agape expands as well; she feels compassion as she contemplates universal blights such as cancer and racism, a social cancer. Amelia's love is valuable even though Lymon does not deserve her attentions.

The narrator's disparaging treatise on love contradicts what McCullers presents as the day-by-day experience of love in Amelia's case. This treatise—again like that of Lysias in Plato's *Phaedrus*—explains that the lover suffers a tremendous narcissistic need for control over the beloved. In Freudian terms, the narrator implies that Oedipal feelings intrude in all love relationships.[30] Just as Amelia acquired an apparent power by assuming masculine roles in her community, in her love life with Lymon she attains the power of "Big Papa" over "Little," the name her father used to call her. But rather than isolating and demeaning the beloved so as always to overpower and possess him (as Lysias predicts the lover will invariably do), Amelia mothers and empowers the effeminate man—actually does "liven [his] gizzard" (9). Indeed she renders him more powerful than herself.

Maintaining Lymon's dependence would have allowed her to control him. Instead, she encourages him to develop into a "chatterer" who struts (39) and finally joins forces with the more powerful Marvin Macy. The effeminate man learns to assert himself. McCullers invites a comparison with the German racist when she presents Lymon as "goose-stepping" (43). The point may be that all love in an aggressive, male-dominated and racist community is self-love wracked by an imbalance of power. Most certainly, we should not see the treatise on love as expressing McCullers's perspective. Indeed, Carr explains in the biography that when autographing a copy of *The Ballad* "on the page containing her famous thesis about love and the relationship between the lover and the beloved . . . she said that her thesis was unadulterated truth only when a person was *not* in love" (428).

The irony that develops because Amelia's behavior does not altogether conform to the narrator's depiction of the lover is very important. Rather than exclusiveness and alienation, the generous Amelia encourages Lymon's sense of community and acceptance of all. The lover as the narrator (and Lysias) paints him is cold, manipulative, and possessive. The lover as McCullers sees him or her suffers "pain, perplexity, and uncertain joy." More particularly, Amelia "swallowed often. Her skin had paled and her large empty hands were sweating" (23). It is the narrator who declares that "the lover is trying to strip bare his beloved" (27). The caregiving Amelia does not behave in this way as she nurtures Lymon and encourages him to assert himself.

Amelia chooses not to belittle "Little" but rather attacks her rival when her attentions and generosity to Lymon backfire. Marvin captures Lymon's affection. Amelia's return to a manly stance is prefigured when, "lifting her skirt" as women do, she forgets "altogether that there were men in the room," revealing "a piece of strong, hairy thigh" (60).

Not that McCullers's treatment of love is altogether positive. The author's ambivalence and cynicism emerge when Lymon does not appreciate

Amelia's attentions, and there is a self-serving undercurrent in Amelia's love for Lymon at times. "Love," the narrator says through his outsider/onlooker mask of the philosopher/moralist, is "a solitary thing," the lover "only a stimulus for all the stored-up love which has lain quiet within the lover for a long time" (26). Love that is not reciprocal is narcissistic and governed by Oedipal feeling. Not that the case is simple, however. The masculine woman to some extent was attracted to the feminine man because he represents a part of herself she represses and wants to control, that is, both her presumed freakishness and her feminine vulnerability. At the start, he is her anima within the animus she had constructed to gain status and power in a male-dominated world. They merge into "one great, twisted shadow of the two of them" (12). Yet is this not also an image of wholeness according to the Platonic model? Ideal love fails to develop because Lymon bleeds Amelia of masculine energy when he takes her checkbook, the key to her cabinet of curios, and handfuls of coins from the cash register.

McCullers's novel may not ultimately affirm the impossibility of love. More important is the depiction of female devotion and the male need to control. As long as one lover demands dominance in a misogynist community, love will fail. But in Amelia's case, McCullers presents an example of love that did revitalize the community, reinforce the pride of each individual, affirm acceptance of "difference," and encourage the community to measure self-worth using means other than money. The value of love is not questioned in McCullers's fictional world: It is "better to take in your mortal enemy than live alone" (60), as Amelia succinctly asserts in the midst of a hopeless situation.

6

The insanity of conforming to an ethical system that denigrates women while admiring materialistic and aggressive behavior in men is the primary issue in this novel. Understatement is a necessary technique for an author such as McCullers—a woman writing in the 1940s about the failure of heterosexual and community love because of misogyny and male-male pairing or "ganging up"—a woman writing about individual abuses of women when abused women were expected not to complain (McCullers's husband threatened to murder her and kill himself).

For the last time, we should consider Sedgwick's brilliant discussion of love triangles and the tendency of men to form homosocial ties with male rivals while trafficking in women.[31] Bonding heterosexually endorses the man's power and masculinity while also ensuring his place in the more important and powerful male collective. Yet "male homosocial desire" is more powerful than heterosexual desire. Bonding heterosexually endorses the woman's dependence while ensuring her a marginal place in the community, especially in the South, where spinsters are marginalized even more consistently—which is another factor behind Amelia's vulnerability to Marvin's advances when he wishes to marry her, to possess her and her possessions.

Even though Marvin eventually abandons Lymon, still the Lymon and Marvin male-male marriage and the chain gang represent a support system women lack. All women are freaks, spinsters, or fallen women in the male-dominated community; women cannot wear the uniform of men. The chain gang ("The Twelve Mortal Men") does not suggest harmony in human relationships but rather homosocial togetherness, destructive male collectives, and the impossibility of true love in a community driven by misogyny.

In a review of *The Mortgaged Heart,* W. G. Rogers makes a "telling comparison between Russian writers and writers from our South" and concludes that "[t]he McCullers genius is left side, mutton soup, Mormon nightgowns. It has never yet been accorded, I think, its full due."[32] James Chappell's translation of Franz Lennartz's argument that McCullers is "a poet with the gift of decoding, unraveling, enciphering the ciphers of fate" (high praise indeed) suggests that using the techniques of poetry rather than biography will help unravel McCullers's fiction.[33] This was evident to a few critics early in McCullers's career. For example, Oliver Evans called the author "a 'writer's writer' and one whose work requires, or at least lends itself to, a considerable amount of explication."[34] Certainly, we should respect V. S. Pritchett's high praise of McCullers's *Ballad:* "She is a regional writer from the South, but behind her lies that classical and melancholy authority, that indifference to shock, which seem more European than American. . . . What she has, before anything else, is a courageous imagination; that is to say one that is bold enough to consider the terrible in human nature."[35] And the terrible in McCullers's *Ballad* is Marvin's bestiality, destructive gender codes, and gangs—evidence of misogyny and homosocial ganging up in America.

Notes

1.   The critics who interpret the chain gang as a positive image are too numerous to cite. A more interesting but related issue may be the critics' reading the chain gang through the paradigm of the male-male marriage. The best example is Todd Stebbins, who senses McCullers's disparaging image of the men "chained together . . . confined," but then reads McCullers's text as a celebration of the classic American story about two male adventurers going off to conquer the wilderness together. Stebbins notes that the men in the chain gang "achieve some harmony in their music," even though the music is "temporary" (37)—then ends his analysis with the observation that "the twelve mortal men . . . can make music, no matter how unlikely the match, as long as they are together: together in a private room, in a town café, roaming the country, or even together on the Fork Falls highway under the wide sky" ("McCullers' *The Ballad of the Sad Café,*" *Explicator* 46, no. 2 [1988]: 38). Barbara C. Gannon seems to follow the trend of romanticizing the chain gang when she sees the first mention

of the prisoners as one of "promise" (59) but rightly notes that, at the end, the "relapse into silence" (60) exposes "the void and the sense of loss" amounting to "a greater misery" after Lymon has wreaked havoc on the town and Amelia's life ("McCullers' *Ballad of the Sad Café*," *Explicator* 41, no. 1 [1982]: 59–60).

2. *The Ballad of the Sad Café* (New York: Bantam, 1971); the novel is hereafter cited in text by page number alone.

3. In *The Member of the Wedding* (New York: Bantam, 1975), McCullers does offer a chorus overcoming gender and racial differences and achieving harmony. Frankie, her white cousin John Henry, and the black servant Berenice sing together and bond as if Berenice were a mother and John Henry, a brother: "they sang a special music that the three of them made up together. . . . [T]heir three voices were joined, and the parts of the song were woven together" (116).

4. Broughton rightly notices that in *The Ballad*, "The human psyche has been split, 'cracked,' if you will, into qualities which are feminine and contemptible on the one hand and masculine and admirable on the other" ("Rejection of the Feminine in Carson McCullers' *The Ballad of the Sad Café*," *Twentieth Century Literature* 20 [1974]: 30).

5. M. M. Bakhtin, *The Dialogic Imagination,* ed. Michael Holquist, trans. Caryl Emerson and Michael Holquist, University of Texas Press Slavic Series, no. 1 (Austin: University of Texas Press, 1981), 277, 276.

6. Is it just a curious coincidence that both Thomas Mann's *Death in Venice* and McCullers's *Ballad* develop bestial characters (in the latter Marvin Macy; in the former the "man standing in the portico above two apocalyptic beasts" [4] whose "ruthless air" inspires the protagonist Aschenbach's "fantasy" of the "terrors of the manifold earth . . . beneath a reeking sky, steaming, monstrous rank" [5], where "the eyes of a crouching tiger gleamed" [6])? Both *Death* and *Ballad* focus on male-male love, depict violent mobs of men, male bands, male troops, male collectives, and male pairs while also defining the relationship between the lover and the beloved (cf. *Phaedrus* and the question of the bestiality of man in *The Works of Plato,* trans. B. Jowett [New York: Dial Press, n.d.]). Mann's "hero," Aschenbach, a fastidious, elderly scholar, stalks his beloved boy, Tadzio. Does not Aschenbach's love for the boy seem suspect given the lover's dream of "[g]angs of men in surly mood [who] made the streets unsafe" (65), the infernal "whirling rout of men and animals [that] overflowed the hillside with flames and human forms," and the "troops of beardless youths [who] ran after goats and thrust their staves against the creatures' flanks" (67), not to mention the fact that the title focuses on *Death,* not love (*Death in Venice and Seven Other Stories,* trans. H. T. Lowe-Porter [New York: Vintage Books, 1954])? McCullers's male-male romance likewise develops in a context of vicious, narcissistic men. Mann would of course refer to "humanity" rather than "men," but the more limited reference to men seems appropriate in the case of McCullers's *Ballad.* Whatever "bestiality" Amelia exhibits seems sadly conditioned by her wish to attain recognition in a misogynist community by imitating the behavior of men. In McCullers's *Reflections in a Golden Eye* (New York: Bantam, 1967), the wife of the Captain responds sarcastically to the officer's threat to murder her with a mock threat: "have you ever been collared and dragged out in the street and thrashed by a naked woman?" (15). The bestiality of women seems hardly worth mentioning in *The Ballad. Newsweek* (7 July 1975) reports that McCullers bought Thomas Mann's *Stories of Three Decades* in 1936.

7. Emily M'Donald, "Carson McCullers Was Ahead of Her Time," *Chattanooga Times,* 6 October 1976, 8. Others have been disturbed by the biographer's lack of sympathy for the author. McCullers's sister Margarita G. Smith refused to help Carr, and Margaret Sullivan, President of "Friends of McCullers," refused Carr's donation of $50 and declared the biographer "no 'friend' of McCullers" (letter to Carr from Sullivan; permission to consult the Carson McCullers Collection for biographical materials donated by Carr was granted by the Archives and Special Collections Division of Otto G. Richter Library, University of Miami, Coral Gables, Florida). Carr does not seem to understand the ailing author's suffering in spite of her mention

of it in the biography. She claims that McCullers did not experience "deep personal grief" when her husband/ex-husband Reeves committed suicide—a claim based on gossip. Moreover, she relates various tidbits regarding McCullers's purportedly rebuffed sexual approaches to fellow writers and friends (e.g., Katherine Mansfield). Carr declares that she has "a love relationship with Carson" as well as with the author's family and friends, specifying that these relationships are strictly "platonic" (*The Atlantic Journal and Constitution*, 5 October 1975, Xerox copy). Yet Carr does not allow McCullers herself Platonic relationships but rather emphasizes the author's declarations regarding being bisexual and the gossip regarding McCullers's promiscuity. Of course, Freud declared us all bisexual. I suspect that if McCullers could have declared herself black, she would have done so. The emphasis on McCullers's sexuality smacks of commercialism. A Doubleday advertisement in the University of Miami Otto G. Richter Library features Carr's biography along with *Lesbian Images* by Jane Rule (Xerox copy, n.d.). At times, Carr reports gossip too eagerly in *The Lonely Hunter: A Biography of Carson McCullers* (Garden City, N.Y.: Doubleday, 1975), 406; this text is hereafter cited in text by page number alone.

8.   *Between Men: English Literature and Male Homosocial Desire* (New York: Columbia University Press, 1985). Sandra M. Gilbert and Susan Gubar argue that *The Ballad* is "overdetermined" (110) and then posit several alternative readings, the last of which coincides with my view. More precisely, they argue that *The Ballad* is "haunted by female anxiety about male social and sexual bonding"; see *No Man's Land* (New Haven: Yale University Press, 1988), 110. They also concur with my argument that misogyny is a crucial factor to consider when reading McCullers's fiction. I worry, however, over their conclusion that Amelia "deserves" the "solitary confinement" she ultimately suffers: "Even in the penitentiary, McCullers implies, men are sustained by their own community while a woman like Miss Amelia—who, even at her most powerful, never had a community of women—has been inexorably condemned to the solitary confinement such a singular anomaly deserves" (112). Both Sedgwick and Gilbert and Gubar are hereafter cited in text by page number alone. The need for an understanding of McCullers's concerns about gender is clearly revealed by Patricia Sweeney, comp., *Women in Southern Literature: An Index* (New York: Greenwood Press, 1986), when the compiler misses Amelia's status as community doctor and instead describes her as "a lonely spinster who runs a small café and *nurses* the people of her community" (38, emphasis mine).

9.   Claire Kahane, "The Gothic Mirror," in *The (M)other Tongue: Essays in Feminist Psychoanalytic Interpretation,* ed. Shirley Nelson Garner, Claire Kahane, and Madelon Sprengnether (Ithaca: Cornell University Press, 1985), 348. Kahane points out that Amelia's "strong hairy thigh . . . signifies male power and the red dress . . . her femaleness within a context of her increasing loss of power" (348).

10.   Criminality and gender—men who are incapable of feeling remorse although perpetrators of crimes and innocent women who are falsely accused or who suffer guilt unnecessarily—are interrelated and important elsewhere in McCullers's fictional world. For example, Frankie Addams in *The Member of the Wedding* suffers guilt because of an early sexual encounter with a boyfriend and feels herself a hopeless criminal for stealing a knife from Sears. Feeling alienated, she ironically envies "glad loud gangs" of soldiers (52) and the "criminals on chaingangs" because they have a "we to belong to" (39). She envies a particular soldier, "a member of the loud free gangs who for a season roamed the streets of town and then went out into the world together." Yet the soldier seems "unjoined" (129) when he nearly rapes her and she "brains" (131) him in order to escape. Then she feels criminal again—herself a murderer. In *The Heart Is a Lonely Hunter* (New York: Bantam, 1953), Mick Kelly feels alienated from her community: "everybody seemed to belong to some special bunch. . . . She wasn't a member of any bunch" (246).

11.   I mean the last grammatically complete sentence of her novel. Although two fragments follow this question in the text, they merely answer the crucial question—more subtly presented because of the fragments.

12.   Lawrence Graver sees McCullers's narrator as a woman (*Carson McCullers,* University of Minnesota Pamphlets on American Writers no. 84 [Minneapolis: University of Minnesota Press, 1969]), but the narrator's stance at the very start of the novel clearly presents him as a male worker/insider. He affirms, "When your shift is finished . . . you might as well . . ." (4). Moreover, he walks "along the main street" (3). Women are confined to the home except for Amelia before her final imprisonment.

13.   McCullers's *Reflections in a Golden Eye* reveals the author's wariness of male collectives, troops, and uniforms: "once a man enters the army, he is expected only to follow the heels ahead of him" (1–2). The least sympathetic character in this novel, "[t]he Captain always wore uniform when away from the post" (10).

14.   Karen Sosnoski identifies the importance of stereotypes in "Society's Freaks: The Effects of Sexual Stereotyping in Carson McCullers' Fiction," *Pembroke Magazine* 20 (1988): 82–88.

15.   See "Toward the Gothic: Terrorism and Homosexual Panic," *Between Men,* 83–96.

16.   Regarding McCullers's narrator, John McNally compares him to Marlow in Conrad's *Heart of Darkness,* also excusing "the apparent authorial intrusions and digressions [which are] no longer flaws in the narrative but actually key passages in the story's curious network of meanings" ("The Introspective Narrator in *The Ballad of the Sad Café*," *South Atlantic Bulletin* 38 [1973]: 41). The assertion that the narrator is a character taking part in the story is a good one; the further point that he alternately reflects community and contradictory authorial attitudes is also crucial. The mini-sermons, I would argue, reflect the authorial perspective; the gossip about Amelia and Marvin's marriage reflects the community perspective (McCullers herself suffered from malicious gossip in Columbus and in New York). Dawson P. Gaillard explains that this inconsistent voice vacillates between using the flat style of a speaker adjusted to the dreariness of the town and the more poetic style of the ballad teller ("The Presence of the Narrator in Carson McCullers' *The Ballad of the Sad Café*," *Mississippi Quarterly* 25 [1972]: 419–28). Mary Ann Dazey points out that the ballad maker is limited to the past tense, the insider/lamenter to the present tense ("Two Voices of the Single Narrator in *The Ballad of the Sad Café*," *Southern Literary Journal* 17, no. 2 [1985]: 33–40).

17.   Concerning the question of ironic tone, Carr offers a paraphrase of McCullers's view: "when one is insensitive to irony or misunderstands it, it is difficult for the author to rationalize the point intended" (*Lonely Hunter,* 237). Carr herself did not seem to understand the irony in McCullers's work or the intellectual milieu of her time. McCullers saw her work as related to the great Continental ironists (Mann, Dostoevsky, Flaubert, Kafka, to name but a few). It is understandable for a foreign critic to miss McCullers's tough ironic tone; unfortunately, such critics have been encouraged in this direction by American criticism (Futin Buffara Antunes declares that "McCullers puts her finger upon man's inner struggles and frustrations with a sentimental and nostalgic note. The gentle and understanding touch of a woman" ["*The Ballad of the Sad Café* and 'The Sojourner': Common Themes and Images," *Estudos anglo-americanos* 3–4 (1979–80): 191]. Richard Gray sees McCullers's fiction as transcending sentimentality—"what Ezra Pound once called that most inhumane of emotions, an indiscriminate sympathy. The unlucky man wallowing in his own bad luck, the account of poverty or suffering that begins and ends in moral posturing." But he then limits McCullers to being dominated by pathos, showing "how tough and really critical an emotion pathos can be," but still as lacking "historical and social context" (see "Moods and Absences" in *Carson McCullers,* ed. Harold Bloom, Modern Critical Views [New York: Chelsea, 1986], 83–84; reprinted from *The Literature of Memory: Modern Writers of the American South* [Baltimore: Johns Hopkins University Press, 1977]).

18.   "Presence of the Narrator," 419–28.

19.   "Carson McCullers' Myth of the Sad Café," *Georgia Review* 21 (1967): 54.

20.   Perhaps the tremendous power of the conditioning to admire strong and aggressive men is shown by the critics who somehow manage to admire Marvin—thus missing the irony

of his portrait. Two examples will suffice, but there are many others: (1) Donna Bauerly rightly notes McCullers's point that "reciprocity is essential to an ideal love," then offers proof of Amelia's inability to love as follows: She "has no desire for the give-and-take of an equal relationship. She makes that quite clear in her rejection of Macy" ("Themes of Eros and Agape in the Major Fiction of Carson McCullers," *Pembroke Magazine* 20 [1988]: 72–76). (2) Louise Westling sees Amelia as "a monstrous creature" (465), a "witch," and an "amazon"—Marvin as "a vigorous normal man" ("Carson McCullers' Amazon Nightmare," *Modern Fiction Studies* 28, no. 3 [1982]: 469). Elaine Ginsberg cites McCullers's *The Member of the Wedding* and *The Heart Is a Lonely Hunter* as evidence that there is a "dearth of adult female roles in American literature" because a woman was expected "to be a redeemer, spiritualizer, and ennobler . . . pure and innocent, forever a child" ("The Female Initiation Theme in American Fiction," *Studies in American Fiction* 3, no. 1 [1975]: 27). Ginsberg might have mentioned Amelia as one of the women characters she cites—seen by society as a "monster," as the critic puts it, on a par with Hester Prynne in *The Scarlet Letter*—"who gained some knowledge in the world [and was] cast in the role of the fallen woman" (28–29). Hawthorne's treatment of the Puritan fathers in "The Custom House" conditions the reader's attitude toward Hester's accusers just as McCullers might have hoped her depictions of the chain gang would encourage the reader to be biased against the town fathers.

21.   "An alleged Ku Klux Klansman called [McCullers] a 'nigger-lover' " (*Lonely Hunter*, 136). Delma Eugene Presley reports in "Carson McCullers and the South" that McCullers refused a request to donate a manuscript to the Columbus public library because of discrimination against blacks (*The Georgia Review* 28, no. 1 [1974]: 19–32). The critic quotes a March 8, 1948, letter to a Columbus newspaper (*Ledger*) written years earlier as the best expression of her views: "Always it has been an intolerable shame to me to know that Negroes are not accorded the same intellectual privileges as white citizens. As an author, represented in the library, I feel it is my duty to speak not only for myself but for the august dead who are represented on the shelves and to whom I owe an incalculable debt. I think of Tolstoy, Chekov, Abraham Lincoln, and Thomas Paine. I would like . . . to say that we owe these (the molders of the conscience of our civilization) the freedom of all citizens regardless of race to benefit by their wisdom, which is our greatest inheritance" (25). One of McCullers's last literary efforts went into writing a civil rights story, "The March" (*Redbook*, March 1967), which was to be the first of a trilogy of stories about blacks (Carr, *Lonely Hunter*, 521). Many reviewers and critics have observed that "McCullers's vision is profoundly affected by the monstrous spectre of racial inequality in the South," as Hugo McPherson puts it in "Carson McCullers: Lonely Huntress," *Tamarack Review* 11 (1959): 28–40, but no one sees the extreme importance of race as a subtle undercurrent clarifying lines of sympathy in *The Ballad*. As recently as 1990 Linda Wagner-Martin declares that "[t]he marginality of the poor, the child, the wife, the slave is a pervasive theme [in] Carson McCullers' *The Member of the Wedding* and *The Heart Is a Lonely Hunter*" but does not mention *The Ballad* in this context (" 'Just the doing of it': Southern Women Writers and the Idea of Community," *Southern Literary Journal* 22, no. 2 [1990]: 19).

22.   Louise Westling argues that Amelia represents "the tomboy grown up, without any concessions to social demands for social conformity"; see her chapter on "Tomboys," in *Sacred Groves and Ravaged Gardens: The Fiction of Eudora Welty, Carson McCullers, and Flannery O'Connor* (Athens: University of Georgia Press, 1985), 119.

23.   Gilbert and Gubar examine the "socially induced dread of female sexuality and the intense misogyny" found in several works of the period, including *The Ballad* (102). See also Dorothy Dinnerstein, *The Mermaid and the Minotaur* (New York: Harper & Row, 1976).

24.   See France Morrow, *Unleashing our Unknown Selves: An Inquiry into the Future of Femininity and Masculinity* (New York: Praeger, 1991).

25.   Carr's innuendos regarding various love triangles in McCullers's life (*Lonely Hunter*) misses the author's capacity for Platonic love. Where did the sick and dying Carson McCullers find sexual energy for all of those affairs suggested by Carr? Her request that friends lie down

in bed with her to talk may be a symptom of the need for intimacy of a Platonic sort, a problem of inordinate physical suffering, and evidence of her fear of death (cf. Lymon's case). The gossipy side of the Carr biography should be ignored. In *The Member of the Wedding*, the adolescent Frankie invites the young boy John Henry to spend the night with her: "she had what she had wanted so many nights that summer; there was somebody sleeping in the bed with her. . . . [F]or now, with somebody sleeping in the dark with her, she was not so much afraid" (13). Carr's emphasis on threesomes is less important than the tradition of the "Doppelgänger"; see McCullers's poem "The Mortgaged Heart," in *The Mortgaged Heart*, ed. Margarita G. Smith (Boston: Houghton Mifflin, 1964). McCullers's interest in "our double nature" (*Mortgaged*, 292), "The Dual Angel" (McCullers's poem, *Mortgaged*, 288), and "a world divided" (*Mortgaged*, 294) places her in the modernist tradition of the double figure. Temira Pachmuss recognizes this when she affirms that "There is a double (internal and external) conflict in the works of Dostoevsky and McCullers" ("Dostoevsky and America's Southern Women Writers: Parallels and Confluences," in *Poetica Slavica: Studies in Honour of Zbigniew Folejewski*, ed. J. Douglas Clayton [Ottawa: University of Ottawa Press, 1981], 120).

26. In her essay "The Flowering Dream," McCullers does say that "[t]he passionate, individual love—the old Tristan-Isolde love, the Eros love—is inferior to the love of God, to fellowship, to the love of Agape. . . . This is what I tried to show in *The Ballad*" (*Mortgaged*, 281). However, McCullers did not believe in God, and she goes on to say that "love is the main generator of all good writing. Love, passion, compassion are all welded together" (*Mortgaged*, 281). We should trust the tale, which implies a valuable, passionate aspect of love even though the author defines the narcissistic sort as well. I do not agree that in McCullers's world "perfect love of the unseen is total abstinence from bodily delights," as Anil Kumar puts it (*Alienation in the Fiction of Carson McCullers, J. D. Salinger, and James Purdy* [Jalandhar City: Guru Nanak Dev University, Amritsar, 1991], 372). Moreover, Frank Baldanza rightly points out that in "A Tree. A Rock. A Cloud," McCullers asserts the value of a "beer-soaked tramp['s] . . . love of a woman"—not placing that love "on the lowest rung on the ladder" as Socrates does ("Plato in Dixie," *Georgia Review* 12 [Summer 1958]: 155).

27. John B. Vickery is unduly negative when he focuses on "delusions of the heart" as the basic theme of *The Ballad* ("Carson McCullers: A Map of Love," *Wisconsin Studies in Contemporary Literature* 1 [Winter 1960]: 13–24).

28. Joseph R. Millichap also considers the value of Amelia's "creative efforts when she was 'together' with Cousin Lymon" ("Carson McCullers' Literary Ballad," *Georgia Review* 27 [1973]: 329–39).

29. I disagree with Margaret B. McDowell that "Amelia lacks any genuine basis for communication with either men or women" (*Carson McCullers*, Twayne's United States Authors series [Boston: G. K. Hall, 1980], 68); cf. McCullers's assertion that "communication is the only access to love" (*Mortgaged*, 281).

30. McCullers certainly would not have missed reading Freud; Carr pinpoints the study of Freud as occurring before writing *Reflections in a Golden Eye* (*Understanding Carson McCullers* [Columbia: University of South Carolina Press, 1990], 37).

31. Sedgwick's introduction to *Between Men* clarifies the basis of her work: "René Girard, Freud, and Lévi-Strauss, especially as he is interpreted by Gayle Rubin, offer the basic paradigm of 'male traffic in women' that will underlie the entire book" (16).

32. *New York Post*, 22 October 1971, 24.

33. Translation in the Otto Richter Library at the University of Miami of *Ausländische Dichter und Schriftsteller unserer Zeit* (Stuttgart: Alfred Kroner Verlag, 1955), n.p.

34. "The Achievement of Carson McCullers," in Bloom, *McCullers*, 21; reprinted from *English Journal* 51, no. 5 (1962).

35. *New Statesman and Nation*, 2 August 1952, 137.

Erasing the "We of Me"
and Rewriting the Racial Script:
Carson McCullers's Two
Member{s} of the Wedding

THADIOUS M. DAVIS*

They are the we of me. Yesterday, and all the twelve years of her life, she had only been Frankie. She was an *I* person who had to walk around and do things by herself. All other people had a *we* to claim, all except her.

—Carson McCullers, *The Member of the Wedding*

It must be terrible to be nothing but black, black, black.

—Frankie, *The Member of the Wedding: A Play*

Race as a familiar sign of social difference figures prominently in modern southern literature, where the cultural network often represents "blackness" as an obverse reflection of the dominant culture's "whiteness." In *The Member of the Wedding,* Carson McCullers's 1946 novel, racialization encodes gender and expands the symbolic possibilities for representing both gender difference and identity formation. McCullers's play, *The Member of the Wedding* (1949, 1951), however, dramatically reveals a narrowing down of an author's vision to suit preconceived racial attitudes and prevalent gender notions of the time, as well as to suit the largest possible audience identification of comfortably familiar characters and stereotypical actions. While McCullers's novel may be read as an intervention in the prevailing mythologies naturalizing whiteness and heterosexuality, her play retreats to an accommodationist position that allows for a smaller register of difference not only for the white girl protagonist, but also for the black adults who partici-

*This essay was written for this volume and is published here for the first time by permission of the author.

pate in her rite of passage into adolescence. The novel, thus, is a project in defamiliarization, whereas the play can be understood as largely an exercise in familiarization.

Carson McCullers battled many of society's limited conceptions of gender, perhaps more consistently than any southern writer of her generation. Her novel *The Member of the Wedding* and her play of the same title telescope her concern with the referential categories of race and gender, with social and cultural difference. Without collapsing the difference of race and gender, McCullers attends in her literary production, with varying degrees of intensity, to race in the representation of women in the South. She assumes the intricate connection of race and gender, particularly in conjoining the two categories and in inscribing race in gender. Perhaps because of the history of the uses to which white males in the South put the iconography of women— the belle or the lady but always white—few southern women writers, whether white or black, whether middle or working class, have been able to contextualize themselves as other than racialized subjects, and as a result, their creative work has been implicitly political.[1]

In a representative April, McCullers establishes the background for her novel: "April came that year sudden and still, and the green of the trees was a wild bright green. . . . There was something about the green trees and the flowers of April that made Frankie sad."[2] Nature in renewal, figured by the natural world and nature's cycle, becomes human nature, that of Frankie's transition from childhood to adolescence, from presexuality to emergent sexuality. Frankie's formation is anticipated in the location of spring as anticipatory to summer.

McCullers sets her primary scene in "that green and crazy summer when Frankie was twelve years old" (1), because she intends to explore the strangeness of a time of transition from childhood to adolescence with its concomitant explorations of sexual awakening, gender awareness, and racial and intergenerational interaction and social belonging all in a small southern community, where "the world seemed to die each afternoon and nothing moved any longer. At last the summer was like a green sick dream, or a silent crazy jungle under glass" (1). The novel proceeds to unfold Frankie's maturation and development from a twelve year old suddenly grown too tall to be a child yet unprepared for the emotional responsibilities of adulthood. At "five feet five and three quarter inches," Frankie wears a size seven shoe and has grown four inches in a year (16). She fears that she will grow to be eleven feet tall: "And what would be a lady who is over nine feet high? She would be a Freak" (16–17). Frankie images herself in the same category as the inmates of the House of Freaks at the Chattahoochee Exposition: The Giant, The Fat Lady, The Midget, The Wild Nigger, The Pin Head, The Alligator Boy, and The Half-Man Half-Woman (17). "Do *I* give you the creeps?" Frankie asks Berenice (18, McCullers's italics). McCullers initiates an unusual angle from which to view her story, and she allows no comfortable touchstones in her language and symbols, her ideas and events. It is a crazy, unpredictable time, or as Frankie says, "The world is certainy [sic] a sudden place" (4).

There is a freshness in the presentation of the age-old emergence into young adulthood, in the rendering of Frankie's search for the "*we of me*" (39, McCullers's italics), for identity and community, for "membership," for inclusion and connection. Her companions, Berenice Sadie Brown, her black surrogate mother, and John Henry West, her six-year-old cousin/surrogate sibling, are inventions that, although immediately striking a chord of familiar reality, have about them a sense of the unexpected in human nature. Berenice, for example, has a "dark and sad" right eye, but a "bright blue glass" left eye: "It stared out fixed and wild from her quiet, colored face, and why she had wanted a blue eye nobody human would ever know" (3). And John Henry wears "around his neck a tiny lead donkey tied by a string," but his chest is "white and wet and naked," and although he is small for his age, he has "the largest knees that Frankie had ever seen, and on one of them there was always a scab or a bandage" (3).

Frankie's independence is represented as isolation; her willful assertion of connection ("we of me"), as perversion. Berenice states that "[w]e all of us somehow caught. We born this way or that way and we don't know why. But we caught anyhow" (113). In particular, puberty for the motherless Frankie is both a social and a sexual condition of in-betweenness: "This summer she was grown so tall that she was almost a big freak, and her shoulders were narrow, her legs too long. She wore a pair of blue black shorts, a B.V.D. undervest, and she was barefooted. Her hair had been cut like a boy's" (2). In contrast to Frankie's appearance, femininity as constructed by southern society and as valorized by Frankie's descriptions of her brother's fiancée is an oasis of frilly dresses, makeup, flirtations, and empty-headed chatter.[3] Indeed, clothing as iconography is as central to the text as it is to the society. Frankie marks her gender confusion by wearing a boy's tee shirt and shorts; later, however, in a movement away from the androgyny of her initial appearance, she assumes an exaggerated feminine guise—a frilly pink dress.

The three central characters are not at all confined to the environment and conventions of life in a southern town during World War II, although they are precisely located in time (1943) and place. Their horizons seem larger in the narrative strategy than the spatial restrictions of the Addams family kitchen, where much of the action takes place, and their actions complement Frankie's becoming first F. Jasmine Addams, who attaches herself to her brother's wedding and anticipates a lasting union of the three J's (F. Jasmine, Jarvis, and his bride Janice), and evolving second into Frances Addams, who finds a new female best friend and a place for herself within a community of "we." Frankie's suppressed identifications throughout the text, however, are with those racialized as black.

Three years after the publication of *The Member of the Wedding*, McCullers completed a play based on her novel. In it she revisioned not Frankie and her cousin John Henry, but the blacks: Berenice, the cook-housekeeper; T. T. Williams, her suitor; and Honey Camden Brown, her foster-brother.[4] Berenice, whose reminiscences of her four marriages in the novel serve both to inform Frankie about the mistaken choices that adults make in trying to replicate a lost happiness and to warn Frankie about the dangers of compulsory heterosexuality, is initially a wise confidante. Although not entirely understanding the depths of Frankie's loneliness or her fears of being "queer" and therefore not "belonging," Berenice nonetheless knows that Frankie's life is in transition, that she is moving from girlhood to womanhood, that physically she is maturing rapidly, and that emotionally she is floundering.

This Berenice in the novel is a woman with a fixed "we of me," which Frankie envies. Berenice has a life of her own outside the Addams household; she has family and a suitor, her organizations and church. She has a social life in which she, T. T., and Honey go out to supper at the New Metropolitan Tea Room. She is secure in her sexual identity, as her revelations about marriage and the treatment of women and wives illustrate.

Berenice is also firmly rooted in her racial identity. Although she does not exaggerate racial differences, she is thoroughly aware of race as a factor of individual identification, as for example when she describes Frankie's brother Jarvis and his fiancée as "a good-looking blond white boy. And the girl is kind of brunette and small and pretty. They make a nice white couple" (27). Blind in one eye, Berenice does not misread the configurations of race in her society; she tells Frankie and John Henry that she is "caught worse" than they "[b]ecause I am black.... Because I am colored.... [T]hey done drawn completely extra bounds around all colored people. They done squeezed us off in one corner by ourself" (113–14). Berenice Sadie Brown is a rounded person with a connected, if not harmonious, past and, implicitly, with a future of her own, for at the end of the novel she is preparing to marry T. T. and has given notice that she will no longer work for the relocating Addams family. The novel ends by complicating received notions of racial difference.[5]

In the play, however, the ideological assumptions maintain racial hierarchies and conventions. There is no intervention in the existing system of representation of blacks, and no disruption of conventional portraits of blacks. There is, instead, a distorting of the lives created in the novel in order to access and claim the expected and the familiar. Berenice's role in assisting Frankie's transformation to adulthood is undermined. In fact, she becomes almost childlike herself. She is coarse, insisting for instance that she has a right to as much fun as anyone, that she has not gone through the change of life. "Fun" is equated with sexual intercourse, and menopause is used to demarcate age and the cessation of sexual pleasure. McCullers emphasized both Berenice's sexuality and her subservience, so that we hear Berenice say that she won't marry T. T. because "he don't make me shiver none" (72), and we watch her upbraid Honey for being impudent to whites and for not addressing her employer Mr. Addams as "sir" (68). Sexualized, racialized, and objectified, Berenice Sadie Brown in the dramatic text cannot become a subject.[6]

Nevertheless, the Berenice of McCullers's novel is still recognizable in the play, but T. T. and Honey are not. T. T. Williams is no longer the prosperous owner of a restaurant, or as McCullers puts it in the novel, emphasizing his racialization, "a well-off colored man who owned a colored restaurant" (35). Instead, he becomes a menial, trivial presence—just another black man who works as a servant for whites. T. T. serves as waiter for the marriage reception, and he is a day-laborer in the homes or businesses of various white men in the community: "Now, Mr. Addams, that's one afternoon I promised to work for Mr. Finny, sir. I can't promise anything, Mr. Addams. But if Mr. Finny change his mind about needing me, I'll work for you, sir" (67). Even more drastically different in the play is his obsequious, bowing, scraping manner. Gone is the mannerly, polite gentleman with a strong sense of propriety. A transformed T. T. "sirs" Mr. Addams no less than four times in a few short sentences (67). Reduced to being subservient and dependent, he bears little resemblance to the T. T. represented in the novel.

Honey Camden Brown is on the surface of the play a different sort of black man from T. T. Williams, yet neither is he the Honey of the novel. There, he is a black man who "could talk like a white school-teacher; his lavender lips could move as quick and light as butterflies" (36), according to Frankie, who seems attracted to Honey not only because of his abilities but also because of his difficulties. Frankie is fascinated by Honey's articulateness and his potential for defying fixed categories of identification. Yet she also observes that Honey is a young man whose options in life are limited; he has injured himself digging in a gravel pit and can no longer do heavy work or be inducted into the army (35). "Honey played the horn, and had been first in his studies at the colored high school" (122). Honey wants a better life and is sensitive to racism in his society because it is the restrictive force circumventing all possible avenues of self-determination.

Frankie recognizes the racist aspects of her society and its debilitating impact on Honey. She identifies with his repressed desires, with his musical talent and linguistic abilities, but she also connects with his outsider condition. She, of course, fancies herself an "outlaw," not only because she has stolen a knife from Sears and Roebuck and broken the law or because she has committed a sexual crime with Barney MacKean and violated moral codes, but mainly because she imagines herself as a nonconformist to society's gender expectations. Frankie suggests that Honey go to Cuba or Mexico, where his light complexion would help him fit in and where his ability to speak well would enable him to learn Spanish quickly, become a Cuban or Mexican, and change his future prospects. She tells Honey: "I don't think you'll ever be happy in this town. I think you ought to go to Cuba. You are so light-skinned and you even have a kind of Cuban expression. You could go there and change into a Cuban. You could go learn to speak the foreign language and none of those Cubans would ever know you are a colored boy. Don't you see what I mean?" (125). After all, Honey is smart, adept at learning; he had "ordered a French book from Atlanta and learned himself some French" (122).

In the representation of Honey and Frankie's identification with him, the interconnections among cultural constructions of race and gender become the most obvious. Because of their appearance and their desires, both Frankie and Honey are culturally androgynous characters. Frankie can subvert her gender identification through the adoption of gender-specific clothing, whereas Honey has the skin coloring and language facility to erase his racial designation. Frankie is not represented in manner or appearance as a "typical southern white preteen girl"; neither is Honey represented as a "typical southern black young man." Moreover, they are not represented as exceptional (in opposition to "typical"); instead, both occupy the space of difference. Applicable here is an observation Trinh T. Minh-ha makes in constructing gender as "a social regular and a political potential for change" that "baffles definition" and "coincides . . . with *difference,* whose inseparable temporal and spatial dynamics produces the illusion of identity while undermining it relentlessly."[7] Frankie's sexual difference (signified by her cross-dressing) is implicated in the representation of Honey's racial difference. As Henry Louis Gates Jr. has concluded:

> The sense of difference defined in popular usages of the term "race" has both described and *inscribed* differences. . . .
>
> Race has become the trope of ultimate, irreducible difference between cultures, linguistic groups, or adherents of specific belief systems which . . . also have fundamentally opposed economic interests. Race is the ultimate trope of difference because it is so very arbitrary in its application.[8]

To be sure, McCullers in "The Flowering Dream: Notes on Writing" states, "In my childhood, the South was almost a feudal society. But the South is complicated by the racial problem. . . . To many a poor Southerner, the only pride that he has is the fact that he is white."[9] Given the material conditions of production, it may not be surprising that McCullers resorted to the specific race ideology and class politics she wrote into her play. Her sensibility in the stage version is conformist. Social relations are structured theatrically so that blacks on stage are "othered," different and distant from Frankie.

In the play, Honey is a "slender, limber Negro boy of about twenty," who is called "Lightfoot" because of his skill in dancing. He plays a horn, which he keeps with him, is ornery toward women and children (specifically Berenice and John Henry), and is characterized as a fun-loving, razor-carrying troublemaker, whose use of reefers (marijuana) causes him to kill a white man with his razor, to run from the law, only to be captured, and to hang himself in a jail cell. This Honey in the play has no history except that of popular images of discontented black men who, although victimized, are rather worthless. He especially appears connected to the characters Sportin' Life and Crown from the 1927 play *Porgy,* adapted by Dorothy Heyward from DuBose Heyward's 1925 novel *Porgy,* and to the same characters in the 1935 opera *Porgy and Bess* (music by George Gershwin). Honey is particularly reminiscent of Sportin' Life, the dapper, nattily dressed dispenser of the drug "happy dust," and given his preoccupations, Honey seems an analogue to the denizens of Catfish Row, whose gambling and drinking, encounters with the law and with death, characterize their lives.

A product as well of the urban novel of low-life, Honey is also presented as childlike. Berenice, for example, refers to his lack of judgment, his getting "high on them reefers," and his having "no more judgment than a four-year-old child" (94). Honey has been in trouble at an earlier point in time when he spent six months on a road gang for swinging at the police (94). In his first appearance in the play, he has been hit by a white MP for pushing a soldier (44), and he laments, "Times like this I feel like I got to bust loose or die" (43). Honey is, as he explains later, "sick of smothering in the nigger hole" (69), so he displays what he calls his "nigger razor" (68) and reiterates that he "can't stand it no more" (69). A malcontent whose motivations are not generated from within the parameters of the stage world in which he functions, Honey has been given no redeeming features, unless his ability to dance and wear flashy clothes can be counted.

Carson McCullers reduces her preexisting, complex characters and actions to the broad outlines of conventional types and simplified forms. She draws upon prevailing popular notions of her times, makes her southern blacks more familiar and predictable for a conflated theater audience—white and primarily northern. Perhaps McCullers conceived of this revisionary process of "blackening" her characters and overdetermining her audience so that she would not have to provide exposition about the characters or the events. Apparently, in depending upon stereotyped behavior and motivation, she took a relatively easy way out in executing her drama. Indeed, in "The Vision Shared," a short article for *Theatre Arts* (April 1950), McCullers reflected on her experience with adapting *The Member of the Wedding* for the stage: "It seemed to me after my first experiences that the theatre was the most pragmatic of all art media. The first question of ordinary producers is: 'Will it get across on Broadway?' The merit of a play is a secondary consideration and they shy from any play whose formula has not been proved a number of times" (*The Mortgaged Heart,* 264). The implication is that an author no less than anyone else in a society is subject to stereotypes, facile language, cultural prejudices, and what Toni Morrison has called "the thunderous, theatrical presence of black surrogacy,"[10] particularly when confronted with issues of marketability, of the play as a commercial property. Clearly, McCullers's observation about the theater contrasts with her comments about the writing of the novel, *The Member of the Wedding:* "It's one of those works that the least slip can ruin. Some parts I have worked over and over as many as twenty times. . . . It must be beautifully done. For like a poem there is not much excuse for it otherwise."[11]

An astute and talented author, as her novel demonstrates, McCullers nonetheless realized the ease with which familiar referents in terms of action, manners, ideas, and portraits can be incorporated into a vision of people and events, a vision that would facilitate responsiveness from a mainstream audience at the end of the 1940s and the start of the 1950s. She perceived, and rightly so, that her audience would be essentially northern whites who would not question the ways in which she represented her characters, those black ones, but also the white ones as well. For example, Mr. Addams takes great offense in the play when Honey does not call him "sir," and he goes on to expound on "uppity niggers" and to stress the word "nigger": "I'll be so glad when the war is over and you biggety, worthless niggers get back to work. And furthermore, you *sir* me! Hear me?" (68, McCullers's italics). In the novel, Addams does not hold the same views, but more significantly, the word "nigger" does not appear in that text at all. In the play, Addams is both paternalistic and patriarchal in acting out his superior position of power and authority; moreover, his use of "nigger" marks Honey as racially inferior, not simply as racially different, based on the dominance and authority of stereotype. Mr. Addams's conceptions and language are geared to a time when whites were frequently uncomfortable with returning black World War II veterans, and most comfortable with rhetoric that put them in their proper place, that is to say, returned blacks to the servile roles whites had constructed for them. The negative representation of both Honey and T. T. reverses the empathetic vision of a nuanced and differentiated black masculinity in the novel and, in the process, eliminates the complicated social positioning of southern black men McCullers depicts there.

The purgation of class stratification among blacks by nullifying a black entrepreneurial class in the play, for example, may not be intended to make the characters more palatable, but rather to provide them with an immediately perceived social history as servants and inferiors that could be an unstated reference point for whites viewing the production. (No need to deal with these characters as equals or to invest in their material realities.) Moreover, with the disappearance of the bourgeoisie, the options for black southern men, such as Honey, become negligible, and mindless self-destructive actions reiterate the potential for violence, or for potential lynch mobs, without the danger of audience identification with or empathy for the character. Because drama is a more public form than fiction, the play depends upon the familiar, that body of social exchanges, representations, and associations that feed on cultural assumptions, ideologies, or predispositions that are not threatening to an audience.

Whereas McCullers's novel is expansive in its empathy and perceptions about human nature and sexual identity, about regional and relational affiliations, about race, gender, and class, the play is restrictive and limiting. It exoticizes both white and black southerners, but especially black. Although both texts are time bound, the play is more closely tied to a temporality and regionality that lessen the significance of the processes of maturation and gender identity for Frankie and the attendant impact of her fellow characters in those processes. Vision and meaning have been realigned to suit available and convenient formations that are prominent in a particular society, to adhere to pervasive tastes and expectations of a defined audience, whose ideological beliefs are anticipated by the drama.

In *Killers of the Dream* (1949), Lillian Smith exposed the "haunted childhood" of every southerner, particularly women of her age, born after the turn of the century.[12] She describes them as "[c]hildren, moving through the labyrinth made by grownups' greed and guilt and fear":

> So we learned the dance that cripples the human spirit, step by step, we who were white and we who were colored, day by day, hour by hour, year by year until the movements were reflexes and made for the rest of our life without thinking. Alas, for many white children, they were movements made for the rest of our lives without feeling. . . . These ceremonials in honor of white supremacy, performed from babyhood, slip from the conscious mind down deep into muscles and glands and become difficult to tear out. (96)

But Smith is quite specific in the connection of her whiteness and her femaleness within her southern community:

> I knew that I was better than a Negro, that all black folks have their place and must be kept in it, that sex had its place and must be kept in it, that a terrifying disaster would befall the South if I ever treated a Negro as my social equal and as terrifying a disaster would befall my family if I ever were to have a baby outside of marriage. (28)

In recounting the contradictions of custom and conscience, Smith attended equally to gender and race in the social matrix and to the separate places each was to have in her world where, in the words told to her by an African-American woman, "It is not legal to be human down here" (40). Smith makes apparent that a southern childhood is a controlling and deflecting trope for racial and gender difference.

In a sense, McCullers operates with a comparable awareness in her fiction. Although she shaped fictive realities in both texts, she did not minimize diversity in human beings and action or maximize any expected, familiar ways of approaching material in her novel. There she seems to have perceived the artist's obligation to break down the barrier of the complacently familiar, to make strange and fresh, to help us see anew human nature, human beings, and human interaction. Interestingly, Marguerite Young in reviewing the novel discerned an aspect of McCullers's vision that is not so easily observed in the play: her "seek[ing] after those luminous meanings which always do transcend the boundaries of the stereotyped, the conventional and the so-called normal."[13]

In her play, however, McCullers seemingly went against her own artistic, imaginative conception of her created people in a given time and place. Perhaps it is that McCullers, less knowledgeable or confident about the conventions of the stage world and less certain about reshaping her fiction into drama, simply took her models from contemporary arbiters of taste and style—whether these were critics, reviewers, or writers, some of whom may have been less informed about black life and southern life than she herself. McCullers admitted that for her "the parallel function of a work of art is to be communicable. Of what value is a creation that cannot be shared? The vision that blazes in a madman's eye is valueless to us. So when the artist finds a creation rejected there is the fear that his own mind has retreated to a solitary uncommunicable state" ("The Vision Shared," in *The Mortgaged Heart*, 263).

Although she knew better, as her novel reveals, McCullers complied with notions of blacks as fighting, stealing, working at menial jobs, believing in superstitions, seeking physical pleasure, and so on. The play after all completed 501 performances on Broadway.[14] At any rate, motivations beyond her artistic impulse and creative imagination clearly influenced how she presented her characters, situations, and themes in the play. Whatever they may have been, these external determinants caused her to take shortcuts to evoke responsiveness but little reflective thinking from her audience.

Let me venture to suggest another reason why McCullers may have succumbed to the then popular images of blacks. If indeed the novel *The Member of the Wedding* struggles with an alternative coming-of-age story, one that constructs the subject as lesbian and southern, then McCullers may well have modified the subject construction in the play by masking the centrality of sexual identification for Frankie and her rejection of the heterosexual romance plot with a focus on the more sensational elements of a staged and stereotypical black southern life. Frankie moves toward bonding with women in the novel. Her sexual and emotional orientation impacts upon her creativity, her imagination, and her consciousness of herself and the rest of her world. Bonnie Zimmerman has posited that "woman-identified writers, silenced by a homophobic and misogynistic society, have been forced to adopt coded and obscure language and internal censorship."[15] McCullers, in writing an emergent lesbian identity, was able to contextualize Frankie as a racialized (white) subject projected against the background of black southerners, and as a result, *The Member of the Wedding* as novel has a marked, though not strident, political content. The objectified ground (Berenice, T. T., Honey, etc.) is specifically racialized black. "The fabrication of an Africanist persona is reflexive; an extraordinary meditation on the self; a powerful exploration of the fears and desires that reside in the writerly conscious," as Toni Morrison has observed. "It is an astonishing revelation of longing, of terror, of perplexity, of shame, of magnanimity."[16]

Indeed, although Frankie in the play still struggles with the problem of difference and the pain of loneliness, she is not defined in her crisis of identity by what Louise Westling calls "the images of sexual freaks in an ambience of androgynous longing, homosexuality, and transvestitism."[17] McCullers first entitled her novel "The Bride" and then "The Bride and Her Brother," but apparently had difficulty grounding a thematic core for her text. Carr recounts an apocryphal incident in which McCullers with Gypsy Rose Lee chased a fire truck for several blocks, then stopped abruptly and said, "Stop! I have it! Frankie is in love with her brother and the bride, and wants to become a member of the wedding!"[18] Whether or not McCullers's clarified conception of her novel was visited upon her in this way, the story codifies the triangular relationship. It inscribes that she gained focus only when she came to understand physical desire and sexual longing in the context of the triangular relationship in which the female (Frankie in *The Member of the Wedding*) is equally attracted to a male and a female and that both attractions are frustrated by social prohibitions against their culmination in a physical relationship; that is to say, Frankie's attraction to her brother is incestuous, whereas her attraction to her brother's bride is homosexual/lesbian. The *ménage à trois*, then, is central both to the narrative and to McCullers's understanding of her narrative focus. As Frankie puts it, "I love the two of them so much. We'll go every place together. It's like I've known all my life, that I belong to be with them. I love the two of them so much" (43). Locating an identity inappropriately in the bond of matrimony is an attempt to construct a different union of three rather than two; and mirroring a single subject in a heterosexual couple is an avoidance of the issue of gender construction and relational identity. In " 'Triangular' Desire," the opening chapter of *Deceit, Desire, and the Novel: Self and Other in Literary Structure*, René Girard argues that the triangle "always allude[s] to the mystery, transparent yet opaque, of human relations."[19] For Frankie, her brother and his bride become representative of two spheres of possibilities for her completion of her self as subject. And it is not surprising that Berenice perceptively names one of the emotions resulting from Frankie's desire: Berenice asks whether Frankie is jealous of her brother's bride.

Although the world of the theater might well provide a more accommodating stage for the dramatization of Frankie's repressed homosocial desires, it could in the aftermath of World War II do so only within the boundaries of "normalcy." The play ends with Frankie and Barney MacKean together anticipating joining Mary Littlejohn (who had been the only friend represented in the conclusion of the novel) and with a plan for the three friends to accompany the movers to Frankie's new house (118). In shifting from Mary to Barney, the play revisions Frankie's entry into adolescence as heterosexual. "Perversion," whether enacted as incest, cross-dressing, or lesbianism, could not assume center stage on Broadway or in "legitimate" theater in the post–World War II years. Such issues could not be commodified and marketed at that time as financially profitable. The answer to representing the kinds of concerns McCullers obviously had in her original text is encoding. On the one hand, the encoding is achieved by obscuring Frankie's flight from the secret sexual encounter with Barney and her longing to be accepted into the tight-knit group of girls, and by making her chosen boy's costume less a function of cross-dressing than an expediency due to the southern heat (that is, shorts and a "B.V. D. undervest" or tee shirt become a "normal" response to the problem of clothing in the August weather). However, on the other hand, and perhaps most significantly here, the encoding is accomplished through the parallel narrative of Berenice, Honey, and T. T., who become exoticized, primitivized, and sexualized in their portraits that supposedly exaggerate to type their "race" traits for a theater audience.

The racial script is rewritten to deny the associative links among Honey, Berenice, and Frankie. Honey's addiction to drugs distances him from Frankie and renders him more threatening to her. Although Frankie, like Honey, occupies the "outlaw" position, she because of her race position can be redeemed, rescued from her outsider criminality, whereas Honey can only die in the play because of his.[20] The dialectic between freedom and imprisonment is played out in Honey's position but just as noticeably in Frankie's recognition of implicatedness: "It must be terrible to be nothing but black, black, black" (70). By equating death metaphorically with the cultural construction of race, McCullers allows a slight comment on the stereotyped racialized characters and actions of her play. The metaphoric veil which W. E. B. Du Bois identified as separating blacks and whites is hardly lifted at all on the stage. Lacking the intersubjectivity of the novel with its production of both Frankie and the trio of blacks (Berenice, T. T., and Honey) as subjects, the play does not allow for their subject construction.[21] Even Frankie, whom the play reconfigures as ultimately "normal," that is, a white, heterosexual southern girl, is objectified, disabled, and held within a typology most familiar and less threatening to the racial and gender social order.

Notes

1. For example, Eudora Welty's photographs from the WPA of the 1930s are a visual imaging of the contours of difference between women in the South that does not depend upon a masculine racial construction or upon a fetishizing of otherness.

2. Carson McCullers, *The Member of the Wedding* (1946; rpt. New York: Bantam, 1975), 20; hereafter cited in the text.

3. As Marjorie Garber suggests, "Gender roles and categories are most vulnerable to critique when they are most valorized, when their rules, code, and expectations are most ardently coveted and admired" (*Vested Interests: Cross-Dressing & Cultural Anxiety* [New York: Routledge, 1992], 51).

4. The members of the Addams family have expanded roles in the play: Mr. Addams, Jarvis and his fiancée, Aunt Pet (Mrs. West, John Henry's mother) all appear. See Carson McCullers, *The Member of the Wedding: A Play* (New York: New Directions, 1951); hereafter cited in the text.

5. Richard M. Cook, for example, observes that when Richard Wright "praised McCullers for being able 'to handle Negro characters with as much ease and justice as those of her own race,' he was praising her for revealing beneath the stereotypes valuable complex human beings—people interesting in the variousness of their contradictions as well as in their suffering" (*Carson McCullers* [New York: Frederick Ungar, 1975], 128).

6. At the same time, however, the stage presence of the actress Ethel Waters, appearing as Berenice in the first New York production (opening January 5, 1950, at the Empire Theater), ameliorated somewhat the stereotyped Berenice of the play. Her performance, although adhering to the type McCullers created for the stage, gave the character a greater stature and more human dimension than the text implied.

7. Trinh T. Minh-ha concludes her 1989 essay, "Difference: 'A Special Third World Woman's Issue,' " with this definition of gender's interaction with difference. See *Woman Native Other* (Bloomington: Indiana University Press, 1989), 116.

8. Henry Louis Gates Jr. makes his observation in "Writing 'Race' and the Difference it Makes," the introduction to *"Race," Writing, and Difference* ([Chicago: University of Chicago Press, 1986], 5), which inserts race into Jacques Derrida's meditations on the sign, *Writing and Difference* (*L'écriture et la différence,* 1978).

9. *The Mortgaged Heart,* ed. Margarita G. Smith (Boston: Houghton Mifflin, 1971), 281; hereafter cited in the text.

10. Toni Morrison, *Playing in the Dark: Whiteness and the Literary Imagination* (Cambridge: Harvard University Press, 1990), 13. Morrison argues that "the self-evident ways that Americans choose to talk about themselves through and within a sometimes allegorical metaphorical, but always choked representation of an African presence" become transparent upon attentive reading (17).

11. Carson McCullers to Reeves McCullers (1945), quoted in Cook, *Carson McCullers,* 60.

12. Lillian Smith, *Killers of the Dream* (1949; rev. ed. New York: Norton, 1961), 25; hereafter cited in the text.

13. Marguerite Young, "Metaphysical Fiction," *Kenyon Review* 9 (1947): 151–55.

14. Virginia Spencer Carr observes that although McCullers's theatrical adaptation of *The Member of the Wedding* had a lengthy, award-winning run in 1950 and "solidified her popular success," it seemingly "had little bearing on her critical reputation," as her second play *The Square Root of Wonderful* (1957) "opened on Broadway and closed in seven weeks" (*Understanding Carson McCullers* [Columbia: University of South Carolina Press, 1990], 4).

15. Bonnie Zimmerman, "What Has Never Been: An Overview of Lesbian Feminist Criticism," in *Making a Difference,* ed. Gayle Greene and Coppélia Kahn (New York: Methuen, 1985), 186.

16. Morrison, *Playing in the Dark,* 17.

17. Louise Westling, *Sacred Groves and Ravaged Gardens: The Fiction of Eudora Welty, Carson McCullers, and Flannery O'Connor* (Athens: University of Georgia Press, 1985), 111. Westling draws upon Patricia S. Box's early treatment of sexual ambivalence in *The Member of the Wedding;* see "Androgyny and the Musical Vision: A Study of Two Novels by Carson McCullers," *Southern Quarterly* 16 (1978): 117–23.

18. Virginia Spencer Carr, *The Lonely Hunter: A Biography of Carson McCullers* (Garden City: Doubleday, 1975), 121. Carr suggests that on Thanksgiving Day 1940, a headlong rush to view the spectacle of a neighborhood fire prompted McCullers's epiphany, which ultimately clarified her conception of the novel in progress.

19. René Girard, *Deceit, Desire, and the Novel: Self and Other in Literary Structure* (Baltimore: Johns Hopkins University Press, 1961), 2–3. Girard also observes that in triangular desire the mediator is always confronted with two competing desires, so that "[t]he mediator can no longer act his role of model without also acting or appearing to act the role of obstacle" (7).

20. Importantly, rather than killing himself as in the play, Honey Brown in the novel attempts to steal more of the "marihuana cigarette[s], . . . something called smoke or snow" by breaking into the "drugstore of the white man who had been selling them to him" and is caught, tried, and sentenced to eight years in prison (149, 151).

21. See Jessica Benjamin, "A Desire of One's Own: Psychoanalytic Feminism and Intersubjective Space," in *Feminist Studies/Critical Studies,* ed. Teresa de Lauretis (Bloomington: Indiana University Press, 1986).

Homoerotics and Human Connections: Reading Carson McCullers "As a Lesbian"

Lori J. Kenschaft*

Every one of McCullers's five novels and novellas contains a significant homoerotic theme. In *The Heart Is a Lonely Hunter,* the unilateral silence between Antonapoulos and Singer provides the type for Singer's relationships with the four characters who cluster around him.[1] Captain Penderton of *Reflections in a Golden Eye* progresses from infatuation with his wife's acknowledged lover to fatal obsession with her unacknowledged one. Jasper of *Clock Without Hands* falls in love with a mixed-race young man who is the key to the mystery of his own family's past. *The Member of the Wedding* centers on a girl's desire for an affianced couple, while *The Ballad of the Sad Café* tells the story of a triangle involving a woman and two men. This recurrent focus on homoerotic bonds—which are never simply represented as a homosexual love story—first suggests that an inquiry into the meanings of homoeroticism in McCullers's writings is essential for understanding those writings.

One cannot, however, simply equate homoeroticism with a homosexual identity that might reasonably be called lesbian or gay.[2] In each of McCullers's texts, the same-sex relationship is never named as homosexual by any of the characters involved, the surrounding characters, or the narrator. With a few partial exceptions, the same-sex nature of these relationships is also disconnected from reflections on individual psychology or personal identity. These relationships float in a social void, unrelated to either a homophobic society or a homosexual subculture. Same-sex love simply exists as a recurrent feature of McCullers's fictional worlds.

Its presence would not, however, be unmarked for a sensitive reader. Time and time again McCullers employs coded descriptions of her characters. For example, not only is Frankie physically masculine in the youthful way canonized in Radcliffe Hall's *The Well of Loneliness*—her legs long, her shoulders narrow, her body awkwardly tall—but her chosen self-presentation is equally so: she wears boys' clothes, sports a boys' haircut, and goes by a boy-

---

*This essay was written for this volume and is published here for the first time by permission of the author. The author would like to acknowledge her colleague Beth Bennett, with whom she discussed several of these ideas.

ish nickname. Frankie's lavender seashell is a provocative symbol of her desire to escape to another world, since lavender is the color most frequently used to signal lesbian/gay content and—perhaps coincidentally, but perhaps not—the smooth, inward-curving surfaces of seashells are suggestive of lesbian erotic imagery.[3] Miss Amelia, invoking similar conventions in a more mature form, is "a dark, tall woman with bones and muscles like a man" who dresses in overalls, prides herself on her muscles, and cares nothing for the love of men. Her marriage is even named a "queer marriage" (198). The constant repetition of the words "queer" and "gay" in conjunction with Cousin Lymon—who has lavender shadows beneath his eyes and a "hunched queer body" (200, 247)—prepares an aware reader for his infatuation with Marvin Macy. "It's so very queer" are also the first words of dialogue in *The Member of the Wedding,* spoken by 12-year-old Frankie about the arrival of her brother and his bride. The word "queer" reappears two more times in the first three pages of the text (257–58). In 1946, when *Wedding* was published, "queer" (like "gay") was a code word known to many "in the life" but few outside; it was frequently used to identify oneself to another discreetly, under the public eye but without public knowledge. As an effective cover, it fully retained its root meanings of "odd," "strange," "off-beat." Nevertheless, a reader who was familiar with the doubled meaning would surely have been sensitized to the possibility that this was, indeed, a queer story.

Such coding is not simply coincidence. *The Ballad of the Sad Café* was written in the summer of 1941; *The Member of the Wedding* was an ongoing project from 1939 to 1946. In 1940 McCullers fell in love with Annemarie Clarac-Schwarzenbach, whom she later considered the greatest passion of her life. According to her biographer, McCullers's husband was already accustomed to her frequent crushes on women. That fall they separated and she moved into a group house. Her housemates included Benjamin Britten and Peter Pears, who were life-long lovers, Christopher Isherwood, and W. H. Auden, whose new lover, Chester Kallman, soon moved in. The next summer at Yaddo, McCullers's men's clothes and boyish haircut made her easily identifiable as a "mannish woman." Said fellow guest Edward Newhouse:

> I was not very good at recognizing a homosexual when I met him. Or her. . . . I was not surprised when Carson told me about herself. She sometimes wore a man's trousers and often a man's jacket, and even I was able to make the connection.[4]

It is not evident, however, just what McCullers told Newhouse about herself. Many years later, Louis Untermeyer said that "Carson's bisexual tendencies were obvious," but McCullers herself told another friend that she was an "invert," and to a third she asserted, "I was born a man."[5]

Although Freudian ideas about homosexuality were beginning to make their way into American circles, McCullers clearly not only knew but also incorporated into her self-understanding and self-presentation the older ideas of sexual inversion. Freudian psychology views homosexuality as a developmental phenomenon: The erotic object is fixed as either male or female at some stage during a child's psychological development.[6] In contrast, the inversion theory earlier popularized by Havelock Ellis holds that sexual object choice is determined before birth and is part of a whole constellation of preferences, attitudes, and aptitudes appropriate to a man or to a woman and unique to that individual. A woman loves another woman because she possesses a man's soul in a woman's body, or vice versa for a man. This theory reflects a belief, common among nineteen-century eugenicists, that behaviors and psychological characteristics are inherited in much the same way as physical traits. It also requires the assumption that men and women are fundamentally different by nature in most, if not all, aspects of their beings. In the case of inverts, by a fluke of nature or of God, the inner being (male or female) does not match the external body (male or female).

McCullers's descriptions of Frankie and Miss Amelia derive directly from this tradition of interpretation, and she was apparently inviting the same interpretation of her own sexuality when she named herself as an invert. For a person of the 1990s, however, McCullers is not easily named a lesbian. She remarried her husband in 1945 and apparently was involved with other men as well. She even playfully propositioned Untermeyer during that summer of 1941.[7] McCullers might well be called bisexual—a term with widely varying connotations depending on context—but it may not always be useful to describe her using an interpretive framework developed in a later time since she did not have access to that framework and therefore formed her self-identity and self-presentation within a different conceptual model. Yet although it may be difficult to attach a label to McCullers herself, her language and her friendships make clear that she was writing within a context in which she would have been quite conscious of lesbian and gay male culture and codes.

These preliminary explorations suggest that both McCullers's texts and their author can reasonably be associated with the word "lesbian" but certainly should not be fully identified with the term. What of their reader? It is well understood that the experiences a reader brings to a text profoundly affect her reading of that text, and lesbian experience should be no different. Most obviously, a reader who was unfamiliar with gay slang circa 1940 would miss certain implications of McCullers's texts, even though those texts could reasonably be read and interpreted without that knowledge. More subtly, what might a lesbian read in the *Sad Café* narrator's description of the experience of a lover?

> He feels in his soul that his love is a solitary thing. He comes to know a new, strange, loneliness and it is this knowledge which makes him suffer. So there is only one thing for the lover to do. He must house his love within himself as best he can; he must create for himself a whole new inward world—a world

intense and strange, complete in himself. Let it be added here that this lover of whom we speak need not necessarily be a young man saving for a wedding ring—this lover can be man, woman, child, or indeed any human creature on this earth. (216)

Anyone may identify with this evocation of loneliness and isolation, but for a lesbian reader in a homophobic society it may seem a particularly poignant portrayal of forbidden love. Indeed, the narrator's pointed reminder that love does not equal heterosexual marriage invites such a reading, as perhaps does the mention of a "human creature" who is neither man, woman, nor child. Margaret McDowell accurately comments: "[L]ove becomes in this novel a force which drives the lover into deeper isolation by driving him in on himself: Love is the dreadful result of an individual's isolation and its intensifier, rather than its cure."[8] One who loves where one may not love does, indeed, often become more isolated by that love. No one associated with a lesbian or gay male community can help but be aware of this fact.

To read as a lesbian, therefore, is not simply to occupy a predefined position. Jonathan Culler points out that the phrase "reading as a woman" implies a disjunction between being a woman (a female reading subject) and a woman's experience, so that reading as a woman is somehow both given and constructed.[9] Both "reading as a woman" and "reading as a man" are shorthand terms for systems of perceiving and processing meanings that are far removed from the grounding in physical bodies to which they refer. These systems are gender coded, but are not automatically achieved by individuals of either gender. So, too, is "reading as a lesbian" a socially and historically produced process: The practice of reading as a lesbian is similarly doubled, and rather more ambiguous. Where one can possibly (though quite arguably) posit that the category "woman" has an origin in a biologically visible distinction, no such marker exists for the "lesbian" who is reading as a lesbian. There is some solid residual sense that "we all know what we mean" when we refer to women: The request for a woman to read as a woman is felt to be divided, not meaningless, because a woman is not only something to be achieved. Such a sense with regard to lesbians, however, can only be misleading. "Lesbian" has something to do with women loving women—exclusively or not, sexually or not, in actuality or not, with men's souls or not, self-consciously or not, as feminists or not—and the debates over these possibilities have at times been quite acrimonious. If the lesbian who is reading is herself a shifting figure, then her reading "as a lesbian" can only be more so.

If we remove our discussion from the individualistic level, however, then reading as a lesbian begins to make a little more sense. Patrocinio Schweickart describes the transition from a woman reading to reading as a woman as "the transfiguration of the heroine into a feminist." She further suggests that reading is an inherently collective activity, since "the production of the meaning of a text is mediated by the interpretive community in which the activity of reading is situated."[10] A woman thus reads as a lesbian whenever she reads in the context of an interpretive community of lesbians, whatever lesbian means in her particular time and place. She reads in light of their experience as well as her own. More specifically (to borrow from Culler), she reads in light of "a reading or interpretation of 'women's [lesbian] experience'—her own and others'—which can be set in a vital and productive relation to the text."[11] There is no term to finish the analogy "woman is to feminist as lesbian is to _____." Nevertheless, that is the meaning I wish to use for the remainder of this paper: To read as a lesbian is to read in the context of a historically grounded and historically changing interpretive community of lesbians.[12]

Such an understanding of reading as a lesbian allows us to escape the question of defining a "lesbian text," which has plagued many attempts to talk about lesbian readings or lesbian criticism. Bonnie Zimmerman, for example, argues that "lesbian criticism begins with the establishment of the lesbian text," an approach that plunges a reader directly into a briarpatch of thorny questions:

> The critic must first define the term "lesbian" and then determine its applicability to both writer and text, sorting out the relation of literature to life. . . . The critic will need to consider whether a lesbian text is one written by a lesbian (and if so, how do we determine who is a lesbian?), one written about lesbians (which might be by a heterosexual woman or a man), or one that expresses a lesbian "vision" (which has yet to be satisfactorily outlined).[13]

Maurice van Lieshout adds the publisher to the process and lists seven possible determining factors, some or all of which may combine to make a piece of "gay or lesbian literature."[14] The endless spawning of unanswered questions is not very fruitful. Another approach, however, is suggested by Gregory Woods: "A gay text is one which lends itself to the hypothesis of gay reading."[15] If reading as a lesbian requires some sort of awareness of a present and past history of women loving women, an awareness that informs and enriches a woman's experience of a particular text, then both text and reader are implicated in the process of reading. The question, therefore, is whether and how a particular text supports a lesbian reading. This question does not reduce to a question of whether a particular author, reader, or central character is lesbian, although any one of these three can certainly increase the likelihood of a lesbian reading. Rather, the question is whether our readings of a text become richer and more satisfying when we entertain the hypothesis of reading as a lesbian. If so, then that hypothesis is appropriate. Its application does not, however, require that the text be labelled "lesbian"—an adjective that is even more problematic when applied to texts than when used with regard to human beings.[16]

But I do not want to weasel out of questions of identification altogether. The very existence of lesbian codes is testimony to the strength of many self-identified lesbians' desire to identify other lesbians. People want to feel that others share their hopes and fears and experiences, and most lesbians feel certain forms of commonality only with other lesbians. Even Michel Foucault argued that sexual identity, although conceptually untenable, is useful if it is not a fact but a function: "a procedure to have relations, social and sexual-pleasure relationships that create new friendships."[17] Readers of all sorts commonly construct an author whose voice may or may not perfectly coincide with the narrative voice of the text, but who is imagined to have a subjectivity that is partially, if incompletely, available to the reader. In a world that is often hostile, and was much more so at the time McCullers was writing, lesbians can be difficult to find. Imagining that the author of a text is lesbian can therefore be a highly pleasurable form of recognition, relationship, and affirmation for a lesbian reader. Nor is it only lesbians who can experience pleasure in imagining this other who is both like and unlike the self—and the discomfort some readers may feel, with or without concomitant pleasures, can also be valuable if it engages them in a challenging but vicarious relationship with the imagined author.

The recent popular and critical attention to women writers, black writers, Native American writers (the list can continue), and to the differences that not being white, male, and middle class makes, indicates that most people retain a residual sense that authorship is significant—the question is how. In a delightfully titled essay, "Believing in Fairies: The Author and The Homosexual," Richard Dyer suggests that authorship be viewed as a form of performance within an interpretive tradition:

> . . . both authorship and being lesbian/gay become a kind of performance, something we all do but only with the terms, the discourses, available to us, and whose relationship to any imputed self doing the performing cannot be taken as read. This may be a characteristically gay (I hesitate to claim lesbian/gay) perception, since for us performance is an everyday issue, whether in terms of passing as straight, signaling gayness in coming out, worrying which of these turns to do, unsure what any of that has to do with what one "is."[18]

Such a model of authorship as performance allows us to address the particularities of the creation of texts without falling into the fallacy that the author gives authority to any one interpretation of those texts. McCullers's biographical experience is relevant because it indicates that she belongs to a specific interpretive community, defined both conceptually and temporally, whose language and ideas shaped her performances of the role of author. As Dyer concludes, "What is significant is the authors' material social position in relation to discourse, the access to discourses they have on account of who they are."[19] We as readers can only imagine McCullers as author, but our appreciation of her performance is deepened if we place her appropriately within the discourses of her and our times. Such enriched possibilities of readings can best be seen by examining specific texts.

* * *

"You mean," Captain Penderton said, "that any fulfillment obtained at the expense of normalcy is wrong, and should not be allowed to bring happiness. In short, it is better, because it is morally honorable, for the square peg to keep scraping about the round hole rather than to discover and use the unorthodox square that would fit it?"

"Why, you put it exactly right," the Major said. "Don't you agree with me?"

"No," said the Captain, after a short pause. With gruesome vividness the Captain suddenly looked into his soul and saw himself. For once he did not see himself as others saw him; there came to him a distorted doll-like image, mean of countenance and grotesque in form. The Captain dwelt on this vision without compassion. He accepted it with neither alteration nor excuse. "I don't agree," he repeated absently.[20]

Ellis's theory of sexual inversion thoroughly informs McCullers's writing. Captain Penderton's soul, not the body that others see, is the essence of his being. It is a doll-like thing: coded feminine. Penderton's sudden insight is provoked by a conversation with Major Langdon about Anacleto, a Filipino servant who is consistently portrayed as effeminate and flighty, "dancing around to music and messing with water-colors." In this moment, Penderton sees a truth within that he accepts fully, "with neither alteration nor excuse." Although the passage parallels Penderton and Anacleto, Penderton's truth within is not the truth of his sexuality alone. Rather, it is the full truth of who he *is*. The sexual connotations are implicit, as are the doubts about who qualifies to be a real man. But to read this truth as only concerning issues of sexuality and gender is overly narrow: The being within is a human with shape and intent. Unlike theories of sexual orientation, which tend to look for an essence of sexuality within each individual, theories of inversion look for an essence of a soul. This soul expresses sexuality as a dimension of its gender, and its gender is intrinsic to its nature, but the soul also possesses an individuality that is not fully defined by gender alone.

McCullers's characters are well known as misfits with peculiar physical and/or psychological characteristics that mark them as alien. Some critics have viewed homosexual attraction as simply one dimension of McCullers's fascination with the freakish: one in a list of "lovers and murderers, impotent homosexuals and gentle perverts, gluttons, idiots, artists, and nymphomaniacs."[21] Such perspectives tend to reify same-sex desire as a quality belonging to "homosexuals"—people defined by a sexual orientation that is far more solid than McCullers's portrayal of multiplicitous, shifting, and often obsessive desires. Few of McCullers's characters are adequately described as homosexual: They are an adolescent girl falling in love with an engaged couple, an Amazonian woman infatuated with a bird-like man, a married man who never consummates the marriage but is entranced by his wife's desire for other men.

M. Segrest suggests a more subtle connection between McCullers's homoeroticism and her recurrent interest in the marginal and alien:

> McCullers, for most of her adult life, acted out what I believe was lesbian alienation (which is to say internalized homophobia) without the political insights into the culture she wrote about. . . . It is little wonder that loneliness and displacement suffuse her writing and are seen as cosmic. I am not saying that all kinds of people are not lonely. But, as a lesbian, I know that we're lonelier than we have to be and that structures of society separate us unnecessarily. This awareness of the way patriarchal power structures limit people is absent in McCullers' writing, making many of her characters—and their creator—embrace the grotesque.[22]

Gayatri Chakravorty Spivak concurs that McCullers's experience of homoerotic desire remained unconceptualized and therefore isolating: "Her homosexuality, like Woolf's, could find no socially collective voice and could not be macro-structurally endorsed like race or class."[23] Although it is always dangerous to read from an author's life into her writing, in this case there does seem to be some connection between McCullers's nonconforming experience of sexuality and her portrayals of human communities.

Theories of sexual inversion define homoerotic desire as an individual pathological flaw. To the extent that McCullers accepted this model, which she largely did, her vision of the nature of homoeroticism remained that of a soul "mean of countenance and grotesque in form." She never portrayed homosexuality as a social or political entity: In her texts, homoerotic interests do not form a basis for human connection and collective activity as they do in many actual lesbian and gay male communities. Perhaps this lack is related to the fact that McCullers was not (contrary to Segrest's and Spivak's implications) herself homosexual. Her heterosexual interests continued to be a formative part of her life and precluded her full adoption of a homosexual identity. This neither-nor position is still alien to many who consider themselves either homosexual or heterosexual and was, if anything, more so for those who thought within the framework of sexual inversion. How could a soul be half female and half male? Furthermore, most of McCullers's participation in gay communities seems to have been in the company of gay men, among whom she as a woman would have been triply alien. Thus McCullers's experience of homoeroticism found no "socially collective voice" partly because of societal negation and internalized homophobia, but also because it did not make sense within either her conceptual model or the small gay community that resisted societal norms.

Perhaps this experience is related to the absence of adult female homoerotic relationships in McCullers's works. By displacing homoeroticism onto men or adolescent girls, McCullers distanced herself from its implications. Her presumably autobiographical figure, Mick, displays many of the characteristic features of the adolescent invert—short hair, masculine nickname, grubby knees, and tomboy ways—but her overt erotic experimentations are heterosexual. The book chronicles Mick's domestication into the role expected of her gender and class, as symbolized by her donning of female clothing and taking a job at Woolworth's (not exactly McCullers's fate). Although Mick resists many aspects of this role, the tide is irreversible. Crucial is her first sexual experience with a neighborhood boy, after which she reflects that "she was a grown person now, whether she wanted to be or not."[24] I agree with Constance Perry that Mick's image of decapitation—"It was like her head was broke off from her body and thrown away. And her eyes looked up straight into the blinding sun while she counted something in her mind" (235)—does not refer to orgasm but rather to Mick's profound alienation from her sexual activity and its implications. It is her "refusal to surrender emotionally to what is occurring and her rejection of it."[25] Mick rebels against heterosexual behavior, but this experience nevertheless initiates her into the constraints of adult womanhood.

McCullers's other adolescent female character is more articulate—and maybe more successful—in her rejection of both femininity and femaleness. When Frankie imagines what she would change if she were the Creator, she plans a world in which "people could instantly change back and forth from boys to girls, whichever way they felt like and wanted" (338). She is both fascinated and horrified by a "morphidite" in the circus House of Freaks who is caught in the middle of this transformation, "divided completely in half"—much like an invert (272). Of the House's eight inhabitants, only this one is named by the text as a "Freak," and he/she haunts Frankie as she fears she will become a Freak herself. Even Frankie's cat, who, with his gray fur and small white spots, is an alter ego to gray-eyed and white-skinned Frankie, is known (at least to Frankie) as both Charles and Charlina (282). Berenice repeatedly affirms the propriety of the world as it is, "insisting that the law of human sex was exactly right just as it was and could in no way be improved," but Frankie remains unconvinced (338).

By the end of the story Frankie goes by the adult form of her name, Frances. She has accepted the prohibitions of the adult world, at least enough to begin to understand them, but she has not necessarily internalized these prohibitions. "Frances" may be less aggressively boyish than "Frankie," but it is nevertheless androgynous when spoken. Although one critic concludes hopefully, "That she might appeal to *male* friends is suggested by the red-haired soldier's interest in her," Frances has firmly repulsed the soldier's overtures: A man's sexual interest in a woman does not, despite all the conventions, imply her reciprocal interest.[26] The text actually ends with Frankie's delight at the arrival of her new *female* friend, Mary Littlejohn. The two girls are planning to spend the night together. Perhaps it is possible to read this text as, among other things, a lesbian coming of age. Frankie learns the discretion that is necessary for survival in a world where she is, indeed, a freak, but she does not in the process renounce her freakishness.

McCullers's systemic linkage of homoeroticism, androgyny, and freakishness thus does not result in a condemnation of homoeroticism—the square peg should be allowed happiness, even if it cannot achieve normalcy. Nor does ambivalence around homosexuality translate into an endorsement of heterosexuality. On the contrary, time and again McCullers's texts challenge the supremacy of heterosexual romance and marriage. Spivak suggests that the relationship between Singer and Antonapoulos in *The Heart Is a Lonely Hunter* be read as a "love-legend *in extremis*." Stripped of all the usual accoutrements of romantic narratives, Singer and Antonapoulos's frustrated non-communication becomes a commentary on traditional romantic ideals. "It can make us begin to suspect that perhaps the 'other' in those canonical and publicized exchanges has always been 'really' like Antonapoulos in this story: mute, muted, distanced, displaced, imprisoned, mysterious, uncommunicative, and so unlike her 'self' that she might as well be mad."[27] A grim reality is reflected in McCullers's funhouse/freakhouse mirror.

Reflections in a Golden Eye is even more a study in the translation of desire: from one object to another, or from love to hate. Penderton, the narrator tells us in the opening pages, "had a sad penchant for becoming enamoured of his wife's lovers" (13). His initial attraction to his wife's acknowledged lover transforms into a ruthless obsession with the young soldier, Williams, who has become infatuated with Leonora. Ultimately Penderton's desire becomes uncontainable: "He thought of the soldier in terms neither of love or hate; he was conscious only of the irresistible yearning to break down the barrier between them" (171). This irresistible yearning comes to its climax when Penderton shoots and kills Williams, whom he has watched entering his sleeping wife's bedroom. Unable to find satisfaction in other ways, desire seeks the final obliteration of the otherness of its object.

This action is also, however, an assertion of the primacy of Penderton's marital relationship: He is performing the role of the angry and outraged husband. Nor is Williams the first in this text to die for the sake of a dysfunctional marriage. Alison Langdon's poorly defined wasting illness is clearly related to her husband's distance and condescension. After the loss of her infant, she cuts off her nipples with a pair of garden shears, thus symbolically neutering herself as she simultaneously rejects the roles of mother-nurturer and female sexual object. When she finally decides to seek a divorce, her husband decides she is crazy: "Not only did he grieve for Alison's sake," the narrator comments, "but he felt ashamed, as though this were a reflection on his own respectability" (151). Two days after he has her incarcerated in an insane asylum, Alison dies of a heart attack. The insistence on marital respectability, combined with the shifting and unacknowledged patterns of desire, results in two deaths and no one's gain.

A different model of intimacy and community is offered in *The Ballad of the Sad Café*. "The meals that are served in the Sad Cafe," says Paula Eckard, "are substitutes for familial love, but they also represent a celebration and a coming together of community."[28] The word "substitutes" implies a lesser satisfaction, but the text suggests that the pleasures of the café are in fact greater than those of family life:

> There is a deeper reason why the café was so precious to this town. And this deeper reason has to do with a certain pride that had not hitherto been known in these parts. To understand this new pride the cheapness of human life must be kept in mind. There were always plenty of people clustered around a mill—but it was seldom that every family had enough meal, garments, and fat back to go the rounds. . . . Often after you have sweated and tried and things are not better for you, there comes a feeling deep down in the soul that you are not worth much. . . . The people of the town . . . washed before coming to Miss Amelia's, and scraped their feet very politely on the threshold as they entered the café. There, for a few hours at least, the deep bitter knowing that you are not worth much in this world could be laid low. (239–40)

The café offers a social existence, one in which life is more than physical. "Family" in this text is a mundane procreative entity linked with the necessities of economic survival, fat back, and the breeding of children. Life is cheap, plentiful, and easily generated, but not easily valued. The café, on the other hand, is transformative: It changes how individuals think and feel about themselves, displaces the physical bonds of family in favor of the social bonds of community, and creates a space in which new forms of relationship may evolve that may finally break through the spiritual barrenness of "normal" existence. Similarly, in *The Heart Is a Lonely Hunter* the café provides a context for human connection that is largely lacking elsewhere in the text. The creative possibilities of the café become fully available to its proprietor, Biff, only after his wife has died, leaving him free to explore non-masculine behaviors and non-heterosexual modes of interaction. The important point is not whether people use their freedom to form homosexual relationships. Rather, these texts present a fundamental critique of a society built around heterosexual couplings and procreative families. In both texts, it is through the café—not through the family or romantic love—that people find self-respect and decent relationship with others.

Everybody loses, therefore, when Marvin Macy reappears and reasserts the primacy of heterosexual marriage. Because of Cousin Lymon, Miss Amelia does not run Marvin Macy off the premises as she had before. Instead, she tries resentfully to compromise with the expectation that she be a woman/wife: "after the day of Marvin Macy's arrival, she put aside her overalls and wore always the red dress she had before this time reserved for Sundays, funerals, and sessions of the court" (238). The compromise is unsuccessful, and Miss

Amelia becomes more and more powerless. Cousin Lymon underlines her impotence and marginalization by mocking her and making her "appear to be a freak"—exiling her from the human community into the shadowy realm of the neither-nor. "There was something so terrible about this that even the silliest customers of the café, such as Merlie Ryan, did not laugh" (245). Terrible indeed, when everyone loses the café that had been the heart of the town. And all, as Kenneth Chamlee accurately explains, because Marvin Macy's "real wish is for a vengeful domination, to subdue her physically in a brawl since he was unable to do so sexually in their marriage bed."[29]

The importance of a social environment is repeated and underlined in the coda: the brief, final story of "Ten Mortal Men" who work in a chain gang and yet sing beautifully together. Todd Stebbins comments, "McCullers is using the twelve mortal men to illustrate the fact that any two people, or a group of people, can make music, no matter how unlikely the match, as long as they are together." He sees the strange epilogue as providing a note of optimism: Despite the disintegration of any given social context, "relationships do occur, harmony can be reached."[30] A new social context will emerge—even if only that of being chained leg to leg—that will enable the creation of something greater than the isolated self can ever achieve. The text clearly focuses on the groupness of the gang, but perhaps Stebbins's inference that *any* two people can make music together, no matter how unlikely other people find the match, is an appropriate final note.

* * *

A hypothesis of reading as a lesbian thus gives new meanings to McCullers's well-known "parade of deformed and confused people seeking human connections."[31] McCullers and others of her time did indeed see lesbianism as a deformity, as many readers and critics still do. McCullers's characters are not, however, simply identifiable as lesbian or gay, identities that would be more culturally explainable than the shifting, neither-nor, multiplicitous desires that McCullers portrays. Much is gained by entertaining the possibility not only that these characters might experience same-sex desires, but that these desires might be linked, through both the text and its historical setting, to a more general rebellion against what it means to be a culturally encoded "woman" or "man." Indeed, such an analysis is essential once we understand that McCullers lived—and struggled—with the theoretical model of sexual inversion, which describes sexuality as a projection of gender. And McCullers's characters are, finally, people seeking human connections. They find these connections not in monogamous romantic love, certainly not in the family, but in broad human communities built on social rather than biological bonds. The text may not be lesbian; the characters may not be lesbian; the author may not be lesbian; the reader may not be lesbian; but reading with the hypothesis that any or all might be reveals new ways of reading these texts.

Notes

1. This book has often been read as a semi-autobiographical account of McCullers's/Mick's coming of age. Although this reading is certainly relevant, Mick hardly meets several of the other primary characters, and the book makes more sense structurally if it is read as centering on Singer. This structural reading seems to be a minority one, however, and it is unlikely if one is trying to avoid acknowledging the primacy of the relationship between the two men.

2. I recognize that there are many difficult issues regarding the connections and disconnections between female and male homoeroticism, between lesbians and gay men. Although I will later consider some aspects of this subject, for now I will simply quote and concur with Eve Kosofsky Sedgwick's third axiom of gay theory: "There can't be an a priori decision about how far it will make sense to conceptualize lesbian and gay male identities together. Or separately" (*Epistemology of the Closet* [Berkeley: University of California Press, 1990], 36).

3. Carson McCullers, *Collected Stories* (Boston: Houghton Mifflin, 1987), 258, 264. This edition, which includes both *The Member of the Wedding* and *The Ballad of the Sad Café,* will hereafter be cited in the text.

4. Virginia Spencer Carr, *The Lonely Hunter: A Biography of Carson McCullers* (Garden City: Doubleday, 1975), 158.

5. Carr, *McCullers,* 110, 159.

6. Although many Freudians have viewed same-sex object choice as pathological, this view is not inherent in Freudian theory. Freudianism does predict, however, that, once object choice has occurred, it is permanent.

7. Carr, *McCullers,* 111.

8. Margaret B. McDowell, *Carson McCullers* (Boston: Twayne Publishers, 1980), 71.

9. Jonathan Culler, *On Deconstruction: Theory and Criticism after Structuralism* (Ithaca, N.Y.: Cornell University Press, 1982) 49.

10. Patrocinio P. Schweickart, "Reading Ourselves: Toward a Feminist Theory of Reading," in *Gender and Reading: Essays on Readers, Texts, and Contexts,* ed. Elizabeth A. Flynn and Patrocinio P. Schweickart (Baltimore: Johns Hopkins University Press, 1986), 49–50.

11. Culler, *Deconstruction,* 63.

12. Perhaps I should note here that I make no claim to *be* a lesbian reading as a lesbian. I rely more on others' lesbian experience than my own, although my own is important, too. I would argue, furthermore, that this is always the case—that people learn more from vicarious experience, from listening to others' stories, than we do from our own direct experience, and the interpretations we use come largely from others. This is part of what it means to belong to an interpretive community.

13. Bonnie Zimmerman, "What Has Never Been: An Overview of Lesbian Feminist Literary Criticism," *Feminist Studies,* 7.3 (Fall 1981): 459.

14. Maurice van Lieshout, "The Context of Gay Writing and Reading," in *Homosexuality, Which Homosexuality? International Conference on Gay and Lesbian Studies,* ed. D. Altman et al. (London: GMP Publishers, 1989), 114.

15. Gregory Woods, *Articulate Flesh: Male Homo-Eroticism and Modern Poetry* (New Haven: Yale University Press, 1987), 4.

16. Actually, this paper relies on a working model of three interrelated but separable modes of lesbian reading:

◊ A lesbian reading can examine how a text utilizes lesbian-identified codes and contexts that originate beyond the text. Such codes may reflect a heterosexual world looking at lesbians, a lesbian world looking at (and, perhaps more importantly, for) each other, or some combination of the two. They position the text as participating in a larger, and historically situated, system of meanings.

◊ A lesbian reading can trace how homosocial and/or homoerotic desire moves within a text. This perspective does not mean a simple labeling of certain relationships as "lesbian" or "homosexual," but rather offers a broader sensitivity to currents, connections, and differences than is possible if heterosexuality is assumed. It enables us to see how texts that might not appropriately be denoted "lesbian" or "gay" may nevertheless reflect their culture's construction of homoerotic and heteroerotic desire.

◊　　　A lesbian reading can analyze how a text supports and/or critiques social-sexual structures. Here the reader views heterosexuality as an institution that attempts to reproduce not just specifically erotic behaviors and desires (although certainly those), but also a whole world of gender-coded identity and relationship.

17.　Bob Gallagher and Alexander Wilson, "Sex and the Politics of Identity: An Interview with Michel Foucault," in *Gay Spirit,* ed. Mark Thompson (New York: St. Martin's Press, 1987), 31.

18.　Richard Dyer, "Believing in Fairies: The Author and the Homosexual," in *Inside/Out: Lesbian Theories, Gay Theories,* ed. Diana Fuss (New York: Routledge, 1991), 187–88. The aspects of performance that Dyer lists as characteristically gay are, indeed, also common experiences among lesbians.

19.　Ibid., 188.

20.　Carson McCullers, *Reflections in A Golden Eye* (New York: Vail-Ballou Press, 1941), 163; hereafter cited in the text.

21.　Ellen Moers, *Literary Women* (New York: Oxford University Press, 1963), 108.

22.　M. Segrest, "Lines I Dare to Write: Lesbian Writing in the South," *Southern Exposure* 9 (1981): 55.

23.　Gayatri Chakravorty Spivak, "Three Feminist Readings: McCullers, Drabble, Habermas," *Union Seminary Quarterly Review* 35 (1979): 20.

24.　Carson McCullers, *The Heart Is a Lonely Hunter* (New York: Bantam Books, 1940), 236; hereafter cited in the text.

25.　Constance M. Perry, "Carson McCullers and the Female *Wunderkind,*" *Southern Literary Journal* 19 (1986): 42.

26.　Dale Edmonds, *Carson McCullers* (Austin: Steck-Vaughn, 1969), 28.

27.　Spivak, "Three Feminist Readings," 18–20.

28.　Paula Gallant Eckard, "Family and Community in Anne Tyler's *Dinner at the Homesick Restaurant,*" *Southern Literary Journal* 22 (1990): 42.

29.　Kenneth D. Chamlee, "Cafés and Community in Three Carson McCullers Novels," *Studies in American Fiction* 18 (1990): 237–38.

30.　Todd Stebbins, "McCullers' *The Ballad of the Sad Café,*" *The Explicator* 46 (1988): 38.

31.　Chamlee, "Cafés and Community," 233.

Index

♦

General Editor

Dr. James Nagel, J. O. Eidson Distinguished Professor of American Literature at the University of Georgia, founded the scholarly journal *Studies in American Fiction* and edited it for 20 years. He is the general editor of the Critical Essays on American Literature series published by Macmillan, a program that now contains over 130 volumes. He was one of the founders of the American Literature Association and serves as its executive coordinator. He is also a past president of the Ernest Hemingway Society. Among his 17 books are *Stephen Crane and Literary Impressionism, Critical Essays on* The Sun Also Rises, *Ernest Hemingway: The Writer in Context, Ernest Hemingway: The Oak Park Legacy,* and *Hemingway in Love and War,* which was selected by the New York Times as one of the outstanding books of 1989 and which has been made into a major motion picture. Dr. Nagel has published over 50 articles in scholarly journals, and has lectured on American literature in 15 countries.